# Hiking Death Valley National Park

D1533073

**Apr 2017**

# Hiking
# Death Valley
# National Park

A Guide to the Park's Greatest Hiking Adventures

Second Edition

**Bill and Polly Cunningham**

GUILFORD, CONNECTICUT

To the thousands of citizens from California and elsewhere, past and present, who laid the groundwork for protection of a large portion of the California desert and to the dedicated state and federal park rangers and naturalists charged with stewardship of California's irreplaceable desert wilderness.

# FALCONGUIDES®

An imprint of Rowman & Littlefield
Falcon and FalconGuides are registered trademarks and Make Adventure Your Story is a trademark of Rowman & Littlefield.

Distributed by NATIONAL BOOK NETWORK

Copyright © 2007, 2017 Rowman & Littlefield
Photos: Polly and Bill Cunningham
Maps: DesignMaps Inc. © Rowman & Littlefield

British Library Cataloguing-in-Publication Information available

The Library of Congress has catalogued the first edition as follows:
1 Names: Cunningham, Bill. | Cunningham, Polly.
2 Title: Hiking Death Valley national park: 36 day and overnight hikes / Bill and Polly Cunningham.
3 Description: Guilford, Conn. : FalconGuides, 2008. | Includes bibliographical
  references and index.
4 Identifiers: LCCN 2007026027 | ISBN 9780762744633 (alk. paper)
5 Subjects: LCSH: Hiking–California–Death Valley National Park–Guidebooks. | Death Valley National Park (Calif. and Nev.)–Guidebooks.
6 Classification: LCC GV199.42.C22 D433 2008 | DDC 796.51/09794/87–dc22 LC record available at https://lccn.loc.gov/2007026027

ISBN 978-1-4930-1653-2 (paperback)
ISBN 978-1-4930-2825-2 (e-book)

∞™ The paper used in this publication meets the minimum requirements of American National Standard for Information Sciences—Permanence of Paper for Printed Library Materials, ANSI/NISO Z39.48-1992.

# Contents

## The Hikes
### Southern Death Valley

### Grapevine/Funeral Mountains

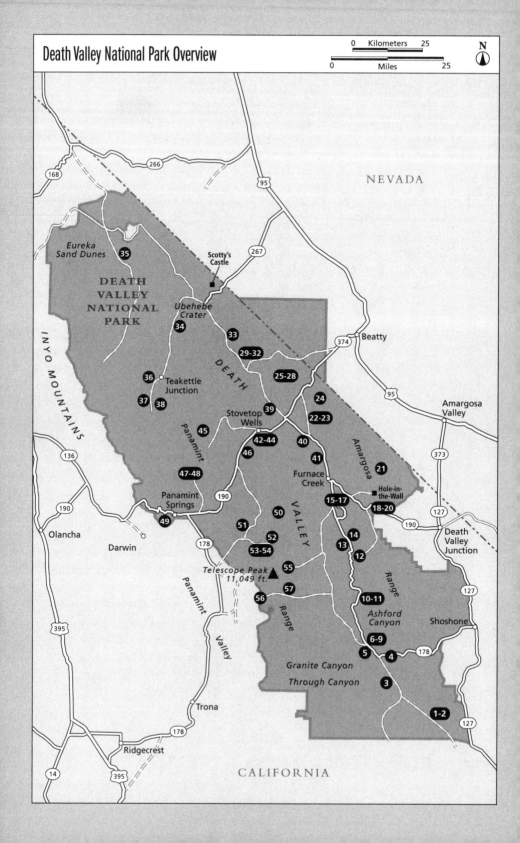

# Acknowledgments

This book could not have been written without the generous assistance from knowledgeable park staff. Special thanks to Charlie Callagan, wilderness coordinator for the park and the leading authority on wilderness hiking in Death Valley. Charlie is a virtual fountain of information and enthusiasm for the park. He provided an in-depth review of our draft material time and again until he was satisfied that we finally had it right. But most of all, Charlie served as friend and guide on several of the exciting new hikes in this book, such as Palmer and Moonlight Canyons. We couldn't have done it without you, Charlie!

During our most recent winter visit to Death Valley, we based out of the Stovepipe Wells Campground and had the pleasure of meeting camp host Phil Bender. Phil strives to help everyone enjoy the best camping experience possible and is truly the Host with the Most. Thanks, Phil!

And thanks to all the hospitable folks who provided advice and insights during our many treks throughout Death Valley. Please know that you are not forgotten.

Our deepest gratitude goes to the incredibly competent (and patient) FalconGuides editors who somehow transformed our roughhewn pile of maps, text, and photos into the book you have before you.

# Introduction

## Death Valley National Park

Death Valley's intimidating name is said to have originated in 1849 when an anonymous member of the forty-niners, after nearly dying while seeking a shortcut to the newly discovered California goldfields, turned around at the final view and exclaimed, "Good-bye, Death Valley!" Now it's our turn to say hello to one of the world's most imposing and contrasting landscapes. The extremes of Death Valley, from soaring snowcapped peaks to North America's hottest, driest, and lowest desert, command respect and entice discovery.

In 1933 President Herbert Hoover proclaimed Death Valley a national monument, a status less protective than that of national park because of mining conflicts. The monument was expanded in 1937 when President Franklin Roosevelt added the 300,000-acre Nevada triangle. In 1952 President Truman added 40 acres of Devil's Hole in Nevada to protect a rare variety of desert pupfish. With mining a major issue in Death Valley, the 1976 Mining in Parks Act is of special significance. This law began phasing out mining in the monument by closing Death Valley to the filing of new claims. The number of old claims has since decreased from 50,000 to zero in 2005 when the last mine closed.

The status of the monument was further elevated in 1984 when the United Nations recognized Death Valley as part of the Mojave and Colorado International Biosphere Reserve. Finally, on October 31, 1994, Death Valley received long-overdue national park classification when President Bill Clinton signed the California Desert Protection Act into law. The 2-million-acre national monument became a more than 3.4-million-acre national park, with 91 percent (3.1 million acres) of the park designated wilderness. In so doing, Death Valley became the nation's largest national park outside Alaska with the largest amount of Wilderness.

As we go to press with this new edition of *Hiking Death Valley National Park*, the National Park Service (NPS) turns one hundred years old. Americans love their national parks, and they consistently rate the agency as among the very best in government. At the same time, however, the permanent workforce of the NPS is fewer than the number of employees at Disneyland. With more than $12 billion in deferred maintenance, the park service budget continues to fall in real dollars. As you lace up your boots to explore Death Valley, please consider celebrating the centennial with service. This can include volunteering at visitor centers and popular trailheads, helping to restore storm-damaged trails and facilities, and donating to nonprofits such as the Death Valley Conservancy and the Death Valley Natural History Association.

## A Long and Complex Geologic Past

The land of extremes that is Death Valley is best dramatized when afternoon shadows from 11,049-foot Telescope Peak are cast across the Badwater Basin, 282 feet *below* sea level. Combine this amazing vertical relief with recent volcanic craters, towering sand dunes, and flood-scoured canyons and you begin to appreciate a long and complicated geologic history.

Death Valley is at the western and youngest edge of the Basin and Range Province (the Great Basin). As such, its relatively youthful topography is extreme, with mountains still growing and basins still sinking. The oldest rocks date back 1.8 billion years but have been too severely changed to be reliably interpreted for geologic history.

Rocks a mere half billion years old are more predictable. The Funeral and Panamint Mountains are made up of these weathered limestones and sandstones. The rocks point to a warm, shallow sea from around 570 million to 250 million years ago. The sea left layers of sediment and a myriad of marine fossils. Between 1933 and 1994 researchers discovered 500 species of fossil plants and animals within the monument. Now that the boundaries have been expanded by 50 percent, the new park may prove to be the most fossil-rich national park in the United States and perhaps in the world.

Death Valley is next to the boundary of two interconnected plates in the earth's crust. When the plates moved slowly in relation to each other, compression folded and fractured the brittle crust. This caused the land surface to push up and the sea to gradually recede west. Most of this faulting took place from 250 million to 70 million years ago. Active mountain building then alternated with inactive periods of mountain-reducing erosion.

Volcanic activity prevailed from 70 million to 3 million years ago. Mountain building stretched and weakened the earth's crust, forming weak spots through which molten material could erupt. This volcanic activity moved westward from Nevada, producing a chain of volcanoes east of the park from Furnace Creek southeast to Shoshone. Eruptions of cinder and ash account for the flamboyant colors of borate mineral deposits at Artist's Palette.

Around 3 million years ago, the floor of Death Valley began to form. Compression was replaced by a pulling apart of the earth's crust, causing large blocks of land to slowly slide past one another along faults. These extensional forces formed parallel north–south trending valleys and mountain ranges. The salt flats of Badwater Basin and the Panamint Range make up one block that is rotating to the east. The valley floor, known as a half-graben, continues to slip down along the fault at the foot of the Black Mountains. This dropping is evident in recently exposed fault scarps near Badwater. Meanwhile, erosion continues with flash floods carrying rocks, sand, and gravel from surrounding hillsides to alluvial fans that spread like gigantic funnels from every canyon mouth. More than 9,000 feet of sediments and salts lie beneath the half-graben floor at Badwater.

Climate has also been a major force in these ongoing changes. During the last major continental ice age, the bottom of Death Valley was covered by a system of huge lakes. As the climate warmed, the lakes disappeared—about 10,000 years ago. A much smaller lake system formed 2,000 years ago during a cold period. This water then evaporated, leaving behind today's salt deposits.

The Ubehebe Craters in the northern end of the park tell the tale of recent volcanic activity of a few hundred years ago. The craters were formed by violent steam explosions caused when molten material mixed with groundwater. Erosion, earthquakes, and subsidence continue to reshape the surface of one of North America's most dramatic and ever-changing landscapes.

## A Tapestry of Life: Don't Let the Name Fool You

More than 1,000 plant species thrive in the incredibly wide range of elevations and habitats found within the park—from dry alkali flats below sea level to the subalpine crests of the highest Panamint summits. These species include nineteen endemics found only within the boundaries of the park, such as telescope bedstraw, Panamint monkey flower, and Eureka Dunes evening primrose. Another twenty-three species have the majority of their range within the park, such as magnificent lupine and Death Valley sage. No fewer than thirteen species of cactus grow within the park. Ironically, this driest of deserts is home to more species of marsh grass than cactus.

Spring wildflowers are a pageant worth waiting for. The white of desert-star, red of Indian paintbrush, pink of desert five-spot, yellow of desert gold, and blue of Arizona lupine are what dreams are made of. But as with everything, there are good years and bad years. A spectacular year for the showy plants of these desert annuals depends on well-spaced rainfall throughout winter and early spring, enough warming sun, and few drying winds. The premier blooming periods in the park are usually late February to mid-April in the lower elevations of valley floors and alluvial fans, early April to early May for midslopes up to 4,000 feet, and late April to early June above 4,000 feet in the Panamints and other mountain ranges.

Death Valley is home to at least fifty-one species of mammals, thirty-six species of reptiles, five species of amphibians, and six species of fishes. Some of the animals, such as desert bighorn sheep, live near springs in inaccessible mountains and canyons. The nocturnal kit fox is common in most of Death Valley. Coyotes may be seen from the salt flats up to the highest mountain plateaus. Some species have been introduced, such as the burro was in the 1880s. The reptile list includes the threatened desert tortoise and the mostly nocturnal Mojave sidewinder rattlesnake. Five species of desert pupfish live in the park, four of which are endemic to Death Valley. These endemics are the Saratoga pupfish, Salt Creek pupfish, Cottonball Marsh pupfish, and the endangered Devil's Hole pupfish. These tiny members of the killfish family vary from 1 to 2.5 inches long. They lived in ancient freshwater lakes during the last ice age. As the climate became drier, the pupfish became isolated in widely separated warm springs and creeks, gradually adapting to higher temperatures and increased salinity.

*Death Valley serves as a backdrop for the remains of the miner's cabin at Keane Wonder Spring (hike 23).*

## Human History

Death Valley has been the site of at least four Native American cultures, beginning about 10,000 years ago with a group of hunter-gatherers known as "the Nevares Spring people." Game was abundant during this wetter period. As the climate became drier, they were replaced by the Mesquite Flat people about 4,000 years later. Then the Saratoga Spring people arrived about 2,000 years ago when the hot, dry desert was similar to today's conditions. These people were skilled hunters who created large, intricate stone patterns in the valley. Nomadic desert Shoshone moved into the valley about 1,000 years ago. Like many people today, they camped near water sources in the valley during winter, then headed up into the cooler mountains during summer to escape searing heat. A Timbisha Shoshone village still exists at Furnace Creek, 0.7 mile north of the Badwater junction.

The first nonnative people to enter the valley were two groups of emigrants on their way to the California goldfields in 1849. From the 1880s to early 1900s, mining was sporadic in the region. Lack of suitable transportation limited mining to only the highest-grade ore. Perhaps the best-known but shortest-lived mine was the Harmony Borax Works, active from 1883 to 1888. It was most famous for its twenty-mule wagons and the *Death Valley Days* radio and television programs. W. T. Coleman built the wagons that hauled the processed mineral 165 miles across the desert to the railroad at Mojave. Gold and silver mining picked up in the early 1900s with such large-scale ventures as the Keane Wonder Mine, but then came the Panic of 1907. Profitable large-scale hardrock mining in Death Valley ended around 1915, although individual miners, like Pete Aguereberry, continued to work their claims for several decades more. During World War II talc was mined here until markets made mining unprofitable. In 1989 these talc-mining claims were bought by the Conservation Foundation and donated to the National Park Service in 1992.

## Weather

The geographer's definition of a desert as a place with less than 10 inches average annual rainfall says little about what a desert really is. Deserts are regions of irregular and minimal rainfall, so much so that for most of the time, scarcity of water is limiting to life.

In the desert, evaporation far exceeds precipitation. Temperatures swing widely between night and day. This is because low humidity and intense sun heat up the ground during the day, but almost all the heat dissipates at night. Daily temperature changes of 50 degrees or more are common—which can be hazardous to unprepared hikers caught out after dark.

Death Valley's land of extremes doesn't end with topography, vertical relief, and a Noah's ark of wildlife. Recorded temperatures range from a sizzling 134°F to a freezing low of 15 degrees. The valley experiences an average annual temperature of 76 pleasant degrees—somewhat deceiving given the summer averages at well above 100°F. Temperatures will be 3 to 5 degrees cooler along with increased precipitation for every 1,000-foot vertical increase in elevation. One balmy July day in 1972, with the air temperature at 128°F, a ground temperature of 201°F was measured at Furnace Creek. With no protective shade, any attempt to hike the salt flats in these conditions could be a terminal experience. For hiking comfort, November to April is hard to beat. Average highs are in the 60- to 90-degree range on the valley floor, cooling considerably at higher elevations. The loftiest mountaintops are often snow covered from November to May.

Precipitation figures can be misleading, as an annual average of less than 2 inches of rain falls in Death Valley. Averages mean nothing in a desert region that may go one or two years without any rain only to receive up to three times the annual average the following year. The mountain ranges can catch torrential downpours, causing flash flooding, road closures, and trail washouts. To check on current road and trail conditions, consult the Death Valley National Park website (www.nps.gov/deva) before heading to the desert.

## Rules to Enjoy the Park

As of 2016 overnight backcountry hikers and campers are required to obtain a permit. Permits are available at the Furnace Creek Visitor Center.

Limited open-desert car camping is allowed at Death Valley, a sprawling park with more than 3 million acres of wilderness and 700-plus miles of dirt roads. The basic rule is that backcountry camping is permitted 1 mile beyond any paved road, day-use-only area, or developed area. Car campers must use preexisting campsites and park immediately adjacent to the unpaved roadway to reduce impact and to avoid violating the wilderness boundary, which, in most cases, closely parallels the road. A high-clearance vehicle is usually needed to travel 1 or more miles from pavement on a dirt road that is open for camping. Camping is not allowed on day-use-only roads, including the Titus Canyon Road, West Side Road, Wildrose Road, and Racetrack Road from Teakettle Junction to Homestake Dry Camp. Camping is also prohibited at three historic mining areas, including the Ubehebe Lead Mine. Actually, the safe thing to do is to avoid camping at any mining area. Backcountry camping is not allowed on the valley floor from 2 miles north of Stovepipe Wells south to Ashford Mill.

Overnight group size is limited to twelve people and no more than four vehicles. Campsites in the backcountry must be at least 200 yards from any water source to avoid disturbing wildlife in these fragile and limited sites. In view of the recent park and wilderness designations at Death Valley, it is important to obtain a copy of the latest backcountry regulations at the Furnace Creek Visitor Center or nearest ranger station.

Off-road vehicle use is prohibited, not only because the land away from roads is wilderness and closed to motorized use, but also because the desert is fragile and painfully slow to recover from damage. Bicycles are permitted on all paved and open dirt roads but are not allowed on trails, off roads, or in park wilderness. Campfires are only allowed in fire pits at developed campgrounds. If you want a fire, bring wood in from outside; gathering the scarce wood here is unlawful. Remember that the park is a museum of undisturbed nature, so removal of any rocks, wood, plants, animals, or historical artifacts is prohibited.

No matter how pitiful the begging coyote may appear, do not feed wildlife. To do so causes them to depend on unnatural food sources, which is tantamount to a death sentence. Speaking of animals, leave your pets at home. They must be restrained at all times and are not allowed off roads, on trails, or in park wilderness.

## Campgrounds, Services, and Fees

Nine developed National Park Service campgrounds with more than 1,500 sites are well distributed in the central to north-central region of the park. Four of these are free, one of which, Wildrose, is open year-round, weather permitting. The Wildrose Campground is reached by way of the rough Wildrose Canyon Road. The other three higher-elevation campgrounds—Emigrant, Thorndike, and Mahogany Flat—are open spring to fall depending on weather conditions. Of the five fee campgrounds,

◀ *Dante's View provides a spectacular panorama of Badwater 6,000 feet below, with the snowcapped 11,049-foot Telescope Peak in the distance (hike 12).*

Furnace Creek and Mesquite Spring are open all year. Texas Spring, Sunset, and Stovepipe Wells are at or below sea level and are open October to April.

The main visitor center and Death Valley Natural History Association (DVNHA) is located at Furnace Creek. The visitor center at Furnace Creek is open from 8 a.m. to 5 p.m. daily year-round. These hours are subject to change, so check online before your arrival. The National Park Service has prepared an excellent series of free hand-outs on such topics as geology, mining history, plants, wildflowers, wildlife, special points of interest, and more. During the high season of November through April, rangers and naturalists present evening talks and guided nature walks.

Check the national park website for current entrance and camping fees.

Food, supplies, and gas can be purchased at Furnace Creek Ranch and Stovepipe Wells. Distances in the sprawling park are vast, so be sure to travel with plenty of gas, water, food, and other necessary supplies.

The few trails in the park that are formally maintained are described in some of the recommended hikes that follow. User trails in drainages may largely disappear after a flash flood. Many of the trailless routes follow natural corridors, such as deep canyons. In the desert, hiking use is generally light with vast distances between trailheads, which, in turn, lead to routes without directional signs. Lack of hiker conveniences found in other, more heavily visited parks and wildernesses is more than made up for by solitude, and by the spirit of adventure that awaits those willing to explore this magnificent park on foot.

## How to Get There

Primary road access to the park from the south is via CA 127 from I-15 at Baker. CA 178 leads west into the park from CA 127 near Shoshone. CA 190 heads west into the park from CA 127 at Death Valley Junction. On the west side, CA 178 takes off from US 395 and enters the park by way of Panamint Valley. CA 190 takes off to the east from US 395 at Olancha, entering the park just west of Panamint Springs. From the north, access is through Lone Pine on CA 136 and then CA 190. The network of roads within the park runs the gamut, from all-weather pavement to a series of rocky washboard ruts that can loosen every bolt and try the patience of even the most determined motorist. The closest large commercial airport is at Las Vegas, about 135 miles southeast of Furnace Creek.

## The Meaning and Value of Wilderness

Visitors to Death Valley and other desert wildlands should appreciate the meaning and values of wilderness, if for no other reason than to better enjoy their visits with less impact on the wildland values that attracted them in the first place.

The most fundamental purpose of the 1964 Wilderness Act is to provide an enduring resource of wilderness for this and future generations so that a growing, increasingly mechanized human population does not occupy and modify every last wild niche. Just as important as preserving the land is the preservation of natural processes, such as naturally ignited fires, floods, landslides, and other forces that shape the land. Before 1964 the uncertain whim of administrative fiat was all that protected wilderness.

The act defines Wilderness as undeveloped federal lands "where the earth and its community of life are untrammeled by man, where man is a visitor who does not remain." At the same time Congress recognized that no land is completely free of human influence, going on to say that wilderness must "generally appear to have been affected primarily by the forces of nature, with the imprint of man's work substantially unnoticeable." Further, a "wilderness" must have outstanding opportunities for solitude or primitive and unconfined recreation, and be at least 5,000 acres in size or large enough to preserve and use in an unimpaired condition. Also, wilderness may contain ecological, geological, or other features of scientific, educational, scenic, or historical value. Death Valley National Park easily exceeds these legal requirements. Any lingering doubts are removed by the distant music of a coyote beneath a star-studded desert sky, or by the soothing rhythm of an oasis waterfall in a remote canyon.

Once designated, the unending job of wilderness stewardship is just beginning. The managing agencies have a special responsibility to administer wilderness in "such manner as will leave them (wilderness areas) unimpaired for future use and enjoyment as wilderness." Unimpairment of wilderness over time can only be achieved through partnership between concerned citizens and the agencies.

Wilderness is the only truly biocentric use of land. It is off-limits to intensive human uses with an objective of preserving the diversity of nonhuman life, which is richly endowed in Death Valley. As such, its preservation is our society's highest act of humility. This is where we deliberately slow down our impulse to mine the last vein of ore or build a parking lot on top of the last wild peak. The desert wilderness explorer can take genuine pride in reaching a remote summit under his or her power, traversing a narrow serpentine canyon, or walking across the uncluttered expanse of a vast desert basin. Hiking boots and self-reliance replace motorized equipment and push-button convenience, allowing us to find something in ourselves we feared lost.

## Wilderness Stewardship

In 2013 the National Park Service adopted a new Wilderness Stewardship Plan for the park. The regulations are now in place, and among the changes is a reduction in the overnight wilderness party size from fifteen to twelve. A mandatory wilderness permit system for overnight backpacking is being slowly phased in. The system will not impose use limits but will include a free online permit to help maintain a quality wilderness experience. A fairly high percentage of the million or so annual visitors to Death Valley get out for at least a short hike. But backpacking is a largely undiscovered treasure in Death Valley.

With the exception of mining areas, the Wilderness boundary is 50 feet from the centerline of almost every dirt road. Some 700 miles of dirt roads are open for car camping within 50 feet of their centerline outside the Wilderness boundary. These roads provide great jumping-off places for Death Valley Wilderness exploration.

## Have Fun and Be Safe

Wandering in the desert has a reputation of being a dangerous activity, thanks to both the Bible and Hollywood. Usually depicted as a wasteland, the desert evokes fear. With proper planning, however, desert hiking is not hazardous. In fact, it is fun and exciting and is quite safe.

An enjoyable desert outing requires preparation. Beginning with this book, along with the maps suggested in the hike write-ups, you need to be equipped with adequate knowledge about your hiking area. Carry good maps and a compass, and know how to use them.

Calculating the time required for a hike in the desert defies any formula. Terrain is often rough; extensive detours around boulders, dry falls, and drop-offs mean longer trips. Straight-line distance is an illusion. Sun, heat, and wind likewise all conspire to slow down even the speediest hiker. Therefore, distances are not what they appear in the desert. Five desert miles may take longer than 10 woodland miles. Plan your excursion conservatively, and always carry emergency items in your pack (see appendix B).

As you consult the equipment list (appendix B), note that water ranks the highest. Carrying the water is not enough—take the time to stop and drink it. This is another reason desert hikes take longer. Frequent water breaks are mandatory. It's best to return from your hike with empty water bottles. You can cut down on loss of bodily moisture by hiking with your mouth closed and breathing through your nose; reduce thirst also by avoiding sweets and alcohol.

Driving to and from the trailhead is statistically far more dangerous than hiking in the desert backcountry. But being far from the nearest 911 service requires knowledge about possible hazards and proper precautions to avoid them. It is not an oxymoron to have fun and to be safe. Quite to the contrary: If you're not safe, you won't have fun. At the risk of creating excessive paranoia, here are the treacherous twelve:

### Dehydration

It cannot be overemphasized that plenty of water is necessary for desert hiking. Carry 1 gallon per person per day in unbreakable plastic screw-top containers. And pause often to drink it. Carry water in your car as well so you'll have water to return to. As a general rule, plain water is a better thirst-quencher than any of the colored fluids on the market, which usually generate greater thirst. It is very important to maintain proper electrolyte balance by eating small quantities of nutritional foods throughout the day, even if you feel you don't have an appetite.

### Changeable Weather

The desert is well known for sudden changes in the weather. The temperature can change 50 degrees in less than an hour. Prepare yourself with extra food and clothing, rain/wind gear, and a flashlight. When leaving on a trip, let someone know your exact route, especially if traveling solo, and your estimated time of return; don't forget to let them know when you actually get back. Register your route at the closest park office, especially for longer hikes that involve cross-country travel.

*Descending Corkscrew Peak with Death Valley Buttes framed perfectly amidst the vast backdrop of Death Valley (hike 26).*

## Hypothermia/Hyperthermia

Abrupt chilling is as much a danger in the desert as heatstroke. Storms and/or nightfall can cause desert temperatures to plunge. Wear layers of clothes, adding or subtracting depending on conditions, to avoid overheating or chilling. At the other extreme you need to protect yourself from sun and wind with proper clothing. The broad-brimmed hat is mandatory equipment for the desert traveler. Even in the cool days of winter, a delightful time in the desert, the sun's rays are intense.

## Vegetation

You quickly will learn not to come in contact with certain desert vegetation. Catclaw, Spanish bayonet, and cacti are just a few of the botanical hazards that will get your attention if you become complacent. Carry tweezers to extract cactus spines. Wear long pants if traveling off-trail or in a brushy area.

## Rattlesnakes, Scorpions, Tarantulas

These desert "creepy crawlies" are easily terrified by unexpected human visitors, and they react predictably to being frightened. Do not sit or put your hands in dark places you can't see, especially during the warmer "snake season" months. In the event of a snakebite, seek medical assistance as quickly as possible. Keep tents zipped and always shake out boots, packs, and clothes before putting them on.

## Mountain Lions

The California desert is mountain-lion country. Avoid hiking at night, when lions are often hunting. Instruct your children on appropriate behavior when confronted with a lion. Do not run. Keep children in sight while hiking; stay close to them in areas where lions might hide.

## Mine Hazards

Death Valley contains many deserted mines. All of them should be considered hazardous. Stay away from all mines and mine structures. All mines are closed to access, whether gated or not. Keep an eye on young or adventuresome members of your group.

## Hantavirus

In addition to the mines, there are often deserted buildings around the mine sites. Hantavirus is a deadly disease carried by deer mice in the Southwest. Any enclosed area increases the chances of breathing the airborne particles that carry this life-threatening virus. As a precaution, do not enter deserted buildings.

## Flash Floods

Desert washes and canyons can become traps for unwary visitors when rainstorms hit the desert. Keep a watchful eye on the sky. Never camp in flash-flood areas. Check with the Furnace Creek Visitor Center (760-786-3200) on regional weather conditions before embarking on your backcountry expedition. A storm anywhere upstream in a drainage can result in a sudden torrent in a lower canyon. Do not cross a flooded wash. Both the depth and the current can be deceiving; wait for the flood to recede, which usually does not take long.

## Lightning

Be aware of lightning, especially during summer storms. Stay off ridges and peaks. Shallow overhangs and gullies should also be avoided because electrical current often moves at ground level near a lightning strike.

## Unstable Rocky Slopes

Desert canyons and mountainsides often consist of crumbly or fragmented rock. Mountain sheep are better adapted to this terrain than us bipeds. Use caution when climbing; the downward journey is usually the more hazardous. Smooth rock faces such as slick pour-offs are equally dangerous, especially when you've got sand on the soles of your boots. On those rare occasions when they are wet, the rocks are slicker than ice.

## Giardia

Any surface water is apt to contain *Giardia lamblia*, a microorganism that causes severe diarrhea. Boil water for at least 5 minutes or use a filter system. Iodine drops are not effective in killing this pesky parasite.

## Leave No Trace Desert Etiquette

The desert environment is fragile; damage lasts for decades—even centuries. Desert courtesy requires us to leave no evidence that we were ever there. This ethic means no graffiti or defoliation at one end of the spectrum, and no unnecessary footprints on delicate vegetation on the other. Here are some general guidelines for desert wilderness behavior:

**Avoid making new trails.** If hiking cross-country, stay on one set of footprints when traveling in a group. Try to make your route invisible. Desert vegetation grows very slowly. Its destruction leads to wind and water erosion and irreparable harm to the desert.

**Keep noise down.** Desert wilderness means quiet and solitude, for the animal life as well as human visitors.

**Leave your pets at home.** In the national park, dogs must be on a 6-foot leash at all times and are not permitted in the backcountry. Not a fun place for your dog. Share other experiences with your best friend, not with the desert.

**Pack it in/pack it out.** This is more true in the desert than anywhere else. Desert winds spread debris, and desert air preserves it. Always carry a trash bag, both for your trash and for any that you encounter. If you must smoke, pick up your butts and bag them. Bag and carry out toilet paper (it doesn't deteriorate in the desert) and feminine hygiene products.

**Never camp near water.** Most desert animals are nocturnal, and most, like the bighorn sheep, are exceptionally shy. The presence of humans is very disturbing, so camping near their water source means they will go without water. Camp in already-used sites if possible to reduce further damage. If none is available, camp on ground that is already bare. And use a camp stove. Ground fires are forbidden; gathering wood is also not permitted.

**Leave your campsite as you found it.** Better yet, improve it by picking up litter, cleaning out fire rings, or scattering ashes of any inconsiderate predecessors. Remember that artifacts fifty years old or older are protected by federal law and must not be moved or removed.

**Treat human waste properly.** Bury human waste 4 inches deep and at least 200 feet from water and trails. Pack out toilet paper and feminine hygiene products; they do not decompose in the arid desert. Do not burn toilet paper; many wildfires have been started this way.

**Respect wildlife.** Living in the desert is hard enough without being harassed by human intruders. Remember this is the only home these animals have. They treasure their privacy. Be respectful and use binoculars for long-distance viewing. Especially important: Do not molest the rare desert water sources by playing or bathing in them.

Beyond these guidelines, refer to the regulations of Death Valley National Park for specific rules governing backcountry usage. Another great source of information is the Leave No Trace website, LNT.org. Enjoy the beauty and solitude of the desert, and leave it for others to enjoy.

# How to Use This Guide

This guide is the sourcebook for those who wish to experience on foot the very best hikes and backcountry trips Death Valley National Park has to offer. Hikers are given many choices from which they can pick and choose, depending on their wishes and abilities. There is no better place in which to actually see the raw, exposed forces of land-shaping geology at work. Those interested in history and paleoarchaeology will have a field day. This book is designed to enhance the enjoyment of all who wish to sample the richness of Death Valley National Park on their own terms. Travel is best done on foot, with distance and destination being far less important than the experience of getting there.

The maps in this book that depict a detailed close-up of an area use elevation tints, called hypsometry, to portray relief. Each gray tone represents a range of equal elevation, as shown in the scale key with the map. These maps will give you a good idea of elevation gain and loss. The darker tones are lower elevations and the lighter grays are higher elevations. The lighter the tone, the higher the elevation. Narrow bands of different gray tones spaced closely together indicate steep terrain, whereas wider bands indicate areas of more gradual slope.

Maps that show larger geographic areas use shaded, or shadow, relief. Shadow relief does not represent elevation; it demonstrates slope or relative steepness. This gives an almost 3-D perspective of the physiography of a region and will help you see where ranges and valleys are.

Begin by referring to the hike locator overview map on page vi, along with the "Hikes at a Glance" matrix for a quick overview of all the hikes presented for the park. After making your selections, turn to the specific hike descriptions for added detail. Each hike is numbered and named and begins with a general description. In many cases the name of the hike is unofficial; you won't find it on any of the listed maps. For example, "Black Point Canyon" is next to the named Black Point, hence the name.

The overview briefly describes the type of hike and highlights the destination and key features.

The "start" is the approximate road distance from a nearby settlement or park visitor center to the trailhead. The idea is to give you a mental picture of where the hike is in relation to your prospective travels.

Hike "distance" is given in total miles for the described route. The mileage is in one direction for a loop, in which you return to the place where you started without retracing your steps, or for a one-way hike, in which you begin at one trailhead and end at another, requiring two vehicles or another driver to pick you up or deposit you at either end. Round-trip mileage is provided for an out-and-back hike, in which you return to the trailhead the same way you came. A lollipop loop combines a stretch of out-and-back with a loop at one end. Mileages were calculated in the field and double-checked as accurately as possible with a GPS and the most detailed topographic maps.

"Hiking time" provides a best guess as to how long it will take the average hiker to complete the route. Always add more time for further exploration or for contemplation.

The "difficulty" rating is necessarily subjective, but it is based on the authors' extensive backcountry experience with folks of all ages and abilities. Easy hikes present no difficulty to hikers of all abilities. Moderate hikes are challenging to inexperienced hikers and might tax even experienced hikers. Strenuous hikes are extremely difficult and challenging, even for the most-seasoned hikers. Distance, elevation gain and loss, trail condition, and terrain were considered in assigning the difficulty rating. There are, of course, many variables. The easiest hike can be sheer torture if you run out of water in extreme heat—a definite no-no.

"Trail surfaces" are evaluated based on well-defined trail standards. Dirt trails have no obstructions and are easy to follow. Rocky trails may be partially blocked by slides, rocks, or debris but are generally obvious and easy to find. Primitive trails are faint, rough, and rocky and may have disappeared completely in places. In the desert some of the best hiking takes place on old four-wheel-drive mining roads that are now closed to vehicular use because of wilderness designation or to protect key values such as wildlife watering holes. Many of the desert hikes are off-trail in washes, canyons, ridges, and fans. "User trails" may form a segment of the route. A user trail is simply an informal, unconstructed path created solely by the passage of hikers.

The "best season" is based largely on the moderate-temperature months for the particular hike and is greatly influenced by elevation. Additional consideration is given to seasonal road access at higher altitudes. The range of months given is not necessarily the best time for wildflowers, which is highly localized and dependent on elevation and rainfall. Nor is it necessarily the best time to view wildlife, which may be near water sources during the driest and hottest summer months.

The maps listed are the best available for route-finding and land navigation: the relevant 7.5-minute topographic map (1:24,000 scale or 2.6 inches = 1 mile) with a 40-foot contour interval. These U.S. Geological Survey maps can usually be purchased at park visitor centers or online directly from the USGS. See appendix C for a listing of other useful smaller-scale maps.

For more information on the hikes in this book, the best available "trail contact" is the Furnace Creek Visitor Center. See appendix D for a complete listing of all agency addresses and phone numbers.

"Finding the trailhead" includes detailed, up-to-date driving instructions to the trailhead or jumping-off point for each hike. For most hikes there is no formal trailhead but rather a starting point where you can park. To follow these instructions, start with the beginning reference point, which might be the park visitor center, a nearby town, or an important road junction. Pay close attention to mileage and landmark instructions. Mileages from the park's visitors map or the Trails Illustrated map were

*The remains of an old talc mine will add an interesting touch of history to your exploration of the Ibex Sand Dunes (hike 1).*

used when available, but in many instances we had to rely on our car odometer, which may vary slightly from other car odometers.

The text following the driving directions is a narrative of the actual route with general directions and key features noted. In some cases interpretation of the natural and cultural history of the hike and its surroundings is included. The idea is to provide accurate route-finding instructions with enough supporting information to enhance your enjoyment of the hike without diminishing your sense of discovery—a fine line indeed. Some of these descriptions are augmented with photographs that preview a representative segment of the hike.

The trail itinerary, "Miles and Directions," provides detailed mile-by-mile instructions while noting landmarks, trail junctions, canyon entrances, dry falls, peaks, and historic sites along the way.

And last, please don't allow our value-laden list of "favorite hikes" (appendix A) to discourage you from completing any of the other hikes. They're all worth doing!

# Death Valley National Park Hikes at a Glance

| Hike and Hike Number | Distance-miles | Difficulty* | Features |
|---|---|---|---|
| Aguereberry Point and | 0.4/1.6 | E/M | vista, mine site |
| Eureka Mine (50) | 1.0 | E | |
| Amargosa Overlook (21) | 7.2 | M | vista, open desert, mine site |
| Artist's Dips (15) | 4.5 | M | canyon, geology |
| Ashford Canyon/Mine (6) | 3.0 | M | mine site |
| Badwater (13) | 2.0 | E | salt flats |
| Black Point Canyon (46) | 5.6 | M | canyon |
| Corkscrew Peak (26) | 8.0 | S | vista |
| Dante's View (12) | 1.0 | E | vista |
| Darwin Falls (49) | 2.0 | E | stream, waterfall |
| Death Valley Buttes (25) | 3.6 | S | vista |
| Desolation Canyon (16) | 4.2 | M | canyon/vista |
| Eureka Dunes (35) | 3.0 | M | sand dunes |
| Fall Canyon (30) | 16.0 | S | dry fall, canyon |
| Foundry Canyon (9) | 5.0 | S | canyon, geology |
| Golden Canyon/ | | | |
| Gower Gulch Loop (17) | 6.5 | M | scenery, geology |
| Grandstand (38) | 1.0 | E | geology, open desert |
| Grotto Canyon (43) | 4.0 | E | canyon |
| Harmony Borax Works (41) | 1.0 | E | historic site, salt flats (option) |
| Hummingbird Spring (53) | 3.0 | M | historic site, vista |
| Hungry Bill's Ranch/ | | | |
| Johnson Canyon (57) | 3.8 | S | historic site, vista |
| Ibex Sand Dunes (1) | 3.0/5.0 | E/M | sand dunes; mine site |
| Kaleidoscope Canyon (4) | 8.0 | S | canyon; geology |
| Keane Wonder Mine (22) | 4.0 | S | mill and mine site |
| Keane Wonder Spring (23) | 2.0 | E | spring, mine site |
| Lake Hill (48) | 3.2 | M | vista, geology |
| Little Bridge Canyon (42) | 7.0 | S | canyon |
| Lostman Spring (27) | 8.6 | M | canyon, geology |
| Marble Canyon (45) | 9.6 | M | canyon, archaeology |
| Mesquite Flat Sand Dunes (39) | 2.0–4.0 | E | sand dunes |
| Monarch Canyon/Mine (24) | 3.0 | E | dry fall, mill site |
| Moonlight Bridge Canyon (33) | 8.2 | M | canyon, geology |
| Mosaic Canyon (44) | 3.6 | M | canyon, geology |
| Mummy (19) | 1.8 | E | canyon, geology |
| Natural Bridge (14) | 2.0 | E | geology, canyon |
| Nemo Canyon (51) | 3.6 | M | canyon |
| Palmer Canyon (31) | 9.6 | S | canyon, geology |
| Panamint Dunes (47) | 9.0 | M | sand dunes |
| Pyramid Canyon (18) | 4.0 | M | canyon, geology |

| Hike and Hike Number | Distance-miles | Difficulty* | Features |
|---|---|---|---|
| Red Wall Canyon (32) | 7.0 | M | canyon |
| Room Canyon (8) | 3.6 | E | canyon, geology |
| Salt Creek Interpretive Trail and Beyond (40) | 0.5/4.2 | E/M | nature trail, vista |
| Saratoga Spring (2) | 1.0/0.8 | E | wetlands, pupfish, historic site |
| Scotty's Canyon (7) | 7.6 | S | canyon, spring |
| Shoreline Butte (5) | 7.0 | S | vista, geology |
| Sidewinder Canyon (10) | 4.4 | M | slot canyons |
| South Fork Hanaupah Canyon (55) | 6.0 | M | mine site, scenery |
| Surprise Canyon to Panamint City (56) | 13.0 | S | stream, canyon, mine/townsite |
| Telescope Peak (54) | 14.0 | S | vista, apex of Death Valley |
| Thimble Peak (28) | 4.0 | S | vista, geology |
| Through-Granite Canyons Loop (3) | 15.0 | S | remoteness, scenery |
| Titus Canyon Narrows (29) | 4.2 | E | canyon, geology |
| Ubehebe/Little Hebe Craters (34) | 1.5 | E | volcanic craters |
| Ubehebe Lead Mine/ Corridor Canyon (36) | 6.0 | M | mine site/canyon |
| Ubehebe Peak (37) | 6.2 | S | vista |
| Upper Hole-in-the-Wall (20) | 11.0 | S | canyon, geology |
| Wildrose Peak (52) | 8.4 | S | vista |
| Willow Canyon (11) | 5.0 | M | canyon |

*E=easy, M=moderate, S=strenuous

# Map Legend

## Transportation

| | |
|---|---|
| =395= | US Highway |
| =190= | State Highway |
| ——— | Local Road |
| ===: | Unpaved Road |

## Trails

| | |
|---|---|
| ------- | Featured Trail |
| ------ | Trail |
| .......... | Off-trail Hike |

## Water Features

| | |
|---|---|
| ⬭ | Body of Water |
| 〰 | River/Creek |
| ⌇ | Intermittent Stream |
| ≋ | Dry Fall/Waterfall |
| ⟳ | Spring |

## Land Management

| | |
|---|---|
| — - — - | State Line |
| — · — | Park Boundary |

## Symbols

| | |
|---|---|
| ✕ | Airport |
| ‖‖‖‖‖ | Boardwalk/Steps |
| ⌣ | Bridge |
| ▲ | Campground |
| ⊓⊓⊓ | Cliff |
| × | Elevation |
| ✕ | Mine |
| ▲ | Mountain/Peak |
| 🅿 | Parking |
| ⟩⟨ | Pass |
| 🛆 | Picnic Area |
| ■ | Point of Interest/Structure |
| 🛈 | Ranger Station |
| 🚻 | Restroom |
| ⋰ | Sand Dunes |
| ○ | Town |
| ❶ | Trailhead |
| 🔍 | Viewpoint/Overlook |
| ❓ | Visitor Center |
| 🌲 | Woodland |

# Southern Death Valley

## 1 Ibex Sand Dunes

These remote sand dunes in a spectacular wilderness setting rise more than 150 feet and are trapped against rugged hills in the extreme southeastern corner of the park. From a distance the dunes appear taller than they are, making them even more impressive. Both the drive and the approach are relatively easy. The dunes are a picturesque and worthy destination in themselves, with added bonuses of expansive views and interesting mining ruins. Their isolation, hidden from paved roads by stark desert mountains, is a key attribute. This all adds up to an enjoyable romp in a giant sandbox.

**Start:** About 72 miles south of Furnace Creek or 40 miles north of Baker

**Distance:** 3.0-mile out and back to the mine ruins (up to 5.0 miles round-trip with side hikes in the dunes)

**Hiking time:** 2 to 4 hours, depending on how much time is spent wandering in the dunes

**Difficulty:** Easy for an out and back to the mine ruins; moderate if climbing the dunes due to steep, loose sand

**Trail surface:** Firm footing on a closed two-track, soft sand in places

**Best season:** November to April

**Fees and permits:** National park entrance fee

**Maps:** NPS Death Valley Visitors Map; Trails Illustrated Death Valley National Park Map; USGS Old Ibex Pass-CA and Saddle Peak Hills-CA

**Trail contact:** Furnace Creek Visitor Center; (760) 786-3200; www.nps.gov/deva

**Special considerations:** On rare occasions a recent rainstorm may cause the Amargosa River to flood portions of the Saratoga Spring Road, rendering it impassable. Dune boarding is destructive and illegal under both park service and wilderness regulations. Drinking water is unavailable, so carry ample water when hiking. Strong winds may reduce visibility with blowing sand. Do not attempt this hike during the heat of the summer or anytime when temperatures exceed 100°F.

**Finding the trailhead:** From Baker on I-15 drive 29.7 miles north on CA 127 to the Saratoga Spring Road, which is marked by the Harry Wade Monument. Turn left (west) on the narrow, sandy gravel road (2WD high-clearance vehicle recommended) and drive 5.3 miles to a dirt road signed "Saratoga Springs 4.4 miles." Turn right (north) and drive 2.6 miles, passing the turnoff to Saratoga Spring. Continue straight (right) on the main road for another 0.9 mile and park next to a large wooden sign that reads "Wilderness Restoration—foot and horse traffic only," marking a vehicular closure of an old road leading to mining ruins east of the dunes. GPS: N35 41.699' / W116 23.602'

If approaching from the Badwater Road (CA 178), take the slow gravel Harry Wade Road 25.7 miles to the signed Saratoga Spring Road.

From Shoshone drive 28.2 miles south on CA 127 to Saratoga Spring Road, marked by the Harry Wade Monument. Turn right (west) and follow the above directions.

# The Hike

From the parking area the dunes rise directly to the east about 1 mile away. You can head straight cross-country on level, open terrain to the low point between the two distinct complexes of sand dunes. Or walk slightly to the left of the wooden sign to pick up the closed two-track that leads to the same gap between the dunes and from there another 0.5 mile to the interesting ruins of a 1950s talc mine. The latter choice is slightly longer. Both routes offer solid footing across a hard-packed desert floor dotted with creosote bushes.

The dunes stretch more than 2 miles on a north–south orientation on the sunset side of the rugged Saddle Peak Hills. At roughly 1,300 acres they are the smallest dunes by area in the park. Their entrapment against high mountains fulfills one of the three conditions for dunes; the others are sand, of which there is an endless supply from nearby washes and canyons, and wind—also endless, especially during spring.

*The Saddle Peak Hills provide a dramatic backdrop to the remote Ibex Sand Dunes.*

# Ibex Sand Dunes

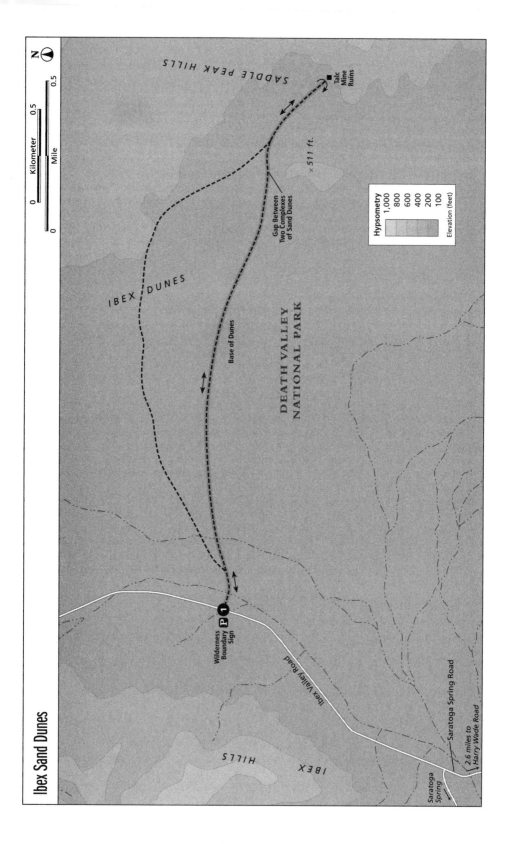

Like all dunes they are ever shifting. At the time of our visit, we climbed what was then the highest dune in the southern complex. Topping out at above 500 feet elevation, we looked down at the talc mine ruins 150 feet below. There are several types of dunes based on their shape. From this vantage point it appeared that most of the Ibex Dunes are crescent-shaped Barchan dunes with arms that extend downwind.

It wasn't easy to reach this point. A narrow ridge with overstepped sides leads to the summit of each dune. The sides are often too steep to negotiate, leaving only the knife ridge for hiking, which is composed of soft sand. The payoff includes sweeping vistas of Death Valley, desert ranges to infinity, and a great feeling of wild, open space.

While traversing the dunes, especially around the edges, be on the lookout for the Mojave fringe-toed lizard. Perhaps they dine on black beetles, of which you'll see lots. You'll also see wind ripples in the sand that resemble ocean waves.

From the dune ridges you can easily drop down to the abandoned talc mill. Like a ghost it hugs the rocky interface between the mountains and the east side of the dunes. The ruins include several very deep and dangerous adits dug into the hillside next to the wooden mill—give them a wide berth. Park regulations, as well as common sense, require that you stay out of these hellacious holes.

For the return you can follow the old mining road that leads north and then west for about 1.5 miles to the parking area. Notice how the dunes are reclaiming and gradually erasing the two-track where it crosses the gap between the north and south dunes. Nature will eventually prevail, but the old talc mill may stand for centuries given the slow rate of decay in the dry desert air.

## Miles and Directions

**0.0** Start at the trailhead off Ibex Valley Road.

**1.0** Reach the gap between the north and south dunes.

**1.5** Arrive at the talc mill mine ruins. Explore, but avoid the deep adits. For a different return route, follow the old mining road that leads north and then west.

**3.0** Arrive back at the trailhead.

*Option:* If you want a longer sandy slog, hike up into the northern complex, which contains larger and slightly higher dunes. From there you'll see your vehicle alongside the Ibex Valley Road. From any point you can return by hiking cross-country 1 to 2 miles west to southwest to the parking area.

# 2 Saratoga Spring

A short stroll takes you to a desert oasis. Saratoga Spring is a spectacular surprise in the arid landscape of southern Death Valley. The spring is a mecca for many birds, including waterfowl, and bird-watchers. There are also a couple of old stone building ruins for those interested in mining history.

**Start:** About 72 miles south of Furnace Creek or 40 miles north of Baker
**Distance:** 1.0-mile loop (or 0.8 mile out and back)
**Hiking time:** 1 to 2 hours, depending on how much you wander along the ponds
**Difficulty:** Easy
**Trail surface:** Old gravel two-track, sand
**Best season:** November to April
**Fees and permits:** National park entrance fee
**Maps:** NPS Death Valley Visitors Map; Trails Illustrated Death Valley National Park Map; USGS Old Ibex Pass-CA

**Trail contact:** Furnace Creek Visitor Center; (760) 786-3200; www.nps.gov/deva
**Other:** There are no trailhead facilities, but there is a wide parking area at the end of the road. This is a day-use only area; no camping is allowed.
**Special considerations:** On rare occasions a recent rainstorm may cause the Amargosa River to flood portions of the Saratoga Spring Road, rendering it impassable. The road to the spring is signed for high-clearance vehicles, but with care a passenger car can make it. If wet, however, the sticky alkaline mud will make the final 1.3-mile track impassable.

**Finding the trailhead:** From Baker on I-15 drive 29.7 miles north on CA 127 to the Saratoga Spring Road, which is marked by the Harry Wade Monument. Turn left (west) on the narrow sandy gravel road (2WD high-clearance vehicle recommended but not required) and drive 5.3 miles to a dirt road signed "Saratoga Springs 4.4 miles." Turn right (north) and drive 2.6 miles to the left turn at the sign for Saratoga Spring. Drive 1.3 miles to the parking area. GPS: N35 40.840' / W116 25.261'

If approaching from the Badwater Road (CA 178), take the slow gravel Harry Wade Road 25.7 miles south to the signed Saratoga Spring Road.

From Shoshone drive south on CA 127 for 28.2 miles to Saratoga Spring Road, marked by the Harry Wade Monument. Turn right (west) and follow the above directions.

## The Hike

At the parking area a sign announces the road is closed to vehicles. The old gravel two-track developed by miners many decades ago is our trail for the first third of the hike. At the top of the rise northwest of the parking area, there is an awesome view of the springs, a series of ponds surrounded by about 15 acres of lush grasses and reeds. The soft green landscape is quite a contrast with the rocky Ibex Hills. This desert wetland creates an inviting habitat for waterfowl and birds, as well as thirsty coyotes and desert bighorn sheep.

*The lush wetlands of Saratoga Spring provide a surprising contrast to the surrounding vast desert.*

Continuing along the path, drop from the rise. The ruins of a small rock building are on the right. These walls are all that's left of what may have been a saloon, or perhaps a store dating from the 1890s development of the talc mine that has left a white scar on the hillside to the north of the riparian area. There is a second similar ruin farther along on the right. In the 1930s Saratoga Spring was briefly the site of a rustic health resort and a water bottling program. Both of these enterprises faded away with gas rationing during World War II.

At 0.2 mile the old roadbed continues north. Here, leave the track and drop toward the pond on your left. Exploring the water's edge is an adventure you don't expect in the desert. If you're stealthy you can spot the shy Saratoga pupfish darting in the shallows. These tiny critters, Cyprinodon nevadensis nevadensis, are a different subspecies from the four other pupfish species elsewhere in the park. In their isolated pools they are on the brink of extinction. This east-side wetland relies on water from the ancient aquifer underlying the Black Range, which is an ever-diminishing resource. Please do not disturb the fish or their sensitive habitat. Stay out of the water.

The muddy shore of the ponds provides fascinating evidence of the many creatures who either visit or live here, leaving their footprints in the soggy, sandy soil.

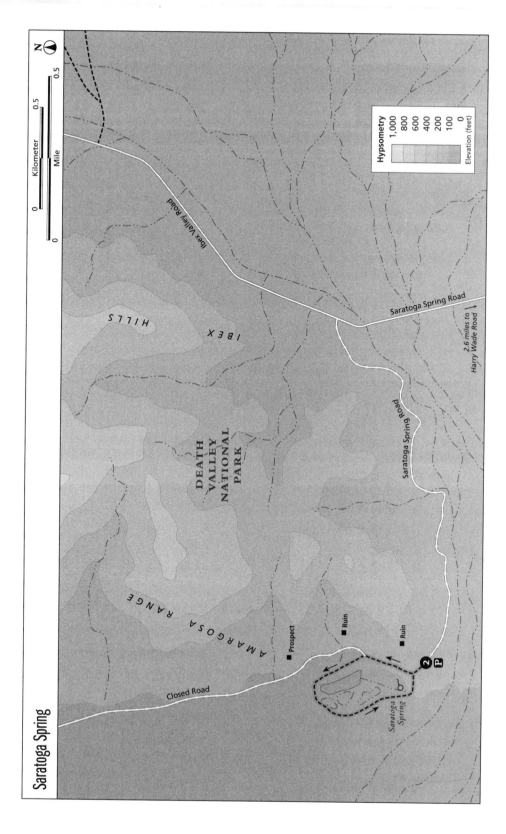

*The remains of this old stone structure add a touch of mining history when visiting Saratoga Spring.*

Instead of the usual silence of the desert, here the sounds of frogs and birds create a lively melody.

The small sandy dunes that surround the wetland create a natural route to travel around the ponds. A user trail takes you back to the main trail at the first overlook. This loop route is slightly longer than the out-and-back route.

Or, if you simply retrace your steps on your way back to the parking area, you might take a side trip to check out the mine adit that you can see from the ponds, up behind the second ruin. Use caution, always, near mines. It was arduous work to dig a mine in these rocky hills. The slag heap that spills down the hillside is evidence of significant excavation. The miners didn't get rich here, but they sure had a lovely view.

After your explorations, return to the parking area by the same route.

## Miles and Directions

**0.0** Start at the parking lot trailhead. After about 50 yards northwest along the gravel two-track, reach the top of a rise.

**0.2** Leave the roadbed and drop toward the pond to the west.

**0.4** Arrive at the northern edge of the pond complex. Continue around the ponds on a user trail. (Option: Retrace your steps to the trailhead for an 0.8-mile hike.)

**1.0** Arrive back at the trailhead.

# 3 Through-Granite Canyons Loop

A long, challenging canyon loop in the wild, lightly visited Owlshead Mountains; these canyons take you to a remote desert range in the southern end of the park.

**Start:** About 54 miles south of Furnace Creek
**Distance:** 15-mile lollipop
**Hiking time:** 8 to 10 hours
**Difficulty:** Strenuous due to distance
**Trail surface:** Off-trail sandy washes, gravelly fans, and canyons with short rocky sections
**Best season:** November through March

**Fees and permits:** National park entrance fee
**Maps:** NPS Death Valley Visitors Map; Trails Illustrated Death Valley National Park Map; USGS Confidence Hills East-CA and Confidence Hills West-CA
**Trail contact:** Furnace Creek Visitor Center; (760) 786-3200; www.nps.gov/deva

**Finding the trailhead:** From Ashford Junction on Badwater Road (CA 178), 26 miles southwest of Shoshone and 48 miles south of Furnace Creek, drive south on the wide gravel Harry Wade Road. After about 5.9 slow miles, look for a wide parking spot alongside the bermed roadway, which will be next to Confidence Wash and about 1 mile before the Confidence Mill site. Driving Harry Wade Road from the south is not recommended because it requires four-wheel drive and is impassable during flooding. GPS: N35 50.754' / W116 34.320'

## The Hike

Upon reaching the jumping-off point for this lengthy desert trek, you'll have driven through a section of Death Valley known as "the Narrows." The brown Confidence Hills to the immediate west are an eroded scarp of the southern Death Valley fault. It was once believed that the adventurous Harry Wade family used the road as an escape route from Death Valley in 1850.

From your parking spot, you can see the prominent rounded hill beyond the Confidence Hills that forms the southern gateway to Through Canyon. A higher range of mountains rises beyond. Begin by hiking southwesterly toward the trailing southern edge of the Confidence Hills. Soon you'll cross the broad, gravelly creosote plain of the normally dry Amargosa River. Skirt around the hills to the lower wash of Granite Canyon. Hike up the wide, high-walled wash to the forks of the wash at about 2 miles. Cross the wash and continue to hike southwesterly toward Through Canyon, reaching the mouth at about 4.3 miles. To the immediate south is the prominent rounded hill that you could see from the trailhead. Look back, to the east, for varied views of fans, buttes, and the jagged teeth of volcanic peaks.

Hillsides bordering the wash are a jumble of volcanic rock with granitic bedrock. In the spring you might see flowering buttercups and the tiny blue flowers of chia along with desert holly, smoke trees, creosote, and saltbush, to name only a few. You'll follow the trails of feral burros for the next couple of miles, with color-banded shades of red, white, and brown rock overhead. The valley splits about 2.3 miles above the

*Looking down the upper reaches of Through Canyon.*

mouth; keep to the right. Another mile brings you to a broad upper basin. The main wash curves left to the horizon. Angle to the right (north) for the crossover to Granite Canyon. Continue right as the valley steepens, reaching a saddle between the two canyons at 7.8 miles.

The route follows a short side canyon down to the floor of Granite Canyon, guarded by great spires and rock columns. From here turn left for a short 0.5-mile round-trip exploration of the narrow upper reaches of Granite Canyon. You'll quickly come to an 8-foot dry fall that can be readily climbed. But the next chokestone, only 50 yards beyond, is more difficult. This is a good turnaround point for the hike back down Granite Canyon. Granite Canyon is steeper and more bouldery than Through Canyon but can be easily negotiated on a mostly sandy wash. After another mile the canyon widens to a valley. Low granite walls on the left side lead up to a colorful red chasm. Overall, Granite is a wonderful contrast to Through Canyon, especially in the upper end, where moderate bouldering and narrow canyons are

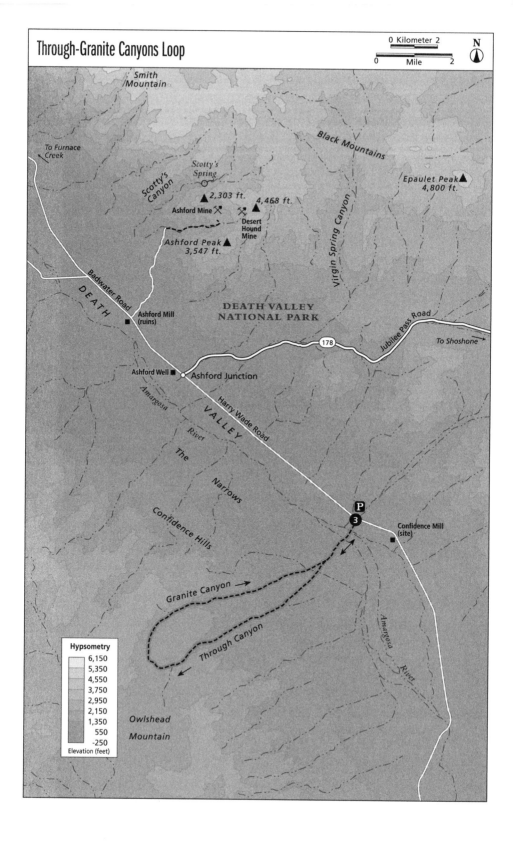

# Through-Granite Canyons Loop

0 Kilometer 2

0 Mile 2

**N**

Smith Mountain

To Furnace Creek

Black Mountains

Scotty's Canyon

Scotty's Spring

▲ 2,303 ft.

Ashford Mine ⚒

⚒ 4,468 ft. ▲

Desert Hound Mine

Epaulet Peak ▲ 4,800 ft.

Virgin Spring Canyon

Ashford Peak ▲ 3,547 ft.

Badwater Road

D E A T H

Ashford Mill (ruins) ■

DEATH VALLEY NATIONAL PARK

Jubilee Pass Road

178

To Shoshone

Ashford Well ■

○ Ashford Junction

Amargosa River

Harry Wade Road

V A L L E Y

The Narrows

Confidence Hills

**P**

**3**

Confidence Mill (site) ■

Amargosa River

Granite Canyon →

Through Canyon

**Hypsometry**

| | |
|---|---|
| | 6,150 |
| | 5,350 |
| | 4,550 |
| | 3,750 |
| | 2,950 |
| | 2,150 |
| | 1,350 |
| | 550 |
| | -250 |

Elevation (feet)

Owlshead Mountain

true delights. Along the way you'll see broken quartz monzonite that is unlike most other places in the park.

After exiting the wide mouth of Granite Canyon at 11 miles, continue down the wash toward the southern edge of the Confidence Hills. When you reach the base of these brown hills in the serpentine steep-walled wash, you'll intersect the stem of this "lollipop" loop. Roughly retrace the first 2 miles of the route in a northeasterly direction back to Confidence Wash, thereby completing this adventuresome 15-mile exploration.

## Miles and Directions

**0.0** Start at the parking area at Confidence Wash on Harry Wade Road. Head southwest.

**2.0** Arrive at the southern edge of the Confidence Hills.

**4.3** Arrive at the mouth of Through Canyon.

**7.4** Angle right (north) to the Granite-Through Canyon divide.

**7.8** Arrive at the divide between the Granite and Through Canyons. Continue down to the floor of Granite Canyon.

**11.0** Arrive at the mouth of Granite Canyon.

**13.0** Arrive again at the southern edge of the Confidence Hills and the close of the loop. Retrace your steps to the start.

**15.0** Arrive back at the parking area at Confidence Wash on Harry Wade Road.

# 4 Kaleidoscope Canyon

Unofficially named, but locally known as Kaleidoscope Canyon, this is one of Death Valley's most beautiful treasures. The canyon is literally a giant natural kaleidoscope with ever changing colorful patterns glowing with ever changing light reflecting off canyon walls and formations. As such, Kaleidoscope is a photographer's and explorer's paradise.

**Start:** About 50 miles south of Furnace Creek
**Distance:** 8.0 miles out and back with 1,850 feet elevation gain/loss
**Hiking time:** 5 to 7 hours
**Difficulty:** Strenuous due to length and elevation gain/loss
**Trail surface:** Firm sandy wash interspersed with gravel and desert pavement, short stretches of bedrock and rock scrambles
**Best season:** October to April
**Fees and permits:** National park entrance fee
**Maps:** NPS Death Valley Visitors Map; Trails Illustrated Death Valley National Park Map; USGS Epaulet Peak-CA

**Trail contact:** Furnace Creek Visitor Center; (760) 786-3200; www.nps.gov/deva
**Other:** For a photographic preview of Kaleidoscope Canyon, check out various blogs on the Internet before your hike.
**Special considerations:** There is no formal parking area or facilities. Nor will you find Kaleidoscope Canyon on a USGS or National Park Service map. There are no signs marking the way. The canyon is in a lightly visited region of the park, so self-reliance and adequate preparation are important. The hike can be done in a half day but can easily be extended to a full-day outing, which you'll want to do if you have time. Carry ample water.

**Finding the trailhead:** Park on a wide spot along the north side of paved Jubilee Pass Road (CA 178) next to milepost 48, which is 48 miles south of Furnace Creek and about 2.5 miles east of Ashford Junction. GPS: N35 54.449' / W116 37.256'

## The Hike

From the parking area cross the wide Jubilee Wash and head straight north across desert pavement toward the left-hand (western) toe of the lower ridge directly in front of you. There is a rounded peak behind the ridge. Upon reaching the toe of the ridge after about 0.5 mile, you'll see a distinctive white-topped hillside far to the north. This white hillside is a key landmark, serving as a beacon, guiding you to the correct Kaleidoscope. Rising above the left side of the canyon, it also marks the approximate turnaround location for the hike.

At this point you've intersected the main wash of the canyon. Follow the wash northward, which for the most part provides good walking. After about 2 miles the side walls close in to form the definite mouth of the canyon. The white-topped hillside is once again visible from the canyon mouth. With the sun to your back you'll be glad that you began hiking during the morning. On the other hand, if you're there in late afternoon you'll likely have better photographic light. The point is that you

*The middle west side of Kaleidoscope Canyon is dominated by huge colorful mounds and pillars.*

can't go wrong whenever you're there, as you'll quickly discover. Turn around every so often for panoramic views to the southwest of Contact Canyon in the Owlshead Mountains.

White rocks litter the canyon floor as it veers sharply to the left, suddenly opening up after a series of tight turns. Within 0.2 mile a small side canyon enters from the left, with the white rock beacon on the right marking the entrance to Kaleidoscope Canyon. The canyon is further marked by a gigantic "canine tooth" formation. Giant fluted rock fins drop to the wide canyon floor on both sides, painted with a profusion of colors, dominated by white. The canyon closes in a bit with a series of 4-foot ledges that are easily climbed.

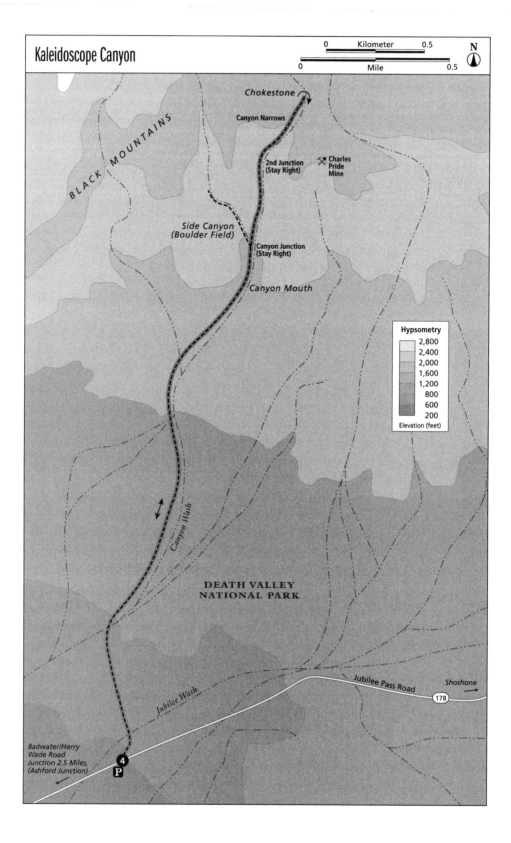

After another 0.25 mile continue climbing steadily up the main canyon to the right. The left side is bound by darker rocks with shades of black, purple, and gray. This is a fascinating wonderland of folded rocks with lines that strike and then dip to form perfect Vs on cliff faces. In turn the faces are adorned with kaleidoscopic brilliance—dazzling splashes of purple, red, black, white, tan, cream, and yellow. These painted rocks would rival any rainbow.

The canyon narrows briefly, followed quickly by a moderate climb of a slanted 15-foot dry fall. After another 0.2 mile a side canyon enters from the left; stay to the right. Once again the canyon opens up and then closes in with the white rock beacon straight ahead. The narrows end quickly at a large chokestone. This wedged rock can be bypassed on the left with some difficulty, but it does mark a good turnaround point for the hike in that you've already traversed the colorful part of the canyon below the narrows.

On the way back down, exercise particular caution in negotiating the sloping dry fall. After all, you're not in a hurry or you wouldn't be exploring Kaleidoscope Canyon in the first place. In particular, by taking your time you'll see shapes, patterns, and colors you missed on the way up. V-shaped strikes and dips reveal phenomenal forces of heat and compression. Suddenly, tilted red rock seems all the more tilted. Note the red spires crowned with darker, more resistant caprock. Hoodoos are encased by weird formations that resemble dollops of Neapolitan ice cream flowing from above.

## Miles and Directions

**0.0** Start at the parking area along Jubilee Wash. Cross the wash and head north.

**0.5** Reach the west side of a low ridge at the entrance to lower Kaleidoscope Canyon Wash.

**2.8** Arrive at the mouth of Kaleidoscope Canyon.

**3.0** Stay right at the junction with a side canyon on the left.

**3.3** Make a moderate climb of a 15-foot dry fall.

**3.5** Arrive at the second canyon junction; stay right.

**3.8** The canyon narrows.

**4.0** Reach the chokestone at the end of the narrows; turn around here and retrace your steps.

**8.0** Arrive back at the parking area.

*Option:* Above the upper narrows lie the shallows, which is where the walls taper away. Up to this point Kaleidoscope has been an amazingly serpentine canyon in a compressed area. If you choose to continue to the north by bypassing the chokestone, you'll find the main canyon blocked by a massive rockslide/boulder field after another 0.1 mile. This obstacle invites further exploration even though you're well past the Kaleidoscope. The rock pile can be easily scrambled, quickly gaining 100-plus feet, to more narrows that reach an unclimbable 20-foot dry fall after 0.3 mile. This 2,100-foot-high turnaround point is about 4.3 miles from the parking area, nearly 2,000 feet below. Carefully pick your way back down the rockslide and chokestone bypass to the floor of the main canyon during your return to the parking area.

# 5  Shoreline Butte

Shoreline Butte, rising from the valley floor at the Narrows, is a solitary 650-foot hill, visible at the south end of Death Valley. From afar the butte is softly rounded, unlike the jagged mountains that stream by on either side. From the summit, the views of the park are panoramic.

**Start:** About 44 miles south of Furnace Creek on Badwater Road, at the Ashford Mill site
**Distance:** 7.0 miles out and back
**Hiking time:** 4 to 5 hours
**Difficulty:** Strenuous due to distance and elevation change
**Trail surface:** Rocky alluvial fan, sandy wash, rocky hillside
**Best season:** October through March
**Fees and permits:** National park entrance fee
**Maps:** NPS Death Valley Visitors Map; Trails Illustrated Death Valley National Park map; USGS Shore Line Butte-CA

**Trail contact:** Furnace Creek Visitor Center; (760) 786-3200; www.nps.gov/deva
**Other:** Trailhead amenities include a spacious parking area, a vault toilet, and picnic tables, as well as the ruins of the mill. The mill was built by optimists who had a substantial amount of concrete to use, but the mill, alas, was never very profitable.
**Special considerations:** The route includes crossing the usually dry Amargosa River, so hikers need to be cognizant of precipitation forecasts in the valley.

**Finding the trailhead:** The trailhead is at the Ashford Mill site, which is between mileposts 43 and 44 on the Badwater Road (CA 178), 43.5 miles south of Furnace Creek, on the west side of the road. GPS: N35 55.135' / W116 40.994'

## The Hike

From the starting point at the parking area, the butte rises to the west. As you will discover, the elusive summit is well behind those foothills you see from the mill site. If you drive toward the butte from the north, take time to stop at the Lake Manley point of interest sign just south of the west-side road junction. The butte from that view has very distinctive wave terraces striping its northern slopes. These are evidence of the rising and falling of the Pleistocene lake that filled Death Valley at the end of the ice age—hence the name of the butte, today so far from a shore. Ironically, the base of the butte is located right on the sea level topo line, so that is another justification for its name in this dry world.

Your cross-country route to the butte goes to the apex of the broad alluvial fan clearly visible from the parking area. Head straight west, dropping from the mill ruins to the river valley. Cross the riverbed. The river is usually only a few isolated puddles (see "Special considerations" for warning). Beyond the river crossing continue west, crossing traces of an old gravel roadbed at you climb up toward the fan.

*A narrow gully on the east side of Shoreline Butte provides an enjoyable descent to the Amargosa River.*

Pick your way up the slope of the fan. If you tire of the plentiful cobbles, you can veer to the right side of the fan where a sandy wash provides more pleasant footing. This can also be your exit route, being easier on your knees, although it's slightly longer.

Nearing the top of the fan, keep the bouldered slope of the butte's foothills on your right (north). The fan narrows to a wash. You'll note that this route is used by wild burros in their wanderings. At 2.5 miles the wash broadens, almost becoming a high hidden valley enjoyed by the burros. Sharp conglomerate walls on the right mark the right-hand ravine that leads toward the summit. This is the first right turn available on the route, so you can't miss it.

Follow this little wash, which grows narrower and steeper until it gets to a ridge. Right below you is a broad gravel area, an ideal resting spot. From here it's easy to wonder which hilltop is actually the summit, 3.5 miles from the mill. Luckily there is a massive cairn visible on the ridge to the southwest, and that's the ridge that leads

*The 650-foot summit of Shoreline Butte offers a commanding view of the Amargosa River Valley and Black Mountains.*

to the summit. Once you're up there the peak is obvious, since a low, less massive cairn marks the spot. Also, there's a peak register under the rocks in a plastic Parmesan cheese bottle. Leave your remarks if you wish.

If you time it right in the spring, you can see flowers galore all along the route, and especially up on the summit ridges, a real *Sound of Music* scene. The view of the surrounding mountains is magnificent. This location at the Narrows is where the Owlshead Mountains and the Black Range curve closer together, and the Confidence Hills rise in the valley to the immediate south. The panorama of Death Valley stretches into the distance. With your Trails Illustrated map you can identify peaks and canyons, even to the Panamint Range to the northwest. It's an eagle's view of the park.

For the descent, return the way you came. Drop to the gravel area and then take the wash downhill. When you emerge at the top of the alluvial fan, the sandy wash is on your left. It is a softer, more benevolent route downward, especially if your knees

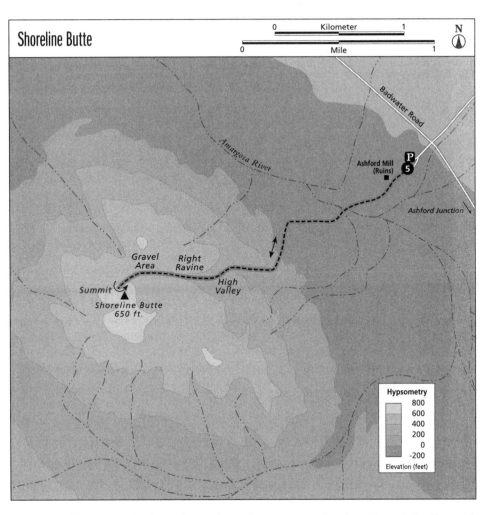

## Shoreline Butte

Ashford Mill
(Ruins)

Badwater Road

Amargosa River

Ashford Junction

Gravel
Area

Right
Ravine

High
Valley

Summit

Shoreline Butte
650 ft.

Hypsometry
800
600
400
200
0
-200
Elevation (feet)

and ankles are tired. Taking the sandy wash puts you at the river about 0.2 mile north of the direct route, so it's slightly longer.

The folks visiting the mill site will want to hear about your trip when you finally climb the slope past the ruins. They probably will be in awe of your strenuous outing.

## Miles and Directions

**0.0** Start at the parking area at the Ashford Mill site. Head southwest.

**0.4** Cross the typically dry Amargosa riverbed.

**2.5** Reach the high valley at the top of the alluvial fan; take the ravine to the right.

**3.2** Reach the gravel area below the summit, a good place for a break.

**3.5** Arrive at the summit, which is marked by a rock cairn. Retrace your steps to the trailhead or, at the fan, take the sandy wash to the north for a slightly longer route back.

**7.0** Arrive back at the parking area.

# 6 Ashford Canyon/Mine

An extensive mine site with several intact buildings lies up a remote and narrow canyon. The rocky mining road has become a hiking trail, leading to the historic early twentieth-century mine site.

**Start:** About 45 miles south of Furnace Creek
**Distance:** 3.0 miles out and back
**Hiking time:** 2 to 3 hours
**Difficulty:** Moderate
**Trail surface:** Rocky old mining road
**Best season:** October through April
**Fees and permits:** National park entrance fee

**Maps:** NPS Death Valley Visitors Map; Trails Illustrated Death Valley National Park Map; USGS Shore Line Butte-CA
**Trail contact:** Furnace Creek Visitor Center; (760) 786-3200; www.nps.gov/deva
**Special considerations:** A high-clearance vehicle is essential for driving the slow, rough road to the trailhead.

**Finding the trailhead:** From CA 127, 1.7 miles north of Shoshone, turn left (west) on CA 178 (East Side Badwater Road/Jubilee Pass Road), which leads to the park boundary. After entering the park, drive 25.1 miles to the signed Ashford Mill Road on the left, 1.9 miles north of Ashford Junction and 26.9 miles south of Badwater. Turn right (east) onto the unsigned Ashford Canyon Road leading northeast directly across from the Ashford Mill site. Follow this high-clearance road for 3 miles to the mouth of Ashford Canyon. Park and hike from here. GPS: N35 57.276' / W116 39.872'

If coming from the north, drive 44.5 miles south of Furnace Creek on Badwater Road to Ashford Canyon Road on the left and follow directions above.

## The Hike

The Ashford (Golden Treasure) Mine was discovered in 1907 and was sold a few years later to supply gold ore to the Ashford Mill. The early years were probably its most productive, since the mine sold for more money than it ultimately yielded. The inefficiency of the mill was at least partly to blame. For more information about the history of mining in Death Valley, visit the Borax Museum (free admission) at Furnace Creek Ranch.

From the mouth of the canyon, the old mining trail climbs steeply up the left side of the deep, narrow Ashford Canyon. Rockslides and erosion are gradually erasing any sign of the trail as nature reclaims the land. But there is still enough evidence of rock construction and built-up roadbeds to make this route fairly easy to follow.

After dropping into the canyon bottom, the road crosses the wash several times. Several steep sections of slanted rock are avoided as the trail pitches right or left. Huge round mine timbers and scattered diggings are found about halfway up. At 1.3 miles the road crosses the wash and contours to the left around the slope, climbs slightly, and then drops to the mining camp.

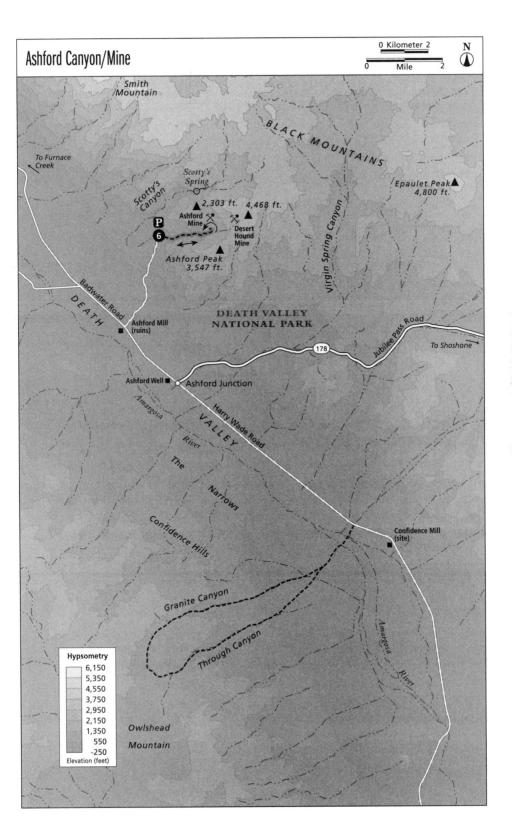

Ashford Canyon/Mine

0 Kilometer 2
0 Mile 2

N

Smith Mountain

BLACK MOUNTAINS

To Furnace Creek

Scotty's Canyon

Scotty's Spring

Epaulet Peak
4,800 ft.

▲ 2,303 ft.     4,468 ft. ▲
Ashford Mine

P
6

Desert Hound Mine

Ashford Peak
3,547 ft.

Virgin Spring Canyon

Badwater Road

DEATH

DEATH VALLEY
NATIONAL PARK

Ashford Mill
(ruins)

178

Jubilee Pass Road

To Shoshone

Ashford Well ■     Ashford Junction

Amargosa

River

VALLEY

Harry Wade Road

The

Narrows

Confidence Hills

Confidence Mill
(site)

Granite Canyon

Amargosa

River

Through Canyon

**Hypsometry**

| |
| --- |
| 6,150 |
| 5,350 |
| 4,550 |
| 3,750 |
| 2,950 |
| 2,150 |
| 1,350 |
| 550 |
| -250 |
| Elevation (feet) |

Owlshead

Mountain

*The Ashford Mine buildings, 1.6 miles up Ashford Canyon, are surrounded by high, rugged peaks.*

The buildings are still somewhat intact, containing some of the furniture and appliances used by the miners. Although they made no effort to clean up their trash, one has to marvel at the incredible determination and optimism the miners must have had to carve such an extensive operation out of such difficult terrain. The miners sure had a view in this southern stretch of the Black Mountains, with Ashford Peak soaring to the south and the rugged canyon below opening to the Owlshead and Panamint Mountains westward. Retrace your route to complete this 3-mile round-trip exploration of some of Death Valley's mining history.

## Miles and Directions

**0.0**  Start at the trailhead at the mouth of Ashford Canyon.

**0.3**  Climb out of the wash (right), bypassing a dry fall/rockslide.

**0.5**  The trail follows the wash up a rough, rocky surface.

**1.3**  The trail crosses the wash and climbs the slope to the left.

**1.5**  Arrive at the Ashford (Golden Treasure) Mine. Return to the trailhead by the same route.

**3.0**  Arrive back at the trailhead.

# 7 Scotty's Canyon

Scotty's is a highly varied canyon—changing from a wide wash to slots to narrows to grottos with small springs guarded by mesquite, alcoves, and sheer cliffs. Moderate rock climbing above the spring allows up-canyon exploration for another 0.5 mile to a rockfall and beyond a short distance to a rock wall. The lack of color in the surrounding brown hillsides is offset by the colorful history of Death Valley Scotty, who once lived in his secluded "Camp Hold-out" in an eroded cave deep in his namesake canyon.

**Start:** About 45 miles south of Furnace Creek

**Distance:** 7.6 miles out and back to rock wall blocking the canyon (6.8 miles out and back to Scotty's Spring)

**Hiking time:** 5 to 7 hours

**Difficulty:** Strenuous due to distance, elevation change, and rock scrambling

**Trail surface:** Variable from a clear singletrack dirt trail to sandy wash to firm gravel canyon floor to solid bedrock

**Best season:** October to April

**Fees and permits:** National park entrance fee

**Maps:** NPS Death Valley Visitors Map; Trails Illustrated Death Valley National Park Map; USGS Shore Line Butte-CA

**Trail contact:** Furnace Creek Visitor Center; (760) 786-3200; www.nps.gov/deva

**Other:** There are no facilities at the parking area, but it does have level space for several vehicles as well as a commanding view of the southwestern horizon from Telescope Peak to the Owlshead Mountains.

**Special considerations:** A high-clearance vehicle is essential for driving the slow, rough road to the trailhead. Some off-trail navigation is needed because Scotty's Canyon isn't visible from the parking area. There is some moderate rock climbing and scrambling on loose rock in the upper end of the hike. The spring may be nothing more than a seep and is not a reliable water source. Carry ample water for this long day hike.

**Finding the trailhead:** From CA 127, 1.7 miles north of Shoshone, turn left (west) on CA 178 (East Side Badwater Road/Jubilee Pass Road), which leads to the park boundary. After entering the park, drive 25.1 miles to the signed Ashford Mill Road on the left, 2 miles north of Ashford Junction and 26.9 miles south of Badwater. Turn right (east) onto the unsigned Ashford Canyon Road leading northeast directly across from the Ashford Mill site. Follow this high-clearance road for 2.8 miles to the end of the road at the mouth of Ashford Canyon. Park and hike from here. GPS: N35 57.276' / W116 39.872'

If coming from the north, drive 44.5 miles south of Furnace Creek on Badwater Road to the unsigned Ashford Canyon Road on the left and follow directions above.

## The Hike

The parking area overlooks Ashford Canyon Wash. Scotty's is the next canyon to the north, about 1 mile distant. Look across the wash to the toe of the first darker rock where it meets a grassy flat. This is where a good, clearly marked trail picks up that

*This chuckwalla lizard in Scotty's Canyon can wedge itself in a tight rock crevice by inflating its lungs.*

leads north to Scotty's Canyon. Drop into the wash and angle slightly downhill (to the northwest) for about 50 yards to the other side. You may see a large rock cairn marking the trail. Either way you'll quickly find it. From here look ahead to the north and you'll spot the trail switchbacking up the far slope. It crosses a low ridge to a colorful red and white side canyon, pocketed with crystal, that leads directly to Scotty's Canyon Wash after about 0.8 mile.

For the return of this out-and-back hike, pay careful attention to the distinctive red rock that defines the mouth of the side canyon. This unsigned junction is the most important turn to remember, as it will lead you to the trail and back to the trailhead, whereas the remainder of the route simply follows the canyon up and back down.

At the mouth of the side canyon turn right and head up the wash. At first the sides appear to close in straight ahead and to the left. After about 0.5 mile the wide-open rocky wash narrows to about 50 feet with rugged brown slopes soaring overhead. Look for a huge funnel-shaped opening on the left (north) slope.

Rock slabs of breccia in the canyon floor resemble concrete with small embedded stones. Over time flash floods have washed away soft sedimentary layers, leaving shallow alcoves framed by horizontal beds of breccia. Canyon edges are dotted with brittlebush, clustered with radiant yellow flowers when in spring bloom. Along the way the canyon bottom varies from 50 yards wide to only a few feet. The walls are low with the adjacent hillsides gradually sloping away to lofty ridges, so despite being in a canyon, the sensation is one of being in wide-open country. The midsection of the canyon contains several shallow slots with low marbleized pour-offs polished by eons of ephemeral runoff.

After hiking nearly 3 miles up the canyon, you'll reach the first grotto at Scotty's Spring. The flow will likely be somewhere between a trickle and seep depending on when the most recent rainfall occurred. The spring is wedged in a tight notch overseen by cliffy alcoves and overhangs. During his early days of prospecting, Death Valley Scotty had a "Camp Holdout" in the large eroded alcove on the right side of the canyon. You're not likely to find any evidence of Scotty's camp. If you do find some small artifact, take only pictures and leave this historical remnant for the next explorers to enjoy. The spring is surrounded by honey mesquite trees and the vines of coyote gourds snaking across the ground. Unlike their domestic cousins these wild squashes are bitter and can be toxic in large quantities.

▶ **You'll learn much more about Death Valley Scotty by taking a walking tour of Scotty's Castle in the northeastern corner of the park, complete with visitor center and museum. At this writing the castle and visitor center are closed due to severe damage from what was described as the 1,000-year rainfall event caused by the October 18, 2015, El Niño storm. Check www.nps .gov/deva for updates.**

A 20-foot-high rock wall blocks the canyon just above the spring. Water drips from an adjacent stair step of rock ledges, producing a soft sound that gently complements calls and wing beats from canyon wrens and other small birds. It is easy to envision Scotty enjoying the tranquility of this remote oasis. Perhaps Native Americans camped here centuries ago. Today the majority of canyon visitors are bighorn sheep, so you'll see their sign. To continue beyond the Camp Holdout grotto, drop back a bit and take a short bypass trail on the right (south) side with an easy descent to the canyon floor above the grotto.

You'll soon come to a second grotto guarded by a thorny mesquite tree and a 20-foot waterfall bound by a large chokestone and sloping rock wall. There are two ways to proceed. One is a bypass trail on the south (right) side of the canyon about 75 yards below the spring. The trail is arduous with a steep, loose rock descent to the canyon floor above the rock wall. The better way is to stay in the canyon and climb up the right side of the sloping rock wall. Begin by sliding face-first against the rock wall on the right side in order to avoid getting poked by the thorny mesquite. Then execute a moderate climb up the sloping wall on the right side, where you'll find good hand- and footholds. After another 0.3 mile a massive rockfall blocks the canyon. This blockage marks a good turnaround point. However, the rockfall can be scrambled, quickly gaining 90 feet in elevation, only to meet an impassable rock wall after only 40 yards. The total elevation gained for the hike at this point is about 1,100 feet.

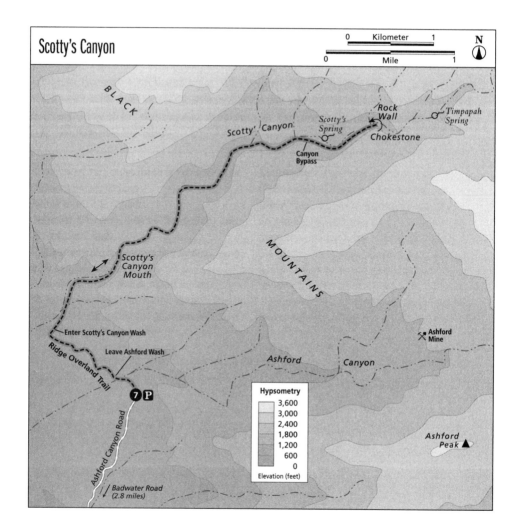

As you head back down the canyon, you're sure to see features you missed on the way up. Perhaps a chuckwalla, inflating itself to twice its normal size in tight cracks to avoid being caught by predators, or maybe an unusual rock or wildflower. The only tricky part of the return route is finding the left-side exit to the correct side canyon that will lead you back to the trailhead. As you approach the spot, look to where red rock meets the south (left) side of the wash. You'll quickly recognize the colorful side canyon that opens to the dirt trail that in turn winds southward to the Ashford Canyon Wash. During your descent into Ashford Wash, you'll see the parking area on the opposite bench above the wash.

Death Valley Scotty was a nationwide celebrity and the West's most famous con artist. Scotty's tallest tales lured wealthy easterners to invest in a bogus gold mine, which he claimed was tucked away in Scotty's Canyon. One of his victims was Albert Johnson, who, despite being conned, became Scotty's close friend, benefactor, and builder of

*Hiking in lower Scotty's Canyon is made all the more interesting with a series of gentle ramps and rocky step-ups.*

Scotty's Castle! You won't find gold up Scotty's Canyon. Its real treasures are whatever discoveries you make there, flavored, perhaps, by a touch of Scotty's engaging spirit.

## Miles and Directions

**0.0**  Start at the trailhead at the mouth of Ashford Canyon.

**0.1**  Locate and follow the trail across the wash to the northwest to Scotty's Canyon Wash.

**0.8**  Reach Scotty's Canyon Wash; turn right.

**1.3**  The wash begins to narrow.

**3.3**  Come to the bypass trail above Camp Holdout on the right (south) side of the canyon;

**3.4**  Arrive at Scotty's Spring/Camp Holdout. Drop back down to the bypass trail (at mile 3.3) to continue up Scotty's Canyon.

**3.5**  Arrive at the chokestone/rock wall climb to the upper canyon. Climb the wall on the right (south) side.

**3.8**  Reach a point where the canyon is blocked by rockfall and, shortly after (if you choose to climb the rockfall), by an impassable rock wall. Turn around here.

**6.8**  Arrive at the side canyon on the left that leads to the trail to Ashford Wash. GPS: N35 57.484' / W116 40.380'

**7.6**  Arrive back at the trailhead at the mouth of Ashford Canyon.

*Option:* If time allows, be sure to check out the Ashford Canyon Mine hike from the same trailhead.

# 8 Room Canyon

Nothing about the view from the Badwater Road suggests the surprises that await you on this canyon hike. This is a unique slot canyon carved out of conglomerate, with boulders to crawl under and climb over. The elevation increase over the 2-mile hike to the turnaround is less than 300 feet, making it one of the flattest canyon hikes available in Death Valley.

**Start:** About 39 miles south of the Furnace Creek junction on Badwater Road
**Distance:** 3.6 miles out and back
**Hiking time:** 3 to 4 hours
**Difficulty:** Easy
**Trail surface:** Cobbled wash, sandy wash
**Best season:** October to April
**Fees and permits:** National park entrance fee
**Maps:** NPS Death Valley Visitors Map; Trails Illustrated Death Valley National Park Map; USGS Shore Line Butte-CA

**Trail contact:** Furnace Creek Visitor Center; (760) 786-3200; www.nps.gov/deva
**Other:** There are no trailhead facilities, but ample parking is available along the Badwater Road.
**Special considerations:** There is danger of flash flooding during heavy rains. Do not attempt this hike during the heat of the summer or anytime when temperatures exceed 100°F.

**Finding the trailhead:** Drive 39 miles south of the Furnace Creek junction on the Badwater Road to milepost 39. Parallel parking is available along the road. GPS: N35 58.571' / W116 43.631'

## The Hike

From the parking area along Badwater Road, the canyon mouth lies directly east. The low foothills below the towering peaks of the Black Range are deceiving. How can an exotic canyon be here? A wonderland awaits you.

Cast aside your doubts and head up the gentle alluvial fan toward the break in the low hills. Your pathway is the main wash coming down the alluvial fan, which provides a pretty clear walking surface. As you approach the hillsides, you may notice a patch of golden outcropping visible on the second row of hills on the right. Use the outcropping only as a marker. Room Canyon is to the north (left) of it.

Entering the opening between the foothills, about 0.7 mile from the road, bear north. The yellow conglomerate is replaced by red adobe on the pinnacles ahead. Just inside the canyon mouth, on the northwest wall, a flock of red pillars rise shakily above you. The group includes one remarkably skinny pillar, reaching like a finger to the sky. A user trail will take you up to the base of the pillars for closer inspection and dramatic photographs. These are reputed to be the tallest free-standing pinnacles in the park!

*Some of the tallest free-standing pinnacles in Death Valley are a unique feature of Room Canyon.*

Continuing on into the canyon, surprises await at every bend. The canyon narrows to less than 10 feet wide almost immediately. Chokestones dangle overhead, or create obstacles on the canyon floor. Children will enjoy the route, but overly large hikers will be challenged by the required crawl through a short tunnel. This is the most difficult maneuver on the hike.

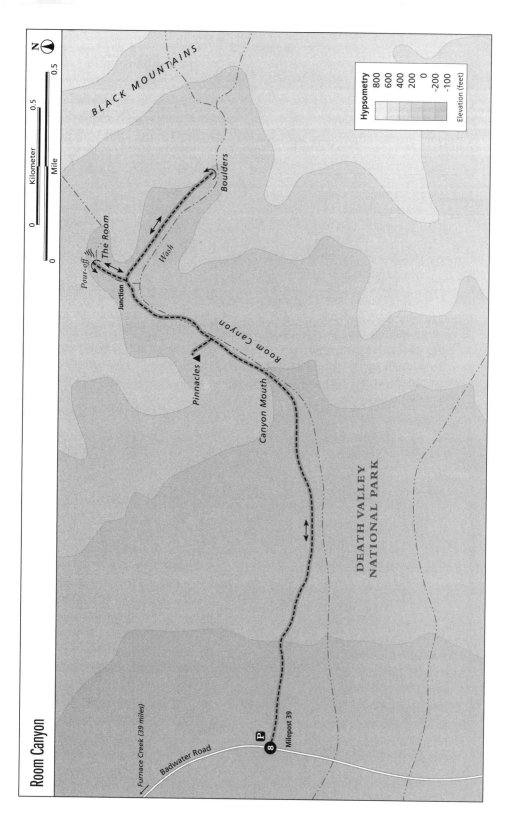

Room Canyon

At a junction about a mile from the road, a wide wash opens to the right. You can check it out on your way back, but your destination for now lies straight ahead. Like the winding streets of a medieval Moroccan village, the red walls lean over the narrow pathway. Huge tilted boulders leave a small space between the high canyon walls. At 1.3 miles from the trailhead lies the large oval room, with majestic cathedral walls rising 300 feet or more on all sides. Just beyond the room a 25-foot stone obstruction blocks further exploration for most hikers, since it requires a Class III scramble to bypass it. This is the turnaround for the casual hiker.

The room is a fascinating spot, and perfect for dining. The silence of the canyon is broken by the twitter of the various birds whose nests ring the upper canyon walls. The power of erosion is everywhere, from the hoodoo spires to the drippy conglomerate stains frozen in rivulets on the canyon walls.

On your way out, take a few moments to explore the open wash to the left at the junction. The entry into the wash is immediately broad, almost panoramic after the close quarters of Room Canyon. A box canyon on the left (north), 0.2 mile up the wash, is blocked by a pour-off. Continue to the southeast where the wash narrows to a canyon. Disorganized boulders litter the narrow canyon floor, creating challenges and obstacles, until you reach the final pour-off at 0.5 mile from the junction. These canyons are subject to constant remodeling.

Retrace your path to the trailhead, enjoying the cool of the canyon before you hit the valley floor.

## Miles and Directions

**0.0**  Start from the Badwater Road trailhead at milepost 39.

**0.7**  Bear north and enter the mouth of canyon.

**0.8**  Take the side trail to the left (north) to reach tall, free-standing pinnacles.

**1.0**  Arrive at a junction with a wash to the right. Continue straight, up the narrow canyon.

**1.3**  Reach the Room; this is the turnaround point.

**1.6**  Arrive back at the junction and turn left into the open wash.

**2.1**  Reach the end of the open wash at a pour-off; turn around here.

**2.6**  Arrive back at the junction.

**3.6**  Arrive back at the trailhead on Badwater Road.

# 9 Foundry Canyon

For the Death Valley canyon collector, this short hike is a must. With dramatic elevation gain and cool labyrinthine slots running deep into a cleft of the Black Mountain range, Foundry Canyon will challenge any hiker's range of adjectives.

**Start:** 39.9 miles south of the Furnace Creek junction on Badwater Road
**Distance:** 5.0 miles out and back with 1,036 feet elevation gain/loss
**Hiking time:** 4 to 5 hours
**Difficulty:** Strenuous due to elevation gain/loss and rock scrambling
**Trail surface:** Cobbled wash, gravel, sand, boulders
**Best season:** Mid-October to mid-March
**Fees and permits:** National park entrance fee

**Maps:** NPS Death Valley Visitors Map; Trails Illustrated Death Valley National Park Map; USGS Shore Line Butte-CA
**Trail contact:** Furnace Creek Visitor Center; (760) 786-3200; www.nps.gov/deva
**Other:** There are no facilities at the trailhead. The nearest vault toilet is about 5 miles south on Badwater Road at the Ashford Mill site.
**Special considerations:** As usual, this hike should not be undertaken during periods of inclement weather due to danger of flash flooding.

**Finding the trailhead:** From CA 127, 1.7 miles north of Shoshone, turn left (west) on CA 178 (East Side Badwater Road/Jubilee Pass Road), which leads to the park boundary. After entering the park, continue on the paved road, turning north at the Ashford Junction with the Badwater Road in the valley. The hike begins at mile 39.9, just north of milepost 40, where the broad sandy wash meets the road on the east side. Park along the road. GPS: N35 57.702' / W116 43.439'
Coming from Furnace Creek, drive south on Badwater Road for 39.9 miles from the CA 190 junction below the Furnace Creek Inn.

## The Hike

From the parking area on the east side of Badwater Road, head up the sandy wash wending its way up the alluvial fan toward the Black Mountain range. With good scouting and a bit of luck, the creosote-dotted path will take you all the way to the canyon mouth, 0.6 mile away. We discovered this route on our way down from the canyon, and it was vastly more pleasant than the heavily cobbled route we stumbled up. The fan forms a narrow S-curve running down from the canyon mouth. Your sandy pathway, though intermittent, avoids the worst of the cobble fields that litter the fan.

The broad fan narrows, with a 30-foot conglomerate cliff face on its south side, and then narrows further. Here, at 1.2 miles and a 300-foot gain from the trailhead, the dark canyon mouth is visible ahead. Finally, in the cool of the canyon, the broad floor continues to narrow while gaining elevation. High vertical walls provide patches of welcome shade, unless it's midday. In the spring an explosion of yellow brittlebushes add color along the canyon walls and provide a lilting perfume to the dry desert air.

*The beginning of Foundry Canyon is deep and dramatic with sculptured rock walls soaring high above.*

At 2.1 miles from the trailhead, and almost 1,000 feet higher than the road, the canyon takes a sharp 90-degree turn to the right (east). The track cuts the corner on the shelf to the right, and suddenly you behold the cleft of the canyon cutting into the massive mountain. It's almost like entering a cave. The dramatic S-slot ahead reveals the convolutions of tectonic shifting and erosion through the granite walls.

The S-turns lead through the narrows to a smooth, marbleized 10-foot waterslide at 2.3 miles from the trailhead. This may be the turnaround for some, but with care you can walk up. Equally important, the slope and the surface of the slide will provide enough friction for a controlled seated descent upon your return trip.

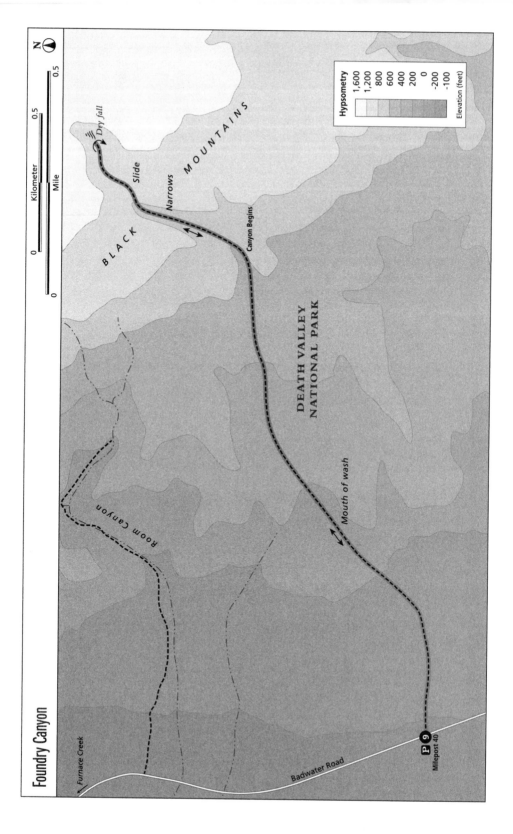

# Foundry Canyon

Hypsometry

| Elevation (feet) |
| --- |
| 1,600 |
| 1,200 |
| 800 |
| 600 |
| 400 |
| 200 |
| 0 |
| -200 |
| -100 |

Dry fall

Slide

Narrows

Canyon Begins

BLACK MOUNTAINS

DEATH VALLEY NATIONAL PARK

Mouth of wash

Room Canyon

Furnace Creek

Badwater Road

Milepost 40

P 9

N

The hikable canyon floor continues almost another 0.2 mile above the slide. A second set of compressed, convoluted narrows twists beneath soaring granite walls. Huge chokestones hang dramatically overhead, caught precariously above the narrow pathway. Finally, another more daunting dry fall, choked with boulders, blocks the path. This is the turnaround point of the hike.

But this is not the end of the drama. As you head back down, enjoying the permanent shade of the slots and the natural air-conditioning of the granite canyon, the view of the plunging canyon floor bracketed by the powerfully eroded granite cliffs, with the skinny strip of sky above, is breathtaking. Since downhill on easy terrain is always relaxing, you can enjoy the scenery created by eons of shifting and erosion.

We usually don't rate our hikes since we like to think they're all outstanding, but Foundry Canyon is definitely a 5-star outing. And the cool, dark canyon is a great relief from the bright desert floor.

## Miles and Directions

**0.0**  Start at the parking area along Badwater Road just north of milepost 40 and head up the sandy wash.

**0.6**  Reach the mouth of wash; continue in a northeasterly direction.

**1.2**  Reach the mouth of canyon.

**2.1**  The canyon narrows and makes a sharp right turn.

**2.3**  Climb a smooth slide and continue up the canyon.

**2.5**  Arrive at a dry fall/boulder jam; turn around here.

**5.0**  Arrive back at the parking area.

*Option:* If energy, water, and daylight are sufficient, consider extending your outing with a hike up Room Canyon, immediately north of Foundry. On your way back down the canyon, cut around to your right (north) at the canyon mouth and skirt the low hills to arrive at Room Canyon. The contrast between the two is astonishing.

# 10 Sidewinder Canyon

This steep, rugged canyon opens to grand vistas of the floor of Death Valley. The canyon out-and-back hike has good highway access and doesn't require a four-wheel-drive vehicle. Narrow tunnels and sheer rock slots require moderate scrambling to dramatic views of Death Valley. Special attractions include several slot side canyons with natural bridges and pour-offs inviting further exploration. The canyon also lies within bighorn sheep habitat.

**Start:** About 33 miles south of Furnace Creek

**Distance:** 4.4 miles out and back in main canyon with 1,000 feet elevation gain/loss (plus about 2.0 miles of short side hikes in several slot canyons)

**Hiking time:** 5 to 6 hours

**Difficulty:** Moderate

**Trail surface:** Dirt path, gravel wash, rocky alluvial fan, short stretches of moderate rock climbing

**Best season:** November through April

**Fees and permits:** National park entrance fee

**Maps:** NPS Death Valley Visitors Map; Trails Illustrated Death Valley National Park Map; USGS Gold Valley-CA

**Trail contact:** Furnace Creek Visitor Center; (760) 786-3200; www.nps.gov/deva

**Finding the trailhead:** From the Furnace Creek Visitor Center, drive 1 mile south to the junction of CA 178 (Badwater Road) and CA 190; turn south on Badwater Road and drive 31.2 miles to an unsigned dirt road that leads 0.2 mile left (southeast). This turn is easy to miss, but it is just before the highway makes a half circle to the west (toward the valley). Proceed on the dirt road for 0.2 mile to a T that contains a short stretch of pavement. Turn right on the T, drive to its end in less than 0.1 mile, and park; this is the trailhead for this hike and the Willow Canyon hike. The mouth of Sidewinder Canyon cannot be seen from the parking area, but it is to the southwest about 0.4 mile up and across a rocky alluvial fan. GPS: N36 03.906' / W116 44.697'

## The Hike

This excursion along the western base of Smith Mountain into the lower end of rugged Sidewinder Canyon provides an exciting introduction to the wild canyon country of the Black Mountains.

Begin by hiking southwest 0.4 mile across a rocky alluvial fan to the mouth of Sidewinder Canyon. On the left you'll see a distinctive low berm that points directly to the mouth of the canyon. The canyon opens to a broad wash high above the salt flats to the northwest. Recent floods have made the fan somewhat rougher and rockier.

At 0.5 mile a side canyon enters from the right. It is a chaotic crumbly mess from loose conglomerate, ending at a 50-foot dry fall after only 0.1 mile. It's best to skip this one because the real treasures lie ahead.

*Overhangs and alcoves abound in upper Sidewinder Canyon.*

A second side canyon enters from the right at 0.7 mile. This steep narrow canyon, full of loose rock, meets a 20-foot dry fall after 0.2 mile. At 1.2 mile in Sidewinder Canyon, the graveled wash widens dramatically to a huge semicircle, presenting a grand view of Death Valley and the Panamint Range beyond. This is where a third side canyon enters from the right with a 10-foot ledge a short ways up that can be climbed with some difficulty. Best to move on up Sidewinder to side canyon 4 at mile 1.3 on the right. This one isn't a slot but is split with the right branch bound by great spires along with granite boulders in the bottom and a huge slant of conglomerate cut by a 40-foot pour spout. The lower left branch of this side canyon is blocked by a massive rockfall. You can crawl or climb through an opening on the left side to a short slot that includes a dark tunnel.

Back to the main Sidewinder, side canyon 5 enters from the right at mile 1.6. This is a real gem, one of the best of the best slot canyons. Its mouth is overseen by an indented rock above the main canyon that resembles an owl's head. The serpentine chasm snakes around for about 0.5 mile to a natural bridge, with a few rock ledges to pull up and over along the way. A 5-foot-high chokestone is wedged just beyond the bridge and can be climbed on the left side, but this is a good turnaround spot.

After returning to the main canyon, you'll come to side canyon 6 at mile 1.7. This slot isn't quite as narrow and dark as the previous one but is well worth exploring.

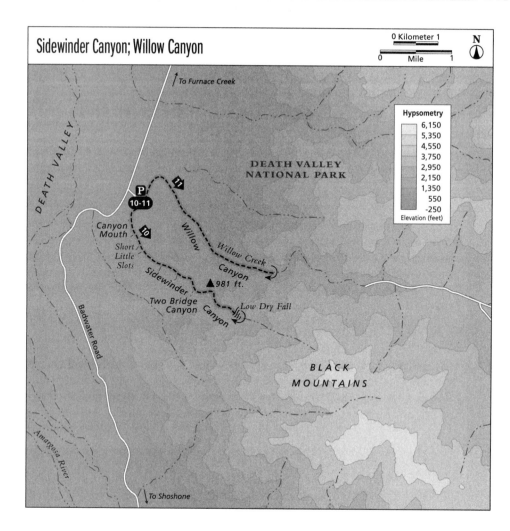

After only 0.1 mile you'll reach two natural bridges close together, so we call this one "Two Bridge Canyon." Continue up another 0.1 mile to a 30-foot crawl under chokestones to a circular room blocked by a massive chunk of the adjoining wall, with "turnaround" seemingly written all over it.

Return to and continue up Sidewinder; the wide wash quickly funnels into a tighter canyon. At 1.8 miles the conglomerate canyon walls are steep with deep overhangs and little alcoves along a narrow passageway. This portion of the canyon is bound by high, rugged mountains with markedly higher rhyolite walls along the face of the main uplift.

At around 2 miles the canyon hosts a series of steep, slanted rocks that can be climbed and descended by anyone with moderate levels of skill and agility. This stretch of Sidewinder has impressive indentations in the rock, with narrows intensifying the canyon experience.

*Three of the six main Sidewinder side canyons are deep, narrow twisting slots.*

At 2.2 miles an 8-foot dry fall is encountered. An experienced rock climber could scale this dry waterfall and continue up the canyon, but most people would have a difficult time pulling themselves over the exposed ledge. The base of this short waterfall is actually an excellent turnaround point for this stimulating round-trip exploration of Sidewinder Canyon and its upper slots. Of the six main side canyons joining Sidewinder from the right side going up, the upper three are the most interesting to explore. They are true slot canyons—deep, dark, and narrow, with hidden chambers, tunnels, and natural bridges.

## Miles and Directions

**0.0**   Start at the trailhead just east of Badwater Road. Head southwest.

**0.4**   Arrive at the mouth of Sidewinder Canyon.

**1.2**   Sidewinder opens to a huge semicircle; continue up the canyon.

**1.3**   Side (slot) canyon 4 enters from the right side.

**1.6**   Side (slot) canyon 5 enters from the right side.

**1.7**   Side (slot) canyon 6 enters from the right side.

**2.2**   Arrive at an 8-foot dry fall in Sidewinder Canyon; this is the turnaround point.

**4.4**   Arrive back at the trailhead.

# 11 Willow Canyon

Seasonal waterfalls provide a suitable home for bighorn sheep in Willow Canyon. The hike is easily accesssible from the Badwater Road.

**See map on page 58.**
**Start:** About 33 miles south of Furnace Creek
**Distance:** 5.0 miles out and back
**Hiking time:** 3 to 4 hours
**Difficulty:** Moderate
**Trail surface:** Sandy canyon floor with rocky sections

**Best season:** November through April
**Fees and permits:** National park entrance fee
**Maps:** NPS Death Valley Visitors Map; Trails Illustrated Death Valley National Park Map; USGS Gold Valley-CA
**Trail contact:** Furnace Creek Visitor Center; (760) 786-3200; www.nps.gov/deva

**Finding the trailhead:** From the Furnace Creek Visitor Center, drive 1 mile south to the junction of CA 178 (Badwater Road) and CA 190; turn south on Badwater Road and drive 31.2 miles to an unsigned dirt road that leads 0.2 mile left (southeast). This turn is easy to miss, but it is just before the highway makes a half circle to the west (toward the valley). Proceed on the dirt road for 0.2 mile to a T that contains a short stretch of pavement. Turn right on the T, drive to its end in less than 0.1 mile, and park; this is the trailhead for this hike and the Sidewinder Canyon hike. The unmarked trail leaves from the northwest corner of the parking lot. GPS: N36 03.906' / W116 44.697'

## The Hike

Although the ratio of hiking the alluvial fan to hiking in the canyon may seem lopsided, this hike features a gem of a canyon. Clearly a bighorn sheep playground, Willow Canyon cuts short your visit at a 70-foot wall with a spectacular ribbon waterfall in season. Prior to that obstacle the canyon winds its narrow way like a street in a medieval city through sheer rhyolite walls, with a tinkling stream intermittently flowing down its center. Small falls, a shelf fall, and finally a long ribbon fall make the passage of the stream a delightful symphony of watery music.

The trip to this canyon follows a user trail that seeks the sandy sections of the fan and wash. Upon leaving the parking area, head northeast, staying below the eroding ash hillsides and their alluvial fans. The sloping forms of these latter features are the southern boundary of the Willow Canyon wash. Beyond their tilting faces, to the northeast, is a vertical wall of the same volcanic ash. This vertical wall is the northern boundary of Willow Canyon wash, and it is clearly seen as you wind your way up the fan following the sandy user trail, which takes you into the wash and on to the canyon itself.

Since you cannot see the canyon from the parking area—only the notch in the mountains beyond the volcanic ash hills suggests it—it is an exciting and abrupt change when the wash enters the canyon. Sheer rust-colored rhyolite walls tower above the gray gravel of the canyon floor. From the brightness of the open wash

*Ribbon falls punctuate the end of the Willow Canyon hike.*

in the valley, you are suddenly enshrouded in cool shadows. The warm wind of the valley becomes a cool breeze within the canyon walls. And, if the season is right, the sound of running water cascading over the eroding canyon floor breaks the silence.

Plentiful sheep sign (tracks, scat, etc.) confirms that this is bighorn sheep habitat, but it is unlikely that you will spot these elusive animals. If lucky enough to do so, please report sheep sightings to park personnel at the visitor center. The presence of water in Willow Canyon makes it a popular spot for the sheep.

Even in season the stream in Willow Canyon is intermittent. At times it disappears underground, only to reappear again as another waterfall. Thus playing a hide-and-seek game, the stream brings visual and aural delight to the hiker. At 2.4 miles the stream drops over an extended shelf of rock in a 3-foot fall (easily climbed via a rock-step to the side). Immediately above the shelf the stream vanishes again. The canyon narrows to less than 15 feet in width as the water-polished walls seem to close the canyon completely. Emerging from the narrows 0.1 mile later, you are confronted with the barricade that terminates the hike: a 70-foot sheer fall rising above you. The stream, when running, comes over this precipice in a silky ribbon. When dry, the fall is also striking for its marbleized, water-smoothed surface.

The return trip from the canyon involves retracing your steps. Leaving the canyon's watery world is done with reluctance; Willow Canyon resembles an oasis at the southern edge of Death Valley.

## Miles and Directions

**0.0** Start at the trailhead just east of Badwater Road. Cross the sandy sections of the alluvial fan to the mouth of the wash.

**0.7** Arrive at the mouth of Willow Canyon.

**2.4** Follow the canyon past a 3-foot fall.

**2.5** Reach the 70-foot dry/wet fall (depends upon season). Turn around here.

**5.0** Arrive back at the trailhead.

# 12 Dante's View

This short, easy hike offers magnificent panoramic views of the highest and lowest points in the continental United States. Surrounded by some of the most dramatic and colorful relief found anywhere, you also enjoy the astounding vertical relief of being nearly 6,000 feet directly above the lowest spot in the nation at Badwater.

**Start:** About 24 miles south of Furnace Creek
**Distance:** 1.0 mile out and back
**Hiking time:** Less than 1 hour
**Difficulty:** Easy
**Trail surface:** Paved road, dirt trail
**Best season:** October through June

**Fees and permits:** National park entrance fee
**Maps:** NPS Death Valley Visitors Map; Trails Illustrated Death Valley National Park Map; USGS Dantes View-CA
**Trail contact:** Furnace Creek Visitor Center; (760) 786-3200; www.nps.gov/deva

**Finding the trailhead:** From CA 190, 11.9 miles southeast of the Furnace Creek Visitor Center and 18 miles west of Death Valley Junction, turn south on the signed Dante's View Road (paved, all-weather). Drive 13.2 miles on this steep, winding road to its end at the Dante's View parking area. The unsigned path to Dante Point takes off to the north from the parking area and is clearly visible from the parking area as it climbs toward Dante Point. GPS: N36 13.238' / W116 43.603'

## The Hike

If at all possible, take this hike in the early morning so that the sun is at your back for better photography and for enhanced enjoyment of the superlative vistas and astounding 5,704-foot drop to the salt flats of Badwater, which sit at 282 feet below sea level. The temperature at Dante's View averages 25 degrees cooler than that of Badwater. This exposed location is usually windy, necessitating a windbreak garment during the hike.

This lofty vantage point in the Black Mountains enables you to almost see, or at least visualize, how the mountains are both slowly moving to the left (south) and rising relative to the surrounding terrain. Looking across Death Valley to the highest point in the park, 11,049-foot Telescope Peak, it is easy to note the major vegetative life zones stretching westward like a giant map. Bristlecone and limber pines thrive high in the Panamint Range. Below is the piñon-juniper zone. Dante's View is situated in a hotter, drier midslope of blackbrush and sage. Floods from the mountains result in graveled alluvial fans with spreading root species such as creosote bush. Freshwater displaces salt from the edges of fans, allowing mesquite to grow. Pickleweed gains a foothold in the brackish water below these edges. The muddy tans and grays of the valley floor grade into white beds of almost pure salt—a chemical desert.

From the parking lot hike north along the road for 0.1 mile to where the Dante Point trail begins a fairly steep climb up the hill. Soon it winds to the left (west) and contours gently along the west slope of the mountain. This contour route provides an

*Dante's View provides breathtaking perspective on the amazing vertical relief between Badwater at minus 282 feet and snowcapped 11,049-foot Telescope Peak in the distance.*

even more impressive view down to Badwater, with an almost overwhelming sense of vertical relief—more than a mile straight down! At 0.3 mile the trail intersects the summit ridge, then climbs the short distance to the 5,704-foot high point. Although unofficial, the trail is clear, well defined, and easy to follow. Return the way you came to complete this 1-mile out-and-back ridge walk—and don't forget your camera.

## Miles and Directions

**0.0** Start at the parking area at the end of Dante's View Road and head north.

**0.3** The trail intersects the summit ridge; go right.

**0.5** Reach Dante's Peak (5,704 feet); turn around here.

**1.0** Arrive back at the parking area trailhead.

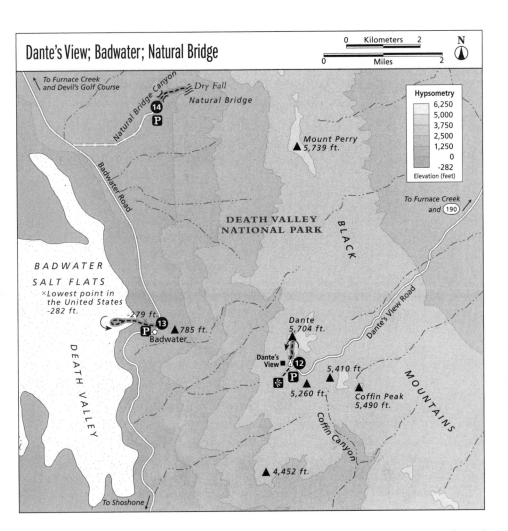

# Dante's View; Badwater; Natural Bridge

0 Kilometers 2
0 Miles 2

N

To Furnace Creek
and Devil's Golf Course

Natural Bridge Canyon

Dry Fall

Natural Bridge

14
P

Badwater Road

**Hypsometry**

6,250
5,000
3,750
2,500
1,250
0
-282
Elevation (feet)

Mount Perry
▲ 5,739 ft.

DEATH VALLEY
NATIONAL PARK

BLACK

To Furnace Creek
and (190)

BADWATER

SALT FLATS
×Lowest point in
the United States
-282 ft.

-279 ft.

P 13 ▲785 ft.
Badwater

Dante
5,704 ft.

Dante's View Road

DEATH VALLEY

Dante's
View ■

12
P

5,410 ft.

▲

5,260 ft.

▲

Coffin Peak
5,490 ft.

▲

MOUNTAINS

Coffin Canyon

▲ 4,452 ft.

To Shoshone

*Option:* For a slightly different and highly worthwhile perspective, hike a well-used path 0.25 mile southwest of the parking area. The rock outcropping at the point of the ridge is especially welcome as a windbreak for setting up a tripod for early morning photography.

# 13 Badwater

This is a perfectly flat hike on a boardwalk that leads you onto the salt flats at the hottest and lowest point in North America and the lowest elevation you can drive to in the Western Hemisphere. This vast bed of salt lies 282 feet below sea level.

**See map on page 65.**
**Start:** About 17 miles south of Furnace Creek
**Distance:** 2.0 miles out and back into the salt flats
**Hiking time:** Less than 1 hour
**Difficulty:** Easy
**Trail surface:** Boardwalk, clear salt flat

**Best season:** November through March
**Fees and permits:** National park entrance fee
**Maps:** NPS Death Valley Visitors Map; Trails Illustrated Death Valley National Park Map; USGS Badwater-CA
**Trail contact:** Furnace Creek Visitor Center; (760) 786-3200; www.nps.gov/deva

**Finding the trailhead:** The large, signed parking area for Badwater is on the west side of Badwater Road, 16.7 miles south of the CA 190 junction at the Furnace Creek Inn. Vault toilets and interpretive signs. GPS: N36 13.823' / W116 46.273'

## The Hike

As bleak as it looks, the popular hike onto the salt flats at Badwater is arguably the ultimate Death Valley experience. If you have been to Dante's View or Telescope Peak, you probably saw the human ants on the white expanse of valley floor and wondered what could be so fascinating. Here you will find individuals, especially families, cavorting like they're at the beach or enjoying a spring snow. To gain a genuine sense of the enormity of the salt flats, hike beyond the heavily traveled boardwalk.

The hike begins at the parking area beneath the cliffs that soar up to Dante's View, 5,755 feet above. There's a sea level sign on the cliff face, high above Badwater, making very clear what minus 280 feet represents. Walk out to the salt flats on the causeway, but continue beyond the well-trod area, depending on the temperature and wind, to a clear area of the flats. Getting away from the highway is essential to get a sense of the magnitude of the salt flats. You'll reach the edge of the 5-mile-wide salt flats at minus 280 feet after only 0.5 mile.

Here salt crystallizes when the groundwater that carries it to the earth's surface hastily evaporates. If you sit on the salt flats, you will find yourself among tiny salt pinnacles, a miniature mountainous world at the bottom of this mountainous basin. In close contact with the surface you will also discover that salt is a tough commodity. The white flooring of the flats is only inches thick, but very firm underfoot. Salt's power as an erosive force is noteworthy in this desert, where it functions much like frost heaves and ice do in a wet climate. Salt crystals grow and force apart boulders, breaking them down to be further eroded by wind and water. The salt crystal crust is sometimes covered with a temporary lake following a rare heavy rainstorm.

*The view to the northeast from the salt flats of Badwater—282 feet below sea level.*

Above the microworld of salt, the world of Death Valley soars. Less than 19 miles to the west is Telescope Peak (11,049 feet), the park's highest point. The difference in elevation between Badwater and Telescope Peak is one of the largest in the United States.

A hike at Badwater is an essential introduction to the expanse of the valley floor. The emigrants and the miners who lived in this environment were a tough lot.

The glare from the salt flats can be as intense as on snowfields at high elevation. Wear sunglasses. Do not hike to the salt flats during the extreme heat of summer. Keep in mind that when the temperature tops 100°F, ground temperatures exceed a sizzling 180°F!

## Miles and Directions

**0.0** Start from the trailhead at the parking area.

**0.5** Reach the end of the boardwalk at the edge of the salt flats. Continue hiking into the flats.

**1.0** Turn around and retrace your steps to the trailhead.

**2.0** Arrive back at the trailhead.

*Option:* The actual lowest point in North America of minus 282 feet is 3.4 miles across the salt flats to the northwest of the Badwater trailhead. This iconic spot may be marked simply by a small rock with the elevation etched in. Don't even consider looking for this otherwise nondescript spot without carrying lots of water. GPS: N36 14.515' / W116 49.535'

# 14  Natural Bridge

An easy, sloped canyon leads to a natural bridge that arches over the trail. The geological phenomena—faults, slipfaulting, chutes and dry fall, natural arch formation—are explained at the trailhead exhibits.

**See map on page 65.**
**Start:** About 13 miles south of Furnace Creek
**Distance:** 2.0 miles out and back
**Hiking time:** 1 to 2 hours
**Difficulty:** Easy
**Trail surface:** Sandy canyon bottom
**Best season:** October through April

**Fees and permits:** National park entrance fee
**Maps:** NPS Death Valley Visitors Map; Trails Illustrated Death Valley National Park Map; USGS Devils Golf Course-CA
**Trail contact:** Furnace Creek Visitor Center; (760) 786-3200; www.nps.gov/deva

**Finding the trailhead:** From the intersection of CA 190 and the Badwater Road in Furnace Creek, drive south on Badwater Road for 13 miles. Turn left (east) on the signed dirt road and drive 1.5 miles to the Natural Bridge parking area. The road is washboardy and rough but is suitable for standard two-wheel-drive vehicles. The trail begins behind the information kiosk. GPS: N36 16.921' / W116 46.069'

## The Hike

Death Valley's fascinating geologic history is featured on the kiosk at the trailhead of the Natural Bridge hike. Bedding and slipfaulting are explained on the board, and understanding the process makes the canyon's display even more impressive. Likewise, differential erosion is explained and illustrated, preparing you for the bridge. Fault caves, metamorphic layers of the Artist's Drive Formation, and mud drips are other topics covered in this condensed version of physical geology. The kiosk is worth a lengthy pause before embarking on the hike.

The canyon floor consists of loose gravel; that feature plus its sharp slope suggests this is a relatively young canyon. The Death Valley floor continues to subside while the Funeral Mountains rise. Geologic forces are still busy here.

The trail begins through deeply eroded volcanic ash and pumice canyon walls. The canyon gradually narrows. At 0.4 mile the bridge stretches over the canyon bottom. An ancient streambed is visible to the north of the bridge, where floods swept around this more resistant section of strata before the pothole beneath it gave way to form the natural bridge.

Beyond the bridge, mud drips, slip faults, and fault caves appear on your journey uphill, reinforcing the information you picked up at the kiosk. A dry fall at 0.8 mile can be climbed with moderate effort, but a 20-foot dry fall blocks travel at 1 mile.

Retracing your steps down the canyon reveals even more examples of geology in action. The shifting light creates iridescent colors. Traveling in the same direction as

*The Natural Bridge—monumental gateway to the upper canyon.*

the powerful flash floods and their load of scouring debris emphasizes the impact of water in this arid environment.

## Miles and Directions

**0.0**  Start at the trailhead at the Natural Bridge parking area. The trail heads northeast.

**0.4**  Arrive at the natural bridge over the trail.

**0.8**  Carefully climb the smaller dry fall.

**1.0**  Where a 20-foot dry fall blocks the canyon, turn around to return to the trailhead.

**2.0**  Arrive back at the parking area.

# 15 Artist's Dips

Close to Furnace Creek and right off the busy Artist's Drive, this 4.5-mile outing takes you swiftly into dramatic solitude, with the vivid strata of colorful volcanic formations rising above the canyons. Review your crayon vocabulary before this hike so you can describe the colors!

**Start:** About 11.5 miles south of Furnace Creek.
**Distance:** 4.5-mile loop
**Hiking time:** 2 to 4 hours
**Difficulty:** Moderate, with two modest dry falls (5 feet and 7 feet)
**Trail surface:** Desert wash, some cobbles, sand
**Best season:** October to April
**Fees and permits:** National park entrance fee
**Maps:** NPS Death Valley Visitors Map; Trails Illustrated Death Valley National Park Map; USGS Devils Golf Course-CA

**Trail contact:** Furnace Creek Visitor Center; (760) 786-3200; www.nps.gov/deva
**Other:** There are no facilities at the parking area along Artist's Drive.
**Special considerations:** Flash flood danger in the washes. Do not attempt this hike if it has rained heavily, is raining heavily, or if it might rain. Do not attempt this hike during the heat of the summer or anytime when temperatures exceed 100°F.

**Finding the trailhead:** From the junction of CA 190 and the Badwater Road below the Furnace Creek Inn, drive south on Badwater Road 8.5 miles. Turn left on the one-way Artist's Drive (signed). There are two large dips (signed Dip) on the road. The first one is at 2.9 miles. That dip is where the hike will start, but the best parking is along the road, 0.4 mile farther, at the top of the rise. The second dip (also signed Dip) will be your exit, so you will walk back 0.1 mile to your car when you finish the hike. GPS: N36 21.131' / W116 47.609'

## The Hike

From the rise between the dips, return southward 0.4 mile to the low point back at the first dip. Turning your back on the lofty Artist's Palette (a volcanic ash formation with a palette of rich blue, violet and green colors), head west, down the wash. The wide mouth becomes narrow and loses elevation quickly, so the presence of the nearby road disappears. Ironically, almost immediately you can spot evidence of an old roadbed on the south (left) canyon wall. Shortly you cross the remnants of old pavement where the former road crossed the wash. This is a marvelous place to pause and observe the impact of pavement and how it accelerates erosion. Continue down the wash. Telescope Peak cuts the skyline straight to the west.

Your descent provides a glorious array of geologic layers, from gravelly conglomerates to multicolored volcanic ash sediments to burnt-umber lava flows. If it is a wet spring, there will be flowers galore. Tenacious desert holly lines the gravel bottom. Gravel ghost erupts where there's enough moisture from rivulets off the canyon walls.

*The down (Dip 1) portion of this colorful hike offers spectacular vistas of the distant Panamint Range.*

Patches of desert five-spot flourish in the sandy bottoms where water exists. Ubiquitous creosote thrives in the middle of the wash.

The dark canyon walls rise as you descend. What initially may have looked like a mundane outing in a wash has now become a dramatic canyon. Continue downward in the canyon. If any junction tempts you to turn, check whether you can see the Death Valley floor ahead in the distance. If you don't see it, don't turn out of the main canyon. Not yet.

The gravel pathway continues to drop. It makes a sharp right-hand turn (north) where fault lines are clearly visibly on the cliff face and the tilted layers are sharply angled. A stretch of narrows extends from 1.2 to 1.5 miles from the road.

At 2 miles from the dip, you can finally see the Death Valley floor far below. The canyon has descended 600 feet since the hike began at Dip 1. Here you take a sharp right turn to head back uphill in the adjacent canyon. Here too a plethora of flowers

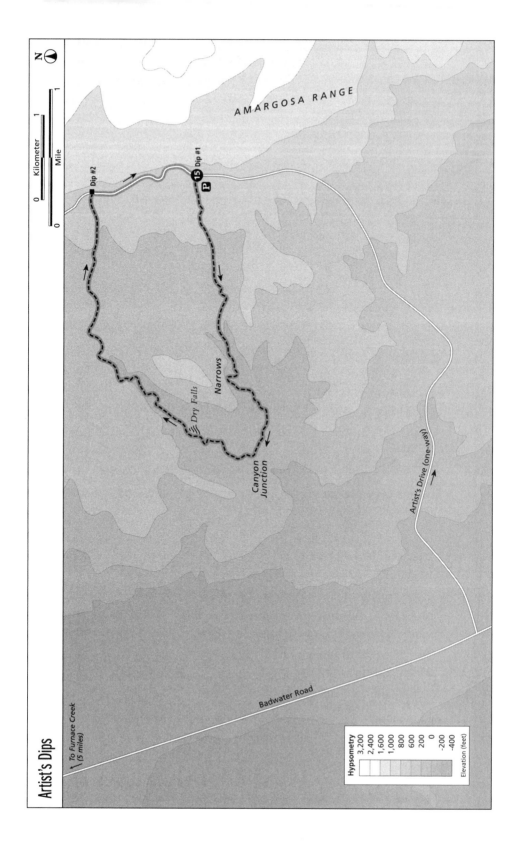

# Artist's Dips

**Hypsometry**

| | |
|---|---|
| 3,200 | |
| 2,400 | |
| 1,600 | |
| 1,000 | |
| 800 | |
| 600 | |
| 200 | |
| 0 | |
| -200 | |
| -400 | |

Elevation (feet)

Badwater Road

Artist's Drive (one-way)

To Furnace Creek
(5 miles)

AMARGOSA RANGE

Dip #2

Dip #1

P

15

Narrows

Dry Falls

Canyon Junction

Kilometer

Mile

N

*Sheer rock walls with astonishing colors abound throughout the Artist's Dips hike.*

blooms in the spring if there has been adequate moisture. Ants are busy harvesting desert holly seeds, leaving a wreath of chaff around their mounds.

Half a mile above the junction, a short 5-foot dry fall is followed by a more challenging 7-foot one. Hand- and footholds make the ascents secure, although a boost from behind can help.

The soaring, fluted red canyon walls, the weeping Navaho red on the vertical pink walls, the walls of green, burnt sienna, and orange—the hike back up to the road at Dip 2 is a visual delight. Be sure to turn around and grab the view down the canyon behind you to get the full dose of dramatic colors, textures, and angles.

The canyon reverts to a wash and flattens as you draw nearer to Artist's Drive. Emerging right below Banish Canyon at Dip 2, you end your hike by turning right (south) and hiking 0.1 mile along the road up to the top of the rise where you left your car.

## Miles and Directions

**0.0** Start at the parking area on Artist's Drive and head south along the road back to Dip 1.

**0.4** Turn right (west) down the wash.

**1.6** The canyon starts to narrow.

**2.4** Reach the canyon junction. Turn sharply right (northeast).

**2.9** Climb two short dry falls in quick succession.

**3.1** The canyon narrows.

**4.4** Arrive back at Artist's Drive. Turn right (south) to your vehicle.

**4.5** Arrive back at the parking area.

# 16 Desolation Canyon

Desolation Canyon is a highly scenic but less crowded alternative to the nearby Golden Canyon. This short hike features moderate canyoneering to a high pass overlooking the Artist's Drive Formation. The deep, narrow, colorful canyon provides a feeling of solitude, with broad vistas from the overlook.

**Start:** About 5 miles south of Furnace Creek
**Distance:** 4.2 miles out and back
**Hiking time:** 2 to 3 hours
**Difficulty:** Moderate
**Trail surface:** Clear wash with 3 short rock pitches
**Best season:** Early November to mid-April

**Fees and permits:** National park entrance fee
**Maps:** NPS Death Valley Visitors Map; Trails Illustrated Death Valley National Park Map; USGS Furnace Creek-CA
**Trail contact:** Furnace Creek Visitor Center; (760) 786-3200; www.nps.gov/deva

**Finding the trailhead:** From the Furnace Creek Visitor Center in Furnace Creek, drive south 1.2 miles to the junction of CA 190 and the Badwater Road; turn right (south) onto Badwater Road and drive 3.7 miles to the unsigned parking area, which is to the left along the east side of the highway. The old road was washed out by the big thunderstorm flood of August 2004. Drive 0.5 mile to the new parking area. The topographic map incorrectly identifies the immediate canyon to the south as Desolation Canyon. In fact, Desolation Canyon is the longer and wider canyon to the immediate southeast of the parking area. GPS: N36 23.728' / W116 50.345'

## The Hike

This is an enjoyable and highly scenic canyon hike for anyone, but it is especially appreciated by those without a four-wheel-drive vehicle in that access is just off the paved highway. Despite its proximity to both the Badwater Road and Artist's Drive, the narrow canyon provides a deep feeling of intimacy and solitude. The entire out-and-back trip offers a superb opportunity to observe the dynamics of badlands erosion, which is everywhere, from mud-filled gullies to bizarre eroded shapes overlooking the canyon.

Because Desolation Canyon involves a short hike at low elevation, the recommended time of day for the hike is mid- to late afternoon when the cooler shadows fill the canyon. Upon return, during late afternoon to early evening, brilliant light can be spectacular on the multicolored east-facing slopes above the canyon.

Begin the hike by following the old washed-out road from the far end of the parking loop. It wraps around the toe of Desolation's west ridge and then leads southeasterly into the broad lower wash of Desolation Canyon at 0.6 mile. At first the wide wash climbs gently, gradually increasing gradient to the first canyon junction. Stay to the right in the main canyon at several junctions that appear during the first mile. Soon the canyon narrows, with even narrower side draws. Desolation isn't a true slot canyon, but in places its walls are close enough to touch both sides at once.

*Hiking up the wash from the mouth of Desolation Canyon.*

The next 0.1 mile brings a couple of stair-step rocks that are easy to climb before the canyon again widens. At around 1.6 miles what appears to be the main canyon to the left ends at a dry waterfall another 0.1 mile up. Continuing up the narrower canyon to the right ends at a steep, unstable rock chute at 2 miles. This is a good turnaround point.

If you've still got the urge and energy to explore, climb up to the right on loose, deep gravel to the 700-foot elevation overlook at 2.1 miles. This relatively lofty vantage point provides a spectacular view of the varied colors of the Artist's Drive Formation to the south. From this point the Artist's Drive road is directly below about 0.3 mile. Return by way of Desolation Canyon to complete this colorful 4.2-mile round-trip badlands/canyon excursion.

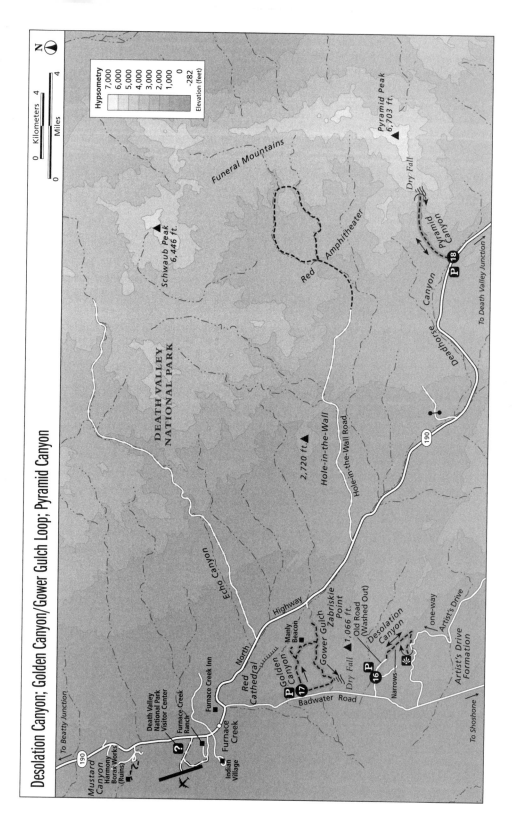

Desolation Canyon; Golden Canyon/Gower Gulch Loop; Pyramid Canyon

# Miles and Directions

**0.0** Start at the trailhead/parking area and follow the old road.

**0.6** At the intersection with the Desolation Canyon wash, turn right up the canyon.

**0.8** Where the canyon splits, stay right.

**0.9** At the canyon junction, stay right up the main wash.

**1.1** The canyon steepens with moderate scrambling.

**1.2** The canyon widens to a junction. Go right up the steeper, less colorful canyon with more stair-step rocks.

**1.6** At the canyon junction, stay right up a narrow gully.

**2.0** The hike ends where the canyon reaches a steep chute. If you don't want to climb to the overlook, this is the turnaround point.

**2.1** Scramble up a very steep, unstable slope (right) to the overlook. Turn around here and return via the same route.

**4.2** Arrive back at the trailhead.

# 17 Golden Canyon/Gower Gulch Loop

A fascinating journey through geologic time passes through rocks of different ages as the elevation increases then loops back down to the floor of Death Valley past borax-mine tunnels. The first section is an educational geology nature trail. The scenery of the extended trip includes a colorful lake bed, exposed strata and alluvial-fan formations, and spectacular scenery of the Panamint Range from below Zabriskie Point.

**See map on page 76.**
**Start:** About 3 miles south of Furnace Creek
**Distance:** 6.5-mile loop (including 2 short side trips)
**Hiking time:** 3 to 5 hours
**Difficulty:** Moderate
**Trail surface:** Sandy trail, rocky wash
**Best season:** November through April
**Fees and permits:** National park entrance fee

**Maps:** NPS Death Valley Visitors Map; Trails Illustrated Death Valley National Park Map; USGS Furnace Creek-CA
**Trail contact:** Furnace Creek Visitor Center; (760) 786-3200; www.nps.gov/deva
**Special considerations:** This is the park's most popular trail, so parking can be difficult at times.

**Finding the trailhead:** From the junction of CA 190 and the Badwater Road, 1.2 miles south of the Furnace Creek Visitor Center, head south on Badwater Road. After 2 miles turn left into the Golden Canyon parking area/trailhead on the east side of the road. There is a vault toilet and an information kiosk at the trailhead. GPS: N36 25.235' / W116 50.820'

## The Hike

An excellent interpretive trail guide to this Golden Canyon nature trail is available for 50 cents at the Golden Canyon trailhead. Ten stops in this geology guide are keyed to numbered posts along the trail.

Golden Canyon was once accessed by paved road. Then in February 1976 a four-day storm caused 2.3 inches of rain to fall on nearby Furnace Creek—one of the driest places on earth where, for example, no rain fell during all of 1929 and 1953. Runoff from the torrential cloudburst undermined and washed out the pavement so that today Golden Canyon is a wonderful place for hikers only. This pattern of drought and torrents follows countless periods of flash floods, shattering rockslides, and a wetter era when the alluvial fan was preceded by an ancient shallow sea—a land in constant flux. In the winter of 2004, heavy rains caused flooding, washing out sections of Badwater Road and further eroding these canyons and gulches.

At stop 2 it is easy to see how the canyon was carved out of an old alluvial fan made up of volcanic rock that predates the origin of Death Valley some 3 million years ago. Layers in the rock tell the tale of periodic floods over the eons. Just above, the canyon displays tilted bands of rock caused by faulting where huge blocks of the earth's crust slid past one another. As you proceed up the canyon, you are literally

*The sharp point of Manly Beacon (left) is complemented by the dramatic amber face of the Red Cathedral (right background).*

passing through geologic time. The Furnace Creek Formation is the combination over time of sediments from a lake bed that dates back around 9 million years. Ripple marks of water lapping over the sandy lake bed hardened into stone as the climate warmed and are evident on the tilted rock. Weathering and the effects of thermal water produced the splash of vivid colors seen today.

Mountain building to the west gradually produced a more arid climate, causing the lake to dry up. At the same time the land tilted due to the widening and sinking of Death Valley and the uplift of the Black Mountains. Dark lava from eruptions of 3 to 5 million years ago slowed down erosion, explaining why Manly Beacon juts so far above the surrounding badlands. These stark badlands rising above the canyon at mile 0.5 are the result of rapid runoff from storms on erodible, almost impermeable rocks.

Several narrow side canyons invite short explorations on the way up Golden Canyon, particularly opposite stop 2, and to the left and just above stops 6 and 7.

The nature trail ends at stop 10, about 1 mile up the canyon at an elevation of 140 feet. For a 0.8-mile round-trip to the base of the Red Cathedral, continue straight ahead up the broken pavement, past the old parking area, to a narrow notch directly below the looming presence of the cathedral, from where the highest point in the park—Telescope Peak—can be seen in the far distance.

Red Cathedral was once part of an active alluvial fan, outwashed from the Black Mountains to the south. The bright red results from the weathering of iron to produce the rust of iron oxide. The cliff faces are made up of the more resistant red rock crowning softer yellow lake deposits.

Upon returning to stop 10 (mile 1.8), follow the signed trail to the left (coming down) up a steep gully well marked with trail posts. The trail climbs across badlands beneath the imposing sandstone jaw of Manly Beacon. At 2.3 miles a high ridge saddle is reached below Manly Beacon. Follow the markers down a side gully to a wash/trail junction at 2.6 miles. The left-hand wash leads eastward up to Zabriskie Point. The right-hand wash/trail descends west to Gower Gulch. If you walk up the main wash, you will quickly come to the artificial cut made in the rock wall to divert Furnace Creek through Gower Gulch. This has resulted in speeding up erosion in the gulch. Note the gray color of the rocks on the bottom of the drainage washed in from Furnace Creek, contrasting with the red and yellow badlands.

Gower Gulch is partially the result of human construction to protect Furnace Creek from serious flooding. For a short side trip toward Zabriskie Point, turn left at the junction and follow the markers for about 0.5 mile to where you can select an excellent overlook of Zabriskie Point, the surrounding badlands, Death Valley, and the distant Panamint Range. Zabriskie Point is another 0.7 mile and 200 feet above and is accessible by road from the other side. It does indeed provide one of the most magnificent views in all of Death Valley, but its proximity to a paved road may detract from the hiking experience on the Golden–Gower loop. Thus the overlook below Zabriskie Point is recommended as the turnaround point for a scenic side trip. Zabriskie Point is a popular starting point for those hiking 3 miles downhill through Gower Gulch then across to the mouth of Golden Canyon.

Back at the trail junction (mile 3.6), there is no marker post leading the way toward Gower Gulch. Simply continue down the wash toward wide, gray Gower Gulch, which drops below mounds of golden badlands. At 3.9 miles a side wash intersects the main wash; continue downward to the right. Early-day miners in search of borax pockmarked the walls of Gower Gulch with tunnels. These small openings are unsecured and potentially dangerous. A mile down, the wide gravel wash bends sharply to the left, narrowing dramatically with the bedding and faulting of red and green rock. The canyon floor then quickly drops 40 feet to below sea level.

At 5.2 miles the wash meets a 30-foot dry fall. A good user trail curves around the rock face to the right. From here the faint but easy-to-follow trail heads north 1.3 miles along the base of the mountains paralleling the highway back to the Golden

Canyon parking area, thereby completing the basic 4.7-mile loop with an additional 1.8 miles of side trips.

## Miles and Directions

**0.0** Start at the Golden Canyon nature trail trailhead at 160 feet below sea level.

**1.0** The nature trail ends at stop 10. Begin the 0.8-mile side trip to the base of the Red Cathedral here.

**1.8** Back to stop 10 and the beginning of the trail toward Manly Beacon.

**2.3** Reach at the high point of the trail below Manly Beacon.

**2.6** Arrive at the trail/wash junction between Gower Gulch and Zabriskie Point.

**3.1** Reach the overlook below Zabriskie Point.

**3.6** Arrive back at the trail/wash junction and begin the hike down Gower Gulch.

**5.2** Gower Gulch reaches a 30-foot dry fall. Take the trail around to the right.

**6.5** Complete the loop and arrive back at the Golden Canyon trailhead.

# Grapevine/Funeral Mountains

## 18 Pyramid Canyon

This is an easily accessible, waterless, out-and-back canyon hike with layered, color-banded mountains. The mountains close into a narrow, dark chasm that is blocked in several places by boulders.

**See map on page 76.**
**Start:** About 14 miles southeast of Furnace Creek
**Distance:** 4.0 miles out and back
**Hiking time:** 2 to 3 hours
**Difficulty:** Moderate
**Trail surface:** Sandy wash with loose gravel and moderate bouldering

**Best season:** October through April
**Fees and permits:** National park entrance fee
**Maps:** NPS Death Valley Visitors Map; Trails Illustrated Death Valley National Park Map; USGS Ryan-CA and Echo Canyon-CA
**Trail contact:** Furnace Creek Visitor Center; (760) 786-3200; www.nps.gov/deva

**Finding the trailhead:** From the Furnace Creek Visitor Center, drive about 14 miles east on North Highway (CA 190). Shortly after passing an information kiosk/pay phone, you'll leave the park boundary on the south side of the highway. Drive another 1.1 miles and look to the north side of the highway for a prominent wash. The trailhead is unsigned, but there is a wide spot alongside the highway on the north side for parking. GPS: N36 22.337' / W116 39.899'

## The Hike

Some of the limestone in the surrounding Furnace Creek Formation is probably travertine that was laid down by volcanic hot springs. Travertine Point rises just east of the trailhead on the south side of the canyon. Pyramid Canyon is not an official place name on the map but is used here to identify the hike. When viewed from the mouth of Pyramid Canyon, the imposing, aptly named massif of Pyramid Peak dominates the skyline to the northeast. After 0.25 mile you'll come to an old, rusted car body halfway buried in the wash—proof positive that you're in the right canyon. Barrel cacti dot the surrounding alluvial-fan conglomerate.

Continue hiking up the wide wash to narrows that define a dramatic gateway beyond. At 1.5 miles the canyon is blocked by a boulder, with dark cliffs ahead. Look back to the southwest for a great view of Telescope Peak. Climb to the left up a slanted rock to get around the boulder. At mile 1.7 reddish, dark cliff walls soar hundreds of feet as the canyon again closes in. The next two boulder blockages occur in quick succession and can be readily climbed. But the fourth blockage at 2 miles is impassable. A gigantic chokestone sits atop a dry fall bound by sheer limestone cliffs. An alcove overhang juts out from the cliff high above the dry fall on the north side of the canyon. Retrace your route to complete this varied 4-mile round-trip canyon hike.

## Miles and Directions

**0.0** Start at the unsigned trailhead/parking area along the north side of the highway (2,560 feet elevation).

**0.25** Look for the old half-buried car body in the wash.

**1.5** At the first rock blockage, the canyon narrows.

**1.7** Arrive at the second rock blockage.

**1.8** This is the third rock blockage.

**2.0** Turn around upon reaching the dry fall/chokestone.

**4.0** Arrive back at the trailhead.

*Option:* For added variety during the return route, look for a low ridge on the right side of the broad wash, about 0.5 mile below the dry-fall turnaround. Angle around the ridge and head up the left (west) fork for about 0.4 mile to a 30-foot dry fall. This two-pronged exploration of Pyramid Canyon adds about 0.8 mile round-trip to the hike.

# 19 The Mummy

This short hike has everything going for it in a compact package. Within only 1 mile you'll see a huge distinctive formation, a small arch, a natural bridge, and a glimpse of history thrown in for good measure. And to top it off, Mummy Canyon is easily accessible from a paved road.

**Start:** About 13 miles southeast of Furnace Creek
**Distance:** 1.8 miles out and back
**Hiking time:** 1 to 2 hours
**Difficulty:** Easy
**Trail surface:** Gravel outwash and sandy canyon bottom with some short rocky sections
**Best season:** October to May
**Fees and permits:** National park entrance fee
**Maps:** NPS Death Valley Visitors Map; Trails Illustrated Death Valley National Park Map; USGS Echo Canyon-CA

**Trail contact:** Furnace Creek Visitor Center; (760) 786-3200; www.nps.gov/deva
**Special considerations:** There is no designated parking area for this unsigned hike. It is important to parallel park next to the busy highway in a safe location. The park entrance sign is a popular photo op so please avoid blocking the view by parking a good distance west of the sign, or just to the east of it.

**Finding the trailhead:** From the CA 190/Badwater Road junction, take CA 190 for 12.3 miles southeast near the edge of the park. On the left (north) side of the highway, park parallel to the road. Find a wide, safe pullout with good visibility in both directions. GPS: N36 22.556' / W116 41.328'

## The Hike

From the parking pullout climb a low berm and drop into the main Furnace Creek Wash. Look down the wash and you'll see a side canyon that enters from the right, bound by brown columnar hillsides. This is Mummy Canyon. You can actually see the backside of the mummy-shaped formation from here, although it blends into the hillside on the far side of the canyon. When you get a lot closer you'll know it when you see it.

Walk down the cobblestone wash as it parallels the road about 0.2 mile to the wide mouth of Mummy Canyon, which is also known as Jensen Canyon. At the mouth take the hairpin right and head straight north toward the canyon. Notice an amazing array of cacti with the most prominent being beavertail, barrel, prickly pear, and silver cholla. The right side of the lower canyon is overseen by a large sphinx-shaped rock next to a small arch.

After about 0.4 mile the canyon begins to narrow dramatically. Striking vertical white streaks of travertine calcium carbonate deposits are embedded into steep slopes

*Although the Mummy soars above the canyon it is best seen from above the canyon mouth on its north side.*

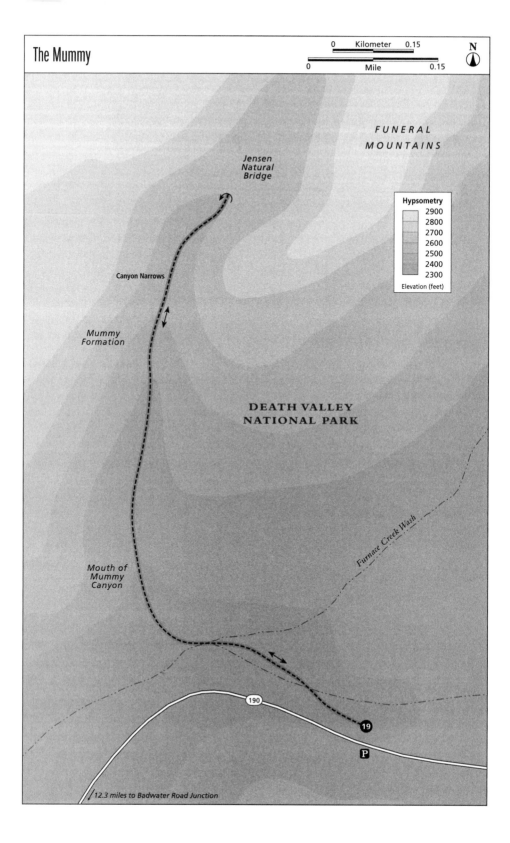

The Mummy

0    Kilometer    0.15

0       Mile       0.15

N

FUNERAL
MOUNTAINS

Jensen
Natural
Bridge

Hypsometry

2900
2800
2700
2600
2500
2400
2300

Elevation (feet)

Canyon Narrows

Mummy
Formation

DEATH VALLEY
NATIONAL PARK

Furnace Creek Wash

Mouth of
Mummy
Canyon

190

19

P

12.3 miles to Badwater Road Junction

of brown conglomerate. Vertical canyon walls have weathered in a honeycomb pattern. Some of the larger chunks of conglomerate in the bottom contain beautiful inlaid pebbles and small rocks glued by quartzite and silica. You'll soon reach a perfect 30-foot-high half-circle alcove that marks the entrance to a second set of even tighter narrows. These narrows end all too quickly at an impassable dry fall over-spanned by a small but very impressive natural bridge. You've reached the turnaround point.

If you stand directly underneath the bridge and look up, you'll have the sensation of gazing straight up into a tunnel. Over the eons floodwaters have poured over the dry fall and through the slot formed by this narrow bridge. This formation, which is probably more durable than it appears, is called the Jensen Natural Bridge. If you missed it on the way up, look carefully on the way down and you'll discover the reason for the name. What you'll find is an authentic glimpse of Death Valley history. Leave it undisturbed so that others can ponder the question: Who was Jensen?

Another point of interest that you might miss on the way to the natural bridge is the Mummy itself, unless you happen to turn around at the right spot. You can't miss it on your return hike back down the canyon. This distinctive formation is a natural likeness of an Egyptian mummy, standing up, on the right (west) side of the canyon going down. The massive rock column towers nearly 200 feet, with detailed facial features looking back up the canyon. Huge arms are folded back up toward the head.

## Miles and Directions

**0.0**  Start at the parking pullout along CA 190 and hike down into the wash.

**0.2**  Reach the mouth of Mummy Canyon.

**0.6**  Reach the first canyon narrows.

**0.8**  Reach the second canyon narrows.

**0.9**  Arrive at Jensen Natural Bridge.

**1.8**  Arrive back at the parking pullout.

# 20 Upper Hole-in-the-Wall

This interesting cross-country canyon trek has lots to see, from marine fossils to grand mountain vistas. Short canyon narrows, geologic wonders, plant species found only in Death Valley, and moderate bouldering add variety to this long loop in the Funeral Mountains.

**Start:** About 12 miles southeast of Furnace Creek
**Distance:** 11.0-mile lollipop
**Hiking time:** 6 to 8 hours
**Difficulty:** Strenuous
**Trail surface:** Sandy, gravelly washes and ridges
**Best season:** Mid-October through mid-April

**Fees and permits:** National park entrance fee
**Maps:** NPS Death Valley Visitors Map; Trails Illustrated Death Valley National Park Map; USGS Echo Canyon-CA and East of Echo Canyon-CA
**Trail contact:** Furnace Creek Visitor Center; (760) 786-3200; www.nps.gov/deva

**Finding the trailhead:** From the junction of CA 190 and the Badwater Road south of Furnace Creek, go southeast on CA 190 for 5.4 miles to the Hole-in-the-Wall dirt road on the left. The road is in the wash, near a sign recommending four-wheel-drive vehicles. The first 3.6 miles of the road is rough and rocky, but is often passable by passenger vehicles with slow, careful driving. Drive 3.6 miles to the Hole-in-the-Wall narrows (Split Canyon) and park there. GPS: N36 24.893' / W116 43.399'

If you have a high-clearance four-wheel-drive vehicle, you can drive another 2.5 miles to the end of the road just before the wilderness boundary. GPS: N36 24.425' / W116 41.164'

## The Hike

At the upper trailhead you'll find remnants of an old travertine quarry. There is another quarry just over the ridge to the north in a small canyon of red sandstone. The quarries produced building stone for the Furnace Creek Inn. From the upper parking area, hike east for about 0.4 mile to the end of the travertine ridge on the left. You might find pictographs in this area. At this point the basin becomes wider and seems strangely remote, despite its proximity to busy Furnace Creek. Plants of this Mojave Desert ecosystem include creosote, rabbitbrush, barrel cacti, and sweetbush favored by bighorn sheep. At 1 mile you'll see a distinctive black rock outcropping on the left. Across to the south a side drainage leads up to an inner basin on the northeast side of Pyramid Peak. Scan the southern skyline for an arch. Schwaub Peak rises to the northeast, uplifted and tilted with almost vertical sedimentary bedding.

At 1.5 mile turn right (east) up a narrow canyon. It's easier to find the correct canyon if you stay on the right side of the broad valley, which is called Red Amphitheater. A sharp pointed peak marks the right entrance of the canyon. At 2.4 miles the canyon is bounded by dark limestone with moderate bouldering. Look for embedded

*Hiking up out of the narrows of the east canyon in the Red Amphitheater.*

marine fossils in the limestone. You'll pass through a canyon narrows with cliff walls marked with eroded ripples. These sedimentary rocks were probably mudstone from the floor of an ancient lake bed.

In the next set of narrows we spotted a perfectly camouflaged horned lizard. This is an uncommon reptile, so it pays to be observant. Death Valley goldeneye and napkinring buckwheat grow together in the wash. This secluded, rugged terrain is heaven for desert bighorn. As you continue up the canyon, you'll see delicate little ferns clinging to rock walls, and you'll wonder how they can survive in this harsh, dry environment.

At 4 miles an arch sits atop tilted cliffs with eroded pockets used by nesting owls. Just beyond is an obvious gap on the left that leads to the next canyon north. At mile 4.8 a major side gully joins the main east canyon from the right. Continue left for another 0.4 mile and look for a route to the left that crosses the ridge to the next canyon north.

After cresting this divide you might spot another arch to the west as you descend to the north canyon. You might also see a light lavender flower with a yellow center known as rock nimulus growing from limestone cracks—these are endemic to Death Valley.

Upon reaching the main canyon floor at around 5.7 miles, turn left (west) and hike down the wash for the return leg of the loop. This stretch contains such wonders as beehive cacti, Death Valley penstemon, marine fossils, and great towering spires and cliffs. Try to avoid the rock nettles or you'll learn the hard way why they're called "velcro" plants. The canyon walls are made of hard, sandy conglomerate, riddled with openings and alcoves. At 7.3 miles the canyon opens, with enticing side canyons to the right that invite further exploration.

When the limestone ridge on the left ends at about mile 8.2, you'll be looking straight south to the Black Mountains. The loop is completed at 9.5 miles. Continue down to the trailhead to finish this varied 11-mile canyon route in Death Valley's Funeral Mountains.

## Miles and Directions

**0.0**  Begin at the upper trailhead/wilderness boundary and head east.

**0.4**  Reach the end of the travertine ridge.

**1.5**  Enter the side canyon to the right (east).

**3.2**  With the low saddle on your left, continue to the right up the main wash.

**4.2**  This is the crossover point for the shorter loop option.

**5.2**  Climb the ridge to the left (north).

**5.7**  At the north canyon, turn left for the downhill (return) leg of the loop.

**9.5**  Complete the basic loop near the canyon junction.

**11.0**  Arrive back at the trailhead.

# Upper Hole-in-the-Wall

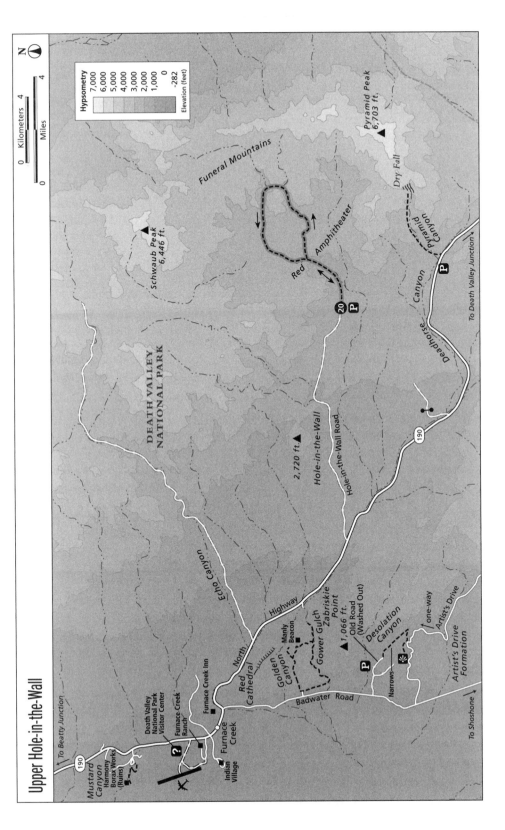

*Options:* The loop can be shortened by 2 or 3 miles by crossing north to the next canyon at about mile 4.2. You can identify the spot by the color of the rocks: red on the left, white to the right, and black limestone straight ahead.

From the upper crossover ridge described in the hike, and before dropping to the next canyon north, climb up the steep ridge to the right (east) for expansive views of Amargosa Valley far into Nevada.

From the Hole-in-the-Wall narrows, 3.6 road miles above CA 190, a short 2-mile round-trip provides desert panoramas, majestic rock formations, and varied terrain. The hike begins at the Hole-in-the-Wall cliffs, which are made of differentially eroded volcanic ash. The narrows are also known as Split Canyon. The multitude of holes form enchanting shapes; some are precise, while others droop. To the north, beyond the alluvial fan, lie the Funeral Mountains. Travel north–northwest using the varnished desert pavement where possible since the wash winds a bit and is loaded with boulders that make hiking difficult. You gain 420 feet in elevation by the time you reach the canyon mouth. Here more towering limestone cliffs display the eyes and mouths of erosion holes. The canyon floor is a wide graveled wash. The canyon narrows and turns at 0.3 mile, only to be blocked by a 40-foot dry fall. The tempting sidehill to the west is too unstable and dangerous for climbing, so this is the terminal point of the canyon hike. At the canyon mouth, hike east 0.2 mile to the next canyon. This one is totally blocked by massive boulders. The return descent to Hole-in-the-Wall features magnificent views of the Artist's Drive Formation at the northern end of the Black Mountains, with Death Valley stretching out beyond. Telescope Peak stands on the far horizon.

# 21  Amargosa Overlook

The drive up Echo Canyon to the trailhead is spectacular, much like Titus Canyon, with a visit to an early twentieth-century mine site to break up the trip. The view from the edge of the Funeral Mountains is breathtaking, a peak experience without the ascent.

**Start:** 13 miles east of Furnace Creek at the end of Echo Canyon Road
**Distance:** 7.2 miles out and back with 660-foot elevation gain/loss
**Hiking time:** 5 to 6 hours
**Difficulty:** Moderate
**Trail surface:** Gravel jeep track, sandy wash

**Best season:** October to April
**Fees and permits:** National park entrance fee
**Maps:** NPS Death Valley Visitors Map; Trails Illustrated Death Valley National Park Map; USGS Echo Canyon-CA and Lees Camp-CA
**Trail contact:** Furnace Creek Visitor Center; (760) 786-3200; www.nps.gov/deva

**Finding the trailhead:** From the Badwater junction below the Furnace Creek Inn, go southeast on CA 190 2 miles to the first left turn, which is the signed Echo Canyon Road. This is a rough four-wheel-drive high-clearance vehicle road. Like at Titus Canyon it twists and turns through spectacular narrows in the lower canyon. At 7.8 miles, in a broad valley, a sign directs you to the right. Follow the arrows to the Inyo Mine and Amargosa turnoff. At 9.1 miles disregard the invitation to turn left for Amargosa. That's a crazy jeep track that descends to the valley. Don't take it. Instead continue straight in the flat valley before you. Right around the bend is the Inyo Mine site (signed). After a break at the mine, continue onward 1.9 miles to the tight turnaround where the road ends at the narrows. GPS: N36 29.750' / W116 41.073'

## The Hike

This hike, with an elevation gain of less than 700 feet spread over 3.6 miles, ends on a peak above the Amargosa Valley. A mountain view without the mountain climb! The drama of Echo Canyon is behind you, but the view ahead is worth the walk.

From the trailhead your pathway lies in the gravel wash through the tight gap. Out of the wash and on the desert floor, the winding route is an old jeep track. If you happen to lose the old roadbed, keep following the drainage and you'll spot it again. The old jeep track wanders but keeps heading east/northeast.

Up over the slanted strata in the bottom, the main canyon bends to the right. At 0.8 mile the jagged end of a ridge rises on the left. Continue on the jeep track. Rolling shrubby hills spread out on both sides.

The 2-mile middle stretch of the hike is in a high, rolling plateau, with little definition. The jeep track shifts from one faint wash to another on the gently rising terrain, often with a cairn to mark the way. Keep alert! On the northeast horizon a large humped promontory becomes visible. That's your destination. Interim ridges may tempt you to stray to peek over the edge, but stay with the jeep track. Enjoy the solitude and silence of open desert hiking. Suddenly you will be rewarded with the

*The Amargosa Overlook appears suddenly on the dramatic edge of the Funeral Mountains high above the Amargosa Desert.*

jaw-dropping view. The eastern edge of the Funeral Mountains drops abruptly to the Amargosa Valley below.

Continue on up to the top of the hump, which also gives you a view of the complex face of the Funerals. To the southeast, far in the distance on the valley floor, you may spot the Ash Meadows National Wildlife Refuge. At the right season it will be a blast of greenery in the desert. The site of the Devil's Hole pupfish, Ash Meadows is an interesting and worthy stop if you're heading to Las Vegas after Death Valley.

Stroll along the Funeral rim as time and daylight permit. At the low point of the precipice, angle southwest to pick up the jeep road. Head back via the same route.

This is a hike for unexpected discoveries. The trip downhill goes much faster.

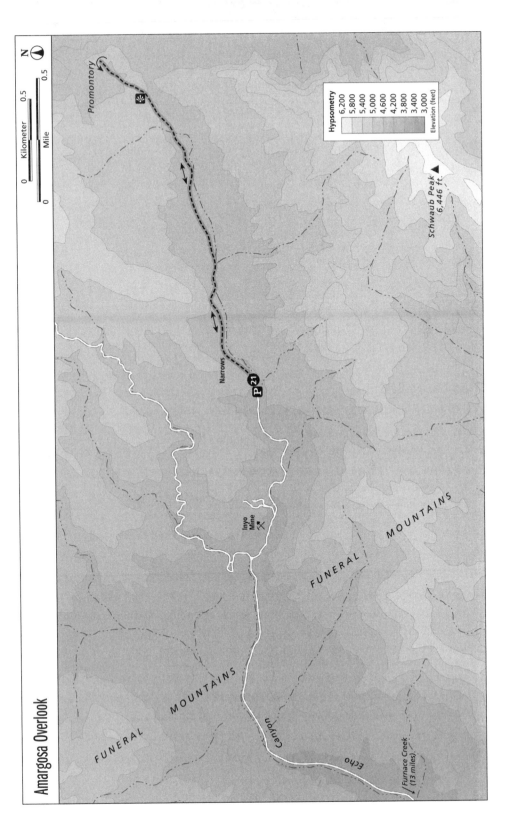

Amargosa Overlook

N

0          0.5
Kilometer

0          0.5
Mile

Promontory

Narrows

P 21

Inyo
Mine ✕

FUNERAL    MOUNTAINS

FUNERAL
MOUNTAINS

Echo    Canyon

Furnace Creek
(13 miles)

Schwaub Peak
6,446 ft. ▲

**Hypsometry**
6,200
5,800
5,400
5,000
4,600
4,200
3,800
3,400
3,000
Elevation (feet)

*Arriving at the edge of the Funeral Mountains, with the huge hump of the Promontory rising in the distance.*

## Miles and Directions

**0.0**  Start at the parking area at the end of the road. Hike in the gravel wash.

**0.5**  Pass through the tilted narrows.

**0.8**  Pass a jagged ridge on the left.

**2.2**  Come to a cairn; turn left to pick up a fainter two-track.

**3.0**  The promontory hump, to the northeast, becomes visible.

**3.4**  Arrive at the brink of the Funeral Range.

**3.6**  Reach the top of the promontory; turn around here.

**7.2**  Arrive back at the parking area.

*Option:* A 0.5-mile loop at the Inyo Mine site is a worthy stop to break up the long drive to the trailhead. This gold mine was a hotbed of activity in the first decades of the 1900s. Several wood structures are still standing, some are leaning, others have collapsed. The compressor to run the mill, as well as the mill itself, is massive. How did they get all this industrial equipment up that sketchy road? Much remains in place. Even the huge bin of the ore crusher is still intact. Scavengers often remove anything of value to recycle elsewhere. Not here. At the Inyo, visitors have set up a display of artifacts on a table for all to enjoy.

Mine openings have been secured by the park service, but it's still important to be careful around mine sites and to keep an eye on adventuresome companions. For more information about the history of mining in Death Valley, visit the Borax Museum (free admission) at Furnace Creek Ranch.

# 22 Keane Wonder Mine

An old mining road in the Funeral Mountains leads to the historic ruins of mines, a mill, and tramways. The route is steep and rocky, and the scenic views down the canyon to Death Valley are dramatic. (See note below; check with the park service to see if the site is open.)

**Start:** About 20 miles north of Furnace Creek
**Distance:** 4.0 miles out and back
**Hiking time:** 2 to 3 hours
**Difficulty:** Strenuous
**Trail surface:** Rocky trail
**Best season:** October through April
**Fees and permits:** National park entrance fee
**Maps:** NPS Death Valley Visitors Map; Trails Illustrated Death Valley National Park Map; USGS Chloride City-CA

**Trail contact:** Furnace Creek Visitor Center; (760) 786-3200; www.nps.gov/deva
**Special considerations:** As of 2016 the Keane Wonder mine has been closed by the park service pending cleanup. When the site has been adequately secured, it will reopen to the public. Check with the Furnace Creek Visitor Center on the status.

**Finding the trailhead:** From Daylight Pass Road at Hells Gate Junction, head south on Beatty Cutoff Road going toward Beatty Junction. After 4.3 miles turn left on the Keane Wonder Mine Road, a good gravel route, and drive 2.8 miles east to the end-of-the-road parking area below the Keane Wonder Mill.

From the visitor center at Furnace Creek, drive north on CA 190 for 11.3 miles to Beatty Cutoff Road and continue right (north) on Beatty-Daylight Pass Cutoff Road for another 5.7 miles to Keane Wonder Mine Road. Turn right and drive the final 2.8 miles to the end-of-the-road parking area/trailhead. GPS: N36 40.073' / W116 54.627'

## The Hike

The Keane Wonder Mine was developed at a time and in a location of hundreds of gold, silver, and lead strikes. The relative success of this venture makes its history and today's ruins all the more intriguing. It all began in 1903 with an almost-unheard-of lucky strike by an unemployed Irish miner named Jack Keane and his partner. After months of futile searching for silver, Keane accidentally stumbled across a huge ledge of gold, calling the find the "Keane Wonder Mine" out of his total astonishment at being so fortunate.

The news spread rapidly, and by 1904 the local gold rush was on. The mine changed hands several times, making a fortune for its original partners, and was capitalized with stocks sold to an eager public. In 1906 Homer Wilson bought the mine and started a consortium that operated the mine for a decade. Wilson ordered a twenty-stamp mill to crush the ore and a gravity-operated aerial tramway nearly 1 mile long. Loaded ore buckets coming down the canyon from the shaft pulled the

*The Keane Wonder Mine aerial tramway terminal overlooks a steep, rugged canyon.*

empty buckets back up. The tram contained thirteen towers, with the longest span being 1,200 feet, and had a vertical drop from top to bottom of 1,500 feet. Lack of water prevented the mill from operating at full capacity. Even so, total gold production from the mine was around $1.1 million, most of which was extracted between 1907 and 1911.

The Keane Wonder Mine was one of the two largest producing gold mines in the Death Valley region, the other being the Skidoo Mine. The artifacts and remnants of this mine have significant historical value and should not be removed or disturbed in any way. For more information about the history of mining in Death Valley, visit the Borax Museum (free admission) at Furnace Creek Ranch.

From the parking area, climb 0.1 mile to the informative kiosk located just below the Keane Wonder Mill ruins. The sign contains a bit of the history of Jack Keane's amazing 1903 gold strike. From the trailhead extensive mining debris can be seen in

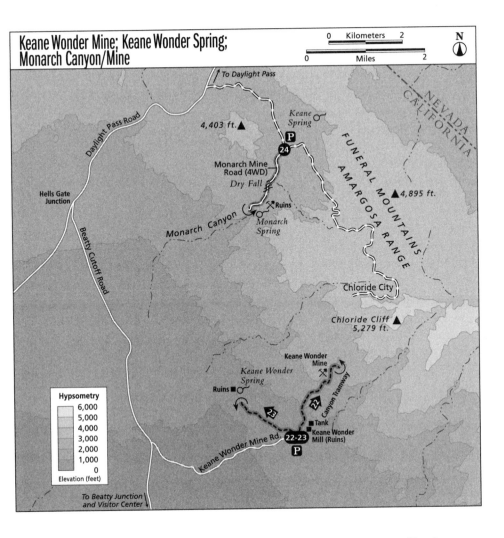

the wash to the left. At 0.4 mile the trail crosses under the tramway and begins a very steep climb straight up the ridge. In just 0.7 mile another 650 feet elevation is gained, at which point the trail contours and climbs more moderately to the right above the tramway canyon leading to the mine. At 1.7 miles the trail reaches the large aerial tramway terminal structure along with several shallow mine shafts.

From here a level trail extends another 0.5 mile around the canyon to an upper mine area containing additional adits. The view down canyon makes this short extension of the hike more than worthwhile. Another narrow trail climbs steeply 0.2 mile to the base of the main mine, which peers from the steep mountainside at around 3,000 feet elevation. Several stone building foundations are passed along the way. Around the bend and at the base of the mine, the area beyond is closed to hiking for public safety. Unsecured mine shafts present hazards and should definitely be avoided. Enjoy them from a safe distance before retracing your route to the trailhead, as you complete this round-trip hiking climb to one of Death Valley's largest and most interesting early twentieth-century mining ventures.

## Miles and Directions

**0.0** Start at the trailhead/parking area.

**0.1** Stop at the kiosk below the Keane Wonder Mill ruins.

**1.7** Arrive at the aerial tramway terminal.

**2.0** View the stone building foundations and mine shafts below the main mine openings.

**4.0** Arrive back at the trailhead.

# 23 Keane Wonder Spring

This nearly level trip takes you to the spring that was essential to the Keane Wonder Mine and mill operations. The area has many traces of mining activities of the last century. Like Keane Wonder Mine, the spring is also closed (2016) pending cleanup by the park service. Check with the Furnace Creek Visitor Center as to its status.

**See map on page 99.**
**Start:** About 20 miles north of Furnace Creek
**Distance:** 2.0 miles out and back
**Hiking time:** 1 to 2 hours
**Difficulty:** Easy
**Trail surface:** Sandy, rocky path
**Best season:** October through April
**Fees and permits:** National park entrance fee

**Maps:** NPS Death Valley Visitors Map; Trails Illustrated Death Valley National Park Map; USGS Chloride City-CA
**Trail contact:** Furnace Creek Visitor Center; (760) 786-3200; www.nps.gov/deva
**Special considerations:** Like the mine, Keane Wonder Spring has been closed to the public, pending cleanup. Check with the visitor center for current status.

**Finding the trailhead:** From Daylight Pass Road at Hells Gate Junction, head south on Beatty Cutoff Road going toward Beatty Junction. After 4.3 miles turn left on the signed Keane Wonder Mine Road, a good gravel route, and drive 2.8 miles east to the end-of-the-road parking area below the Keane Wonder Mill.

From the visitor center at Furnace Creek, drive north on CA 190 for 11.3 miles to Beatty Cutoff Road and continue right (north) on Beatty-Daylight Pass Cutoff Road for another 5.7 miles to Keane Wonder Mine Road. Turn right and drive the final 2.8 miles to the end-of-the-road parking area/trailhead. The trail to the spring begins at the northeastern corner of the parking area and heads north. GPS: N36 40.073' / W116 54.627'

## The Hike

The Keane Wonder Mine complex was at its height in the gold boom from 1906 to 1912. It was resuscitated by optimistic prospectors and investors several times. The most recent renaissance was in 1935–1937 when cyanide leaching of the mine tailings took place on the site. The tanks used for that operation still stand below the parking area.

Where the mine trail goes directly up the hillside, the user trail to Keane Wonder Spring goes left. The trail begins after you drop into the debris-strewn wash just north of the parking area. Emerging from the wash above the pair of settling tanks nestled together, you pick up the well-traveled trail. A broken pipeline lies 50 yards below on the hillside; it will lead you to the spring.

The trail travels by numerous mine openings and scenic travertine rock outcroppings. At 0.6 mile the trail merges with a trail coming up from lower on the hillside; you'll return to the parking area via this trail on the hike back. More mine openings

*Salt grass thrives in the marsh at Keane Wonder Spring.*

and a stone foundation are nearby. The trail is meticulously bordered with rocks for most of the way.

Continuing northward, soon your nose will detect the scent of sulfur, even on a windy day. There, at 0.8 mile, the trickling stream from the spring crosses the road. Above the trail take a side trip to the spring. The salt grass marsh flourishes in the salt-encrusted soil 30 yards above the trail. A sign posted by the National Park Service warns of gas hazards in the mine shaft immediately above the spring. The area has many mine shafts, some flooded, all dangerous.

This mining wasteland is also full of wildlife. Heavy bighorn sheep use is evident from the droppings on the damp spring banks. Birds and crickets create a symphony of sound in the desert stillness.

Continuing northward, the trail follows a crude aqueduct and curves around, now totally out of sight of the parking area and industrial sprawl there. More of the ubiquitous mine sites and another sulfurous spring bracket the trail. At your destination at 1 mile, you'll find a mine chute and a miner's cabin. Rusty cans, pieces of pipe, and the usual pieces of nondescript rusty artifacts litter the ground. In the dry desert air, the cabin is so well preserved it appears the miner left recently. Across the shallow gully to the west is a large rock outcropping atop a hill. Notice the stone walls built under the natural overhang. Did wind, heat, or both drive the miner to take refuge in such a primitive rock shelter?

Return the way you came, continuing on the wide rock-lined trail at the junction you passed on the way in. In sight of the parking area, the trail dissipates in the mine debris in the gully near the largest of the remaining tanks. From there you have to pick your way back to your vehicle.

The amazing thing about the Keane Wonder Spring hike is its plethora of mine sites. The Keane Wonder Mine was heralded to be the richest gold strike in Death Valley, attracting a multitude of hopeful miners. At its height nearly 500 prospectors were working in the area. Thus everywhere you look there's another mine mouth with its tailings dripping down the hillside. Mine tunnels like rabbit holes cut through the ridges and disappear into the mountainside. Curious children and adults should avoid all mines.

For more information about the history of mining in Death Valley, visit the Borax Museum (free admission) at Furnace Creek Ranch.

## Miles and Directions

**0.0** Start at the end-of-the-road trailhead; the trail heads north above the pair of settling tanks.

**0.3** The trail crosses a wash and continues following the contour of the hillside.

**0.6** The trail merges with another trail from the lower hillside. Continue on the trail to the spring/mine site.

**0.8** The first spring crosses the trail. An aqueduct ditch parallels the trail.

**1.0** Arrive at a mine chute and cabin and another sulfur seep. Turn around here.

**2.0** Arrive back at the trailhead.

# 24 Monarch Canyon/Mine

This out-and-back hike takes you down a rocky canyon in the Funeral Mountains to an 80-foot dry fall, a well-preserved stamp mill, and a desert spring.

**See map on page 99.**
**Start:** About 27.5 miles north of Furnace Creek
**Distance:** 3.0 miles out and back
**Hiking time:** 2 to 3 hours
**Difficulty:** Easy
**Trail surface:** Four-wheel-drive road, rocky trail, clear wash

**Best season:** October through April
**Fees and permits:** National park entrance fee
**Maps:** NPS Death Valley Visitors Map; Trails Illustrated Death Valley National Park Map; USGS Chloride City-CA
**Trail contact:** Furnace Creek Visitor Center; (760) 786-3200; www.nps.gov/deva

**Finding the trailhead:** From NV 374/Daylight Pass Road 3.4 miles northeast of Hells Gate Junction in Boundary Canyon and 15.8 miles southwest of Beatty, Nevada, look for a road to the south that is marked only with a small sign recommending four-wheel drive. Carefully driven high-clearance two-wheel-drive vehicles can negotiate this road for 2.2 miles to the bottom of upper Monarch Canyon. High-clearance four-wheel drive is required for vehicular travel beyond this point to Chloride City. The rough Monarch Mine Road takes off south from this point. This road junction can serve as the trailhead for the hike down Monarch Canyon. However, the hike can be shortened by 1.2 miles round-trip by driving down Monarch Mine Road to a point just above the dry fall. GPS: N36 44.216' / W116 54.736'

## The Hike

Hikers can start at the unsigned junction between the rough Chloride City Road and four-wheel-drive Monarch Mine Road (3 miles round-trip to Monarch Spring) or at the end of the Monarch Mine Road (1.8 miles round-trip). From the Chloride City Road junction, the trip starts out in rounded, low-lying hills. The four-wheel-drive road descends southwesterly, entering a rocky canyon after 0.3 mile.

At 0.6 mile the road ends above a striking 80-foot dry fall. A major side canyon enters from the left, bounded by high cliffs marked by folded, multicolored bands of rock. Continue left around the falls on the old mining trail. After another 0.1 mile the trail drops to the wash, which is covered with horsetails and Mormon tea. This is favored habitat for quail and other birds. The base of the dry fall is definitely worth visiting, so turn right and walk 0.1 mile up to the precipice. In addition to the main wide falls, another smaller but equally high falls guards the canyon bowl to the left. The canyon walls are distinguished by shelf rock catch basins, overhangs, and contorted layers of colorful, twisted rock.

Proceeding back down the sandy canyon wash, an eroded mining trail crosses to the right and then drops back to the canyon floor at 1 mile. Rock cairns are in place for the return trip. At 1.2 miles the wood and cement ruins of the Monarch Mine

*The base of the Monarch Mine stamp mill.*

stamp mill are reached on the left. The ore chute to the mill extends up an almost vertical rock face.

To further experience the rugged grandeur of Monarch Canyon, continue down the wash another 0.3 mile to the brushy bottom just below Monarch Spring. Here the canyon bends sharply to the right and begins to narrow. Hiking below the spring would be difficult due to dense vegetation and loose, rocky side slopes. Retrace your route back to your vehicle.

For more information about the history of mining in Death Valley, visit the Borax Museum (free admission) at Furnace Creek Ranch.

## Miles and Directions

**0.0** Start at the trailhead at the junction of Chloride City Road and Monarch Mine Road in upper Monarch Canyon.

**0.6** Arrive at an 80-foot dry fall at the end of Monarch Mine Road.

**0.7** The mining trail drops to the bottom of a canyon wash.

**0.8** Walk up the wash to the base of the dry fall.

**1.2** Arrive at the Monarch Mine stamp mill ruins.

**1.5** Arrive at Monarch Spring. Return to the trailhead by the same route.

**3.0** Arrive back at the trailhead.

# 25 Death Valley Buttes

This is a short but challenging hike/scramble to the summits of two of the three prominent Death Valley Buttes at the southern foot of the Grapevine Mountains. The vistas are among the most dramatic in the Park.

**Start:** About 14 miles northeast of Stovepipe Wells Village
**Distance:** 3.6 miles out and back to Red Top with 1,300 feet elevation gain/loss (2.0 miles out and back to easternmost Death Valley Butte)
**Hiking time:** 4 to 5 hours
**Difficulty:** Strenuous to Red Top due to exposed, narrow summit ridge with loose rock and steep drop-offs (moderate to the eastern Death Valley Butte)
**Trail surface:** Sandy wash, good user trail, rugged route-finding with rock scrambling
**Best season:** Late October to early April
**Fees and permits:** National park entrance fee

**Maps:** NPS Death Valley Visitor's Map; Trails Illustrated Death Valley National Park Map; USGS Chloride City-CA and Stovepipe Wells NE-CA
**Trail contact:** Furnace Creek Visitor Center; (760) 786-3200; www.nps.gov/deva
**Other:** There are no facilities at the parking area. There is a vault toilet at Hells Gate 0.7 mile to the north.
**Special considerations:** Proceed slowly and carefully through a rough and rocky 0.3-mile stretch just below the summit of Red Top. Carry adequate water and be especially cautious on the exposed ridge during times of high wind.

**Finding the trailhead:** Some hikers start at Hells Gate, 22 miles northeast of Furnace Creek. Hells Gate is certainly a good vantage point for an overview of this up-and-down hike, and, if you look carefully, you can spot the user trail climbing the extreme east end of Death Valley Buttes. However, to avoid walking the 0.5 mile of alluvial fan and wash next to the highway, drive 0.7 mile south of Hells Gate and park at mile 6.1 (0.1 mile north of milepost 6) alongside the Daylight Pass Road. Look for a safe wide spot on the west side of the highway atop a small rise about 50 yards south of the wash that crosses the road. GPS: N36 42.912' / W116 58.915' (elevation 2,000 feet)

## The Hike

This is an adventuresome hike where looks can truly be deceiving. As you drive past the south side of the buttes, their ascent appears quick, easy, and straightforward. Not so. The trek to the summit of Red Top is a serious one and should only be attempted by those experienced in off-trail route-finding on steep, rough terrain.

From the parking area hike back up the highway (toward Hells Gate) about 50 yards to the wash and turn left (north) up the wash. After about 100 yards you'll reach the rocky eastern base of Death Valley Buttes where it meets the wash. Continue another 20 to 30 yards to a distinct user trail that climbs the rocky slope up to the buttes. Although faint in places the user trail becomes more prominent the farther

*From the summit of Red Top, high point of Death Valley Buttes, looking across Death Valley to the Cottonwood Mountains far to the west.*

up you go and is easy to follow for about 1.4 miles to the rugged northeast buttress of Red Top.

From the parking area the first high point on the main ridgeline is reached at 0.6 mile. Beyond to the west the user trail remains visible. There are several rocky spires to work around before the 2,750-foot top of the eastern Death Valley Butte at 1 mile. Little remains of a metal marker that once stood atop the butte. East Butte is a great destination in its own right with superb views all around, except to the immediate southwest, which is blocked by the higher Red Top.

From the eastern butte the user trail veers left and quickly loses 260 vertical feet before leveling out on a long, fairly smooth stretch of the ridge. From the saddle the trail drops off the ridge to the right (north) side and contours for about 0.4 mile to the rocky base of the rugged northeast face of Red Top. This is where the real climb begins.

The final push to the 3,017-foot apex of Red Top is difficult, with 300 feet of elevation gain over 0.3 mile of rock scrambling. One short segment of steeply slanted bedrock is especially tricky due to serious exposure for about 10 feet. Hand-over-hand rock work is necessary in some places. Red Top isn't for everyone. Many hikers would be satisfied with just climbing the eastern butte, which is only 267 feet lower.

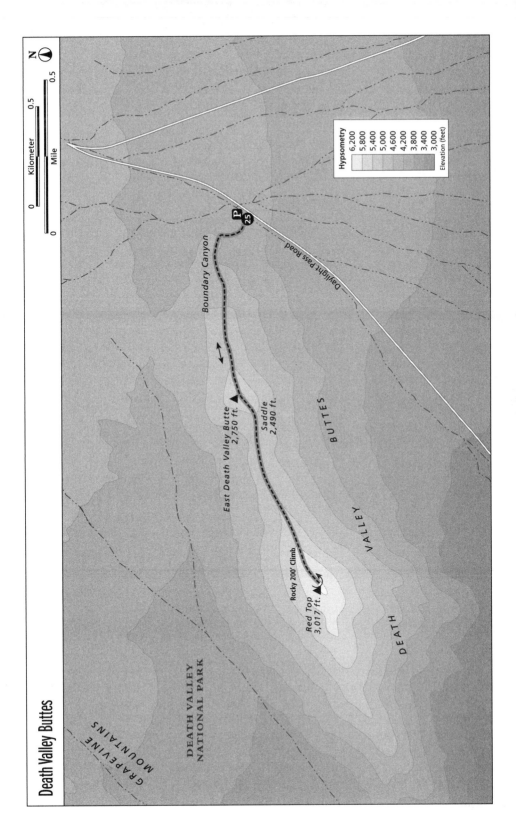

Death Valley Buttes

This upper rock climb portion of the hike is marked by an occasional cairn, and in one place by a rock alignment, to help guide the route. Still, careful route-finding is essential, and there is no obvious best way. This isn't a technical climb requiring special equipment, but every move must be calculated to ensure safety.

The summit ridge levels out at the top of the rock scramble with an easy 0.1-mile stroll to Red Top, marked by a brass benchmark. The ridge is sparsely dotted with creosote, Mormon tea, and spruce bush. Red rock, colored by oxidized iron, covers the ground. The 360-degree panorama from Red Top is spectacular—exceeded only in this part of the park by the views from Thimble and Corkscrew Peaks, which rise prominently to the northwest. Perhaps most impressive are the views southward of Death Valley overseen by Telescope Peak and the entire vast complex of the Mesquite Flat Sand Dunes to the southwest.

Before getting to Red Top you might be thinking of two possibilities: continuing on to the westernmost of the three major Death Valley Buttes (2,068 feet) or dropping off the side of Red Top for a loop hike. Both options are not recommended. The westernmost butte isn't even connected to Red Top. It stands alone, separated by a major wash. After ascending Red Top you definitely won't feel like dropping some 1,800 feet on dangerous rock and then climbing another 700 feet, condensed within 1 horizontal mile. Dropping off either side of Red Top on steep, unstable rocks is an equally bad idea.

The most reasonable and enjoyable choice is to retrace your route back down to the parking area. Picking your way down the steep, rocky northeast face of Red Top will be challenge enough.

## Miles and Directions

**0.0**  Start from the wash that crosses Daylight Pass Road near milepost 6 (2,000 feet). Head 50 yards up the highway and turn left at the wash.

**0.1**  Pick up the user trail at the eastern base of the buttes.

**1.0**  Reach the top of the eastern Death Valley Butte (2,750 feet). (***Option:*** Turn around here for the short hike.)

**1.4**  Arrive at the base of Red Top.

**1.8**  Reach the summit of Red Top (3,017 feet).

**3.6**  Arrive back at the parking area.

# 26 Corkscrew Peak

This is a challenging full-day hike with an elevation gain of 3,200 feet to the apex of an iconic, aptly named peak in the southern Grapevine Mountains.

**Start:** About 22 miles north of Furnace Creek
**Distance:** 8.0 miles out and back with 3,200 feet elevation gain/loss
**Hiking time:** 7 to 9 hours
**Difficulty:** Strenuous due to distance, steepness, and elevation gain
**Trail surface:** Gravel wash, good user trail, moderate rock scrambling near the summit
**Best season:** October to April
**Fees and permits:** National park entrance fee
**Maps:** NPS Death Valley Visitors Map; Trails Illustrated Death Valley National Park Map;

USGS Chloride City-CA, Daylight Pass-CA, and Thimble Peak-CA
**Trail contact:** Furnace Creek Visitor Center; (760) 786-3200; www.nps.gov/deva
**Other:** There are no facilities at the parking area, but the wide level spot next to the highway has room for several vehicles.
**Special considerations:** There is no official trail and recent flooding has erased portions of the user trail, especially in the wash near the parking area. Carry more water than you think you'll need for the arduous long climb to the summit.

**Finding the trailhead:** About 1 mile northeast of Hells Gate and 17 miles southwest of Beatty, Nevada, park alongside the Daylight Pass Road next to the Corkscrew Peak sign next to milepost 8. GPS: N36 44.341' / W116 58.090'

## The Hike

From the parking area Corkscrew Peak dominates the skyline several miles away to the northwest. The route begins toward the right (east) side of the peak. There isn't an official trail, but most of this popular climb is served by an easy-to-follow user-created trail, except at the very beginning. Recent flooding has erased portions of the trail in the Boundary Canyon wash.

From the parking area hike north to northwest about 0.4 mile, aiming toward a mountain with banded rock. Head toward the ridge on the right side of the first side wash and then enter the left side of the second side wash. Continue up the wash toward brown boulders with splashes of oxidized red and white rocks. The wash narrows and climbs to a low ridge above a mesquite thicket at around 0.6 mile with the way occasionally marked with a cairn. At this point you'll pick up a good user trail that leads around low ridges and gullies to a wide wash at 0.9 mile.

Turn right (north) up this main wash, which provides good walking on a hard-packed pebbly surface. The user trail varies from distinct to faint to nonexistent, but you don't really need a trail in the wide-open wash. After about 1 mile the canyon closes in on the left side of the wash, marked by a large boulder. A dark rock band

*Huge volcanic rocks frame a square window on the main south ridge of Corkscrew Peak just below the summit.*

marks the right side. Enter this left side canyon at 1.9 miles and continue up a short distance to an alignment of rocks that spans the 25-foot-wide canyon floor.

If you continue straight up the wash, you'll find a narrowing canyon with 50-foot-high corrugated walls. Instead, turn left at the rock alignment and climb a short side canyon with an easy 4-foot-high ledge. The trail follows a knife ridge northward with the exit canyon wash directly below on the right. The imposing southern buttress of Corkscrew Peak looms ahead and far above.

After about 0.4 mile of moderate incline up the open ridge, the trail begins climbing more steeply through a mostly rocky section of outcroppings that resemble dinosaur fins. Then the trail zigzags through the rocks toward two distinctive cliff bands that guard the southeast face of the peak. A bighorn sheep trail veers to the left. The main user trail remains visible to the high western horizon and at times is brutally steep. A striking maroon-colored ridge lies to the right (northeast). A dramatic series of pointed spires and columns highlight the continued ascent to where the

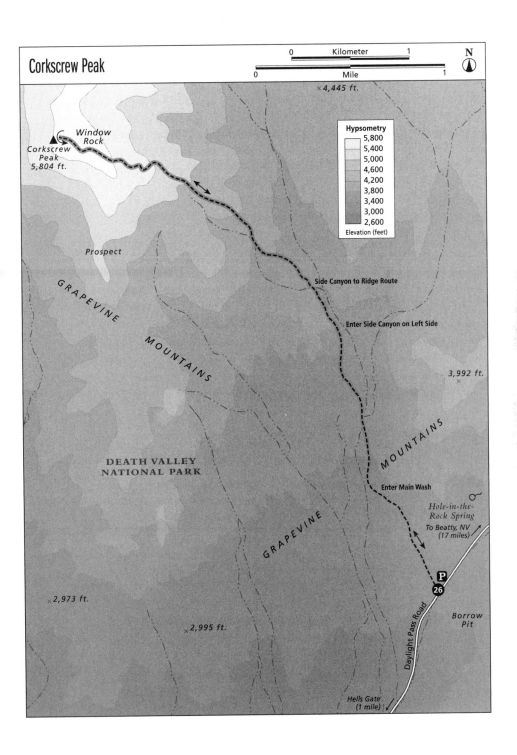

Corkscrew Peak

Kilometer
0          1
Mile
0          1

N

× 4,445 ft.

**Hypsometry**
5,800
5,400
5,000
4,600
4,200
3,800
3,400
3,000
2,600
Elevation (feet)

Window
Rock

Corkscrew
Peak
5,804 ft.

Prospect

G R A P E V I N E

M O U N T A I N S

Side Canyon to Ridge Route

Enter Side Canyon on Left Side

3,992 ft.
×

DEATH VALLEY
NATIONAL PARK

M O U N T A I N S

Enter Main Wash

Hole-in-the-
Rock Spring

To Beatty, NV
(17 miles)

P
26

G R A P E V I N E

× 2,973 ft.

Borrow
Pit

× 2,995 ft.

Daylight Pass Road

Hells Gate
(1 mile)

trail intersects the northern edge of the highest and largest cliff band. Along the way clusters of cotton top cacti dot the landscape.

The final pull from the lower rock band to the main south ridge of the peak gains 600 vertical feet in not much more horizontal distance. But upon reaching this ridge you've all but bagged the peak, so you can savor a well-earned break next to a feature that resembles an arch but is actually a large opening formed by the placement of horizontal and vertical rocks. We'll call it Window Rock for lack of a formal name.

From Window Rock the trail up is clearly visible, gaining about 250 feet in 0.1 mile along a bony spine to the summit. The apex offers lots of places to perch, photograph, and take in much of the eastern half of the park. Perhaps your breath was taken away on the way up, but brace yourself for views that will once again take your breath away! Corkscrew is surrounded by jagged, cathedral-like pinnacles, spires, and columns. Especially impressive are the views northwest to much higher Thimble Peak, beyond to Palmer Peak, and southward to Death Valley and surrounding mountain ranges as far as the eye can see. Be sure to orient your park overview map for this fabulous panorama of Death Valley geography.

It's worthwhile to read the peak register that is wedged in a rock pile, if for no other reason than to compare your experience with that of previous visitors. For example, one prior hiker wrote: "What a fabulous hike! Death Valley has so much to offer. Thankful to spend Thanksgiving here with some great people."

On the way back down, upon reaching Window Rock, you might be tempted to create a loop route by descending the rugged backside of the cliff wall on the main south ridge. This is definitely not recommended due to dangerous loose footing. It is far safer and more enjoyable to make this hike an out and back by retracing the user trail back to the parking area. You'll see things you missed on the way up and be treated to equally fabulous vistas all the way down.

As you hike back down the main wash, be on the lookout for the trail you came up on that climbs out of the wash to the left, reaching the parking area after about 0.9 mile.

## Miles and Directions

**0.0** Start from the parking pullout alongside Daylight Pass Road next to milepost 8 (2,580 feet). Hike north to northwest for about 0.4 mile.

**0.6** The user trail becomes more evident along a low ridge.

**0.9** Enter the main wash.

**1.9** Enter the side canyon on the left side of the wash.

**2.1** Reach a rock alignment; turn left (northwest) to climb the ridgeline user trail.

**3.5** Steep, rocky section of trail.

**3.9** Arrive at Window Rock on the south summit ridge.

**4.0** Reach the summit of Corkscrew Peak (5,804 feet).

**8.0** Arrive back at the trailhead on Daylight Pass Road.

# 27 Lostman Spring

This is an unusual Death Valley hike—it starts high (4,660 feet) and goes down (to 3,088 feet). The basalt formations are spectacular, offsetting the faded spring that is the destination.

**Start:** 18 miles west of Beatty, Nevada, on the Titus Canyon Road
**Distance:** 8.6 miles out and back with 1,600 feet elevation loss/gain
**Hiking time:** About 6 hours
**Difficulty:** Moderate, all downhill for 4.3 miles, then all uphill
**Trail surface:** Sandy streambed, gravel wash, rocky in spots
**Best season:** Mid-October to early April
**Fees and permits:** National park entrance fee

**Maps:** NPS Death Valley Visitors Map; Trails Illustrated Death Valley National Park Map; USGS Thimble Peak-CA
**Trail contact:** Furnace Creek Visitor Center; (760) 786-3200; www.nps.gov/deva
**Special considerations:** There's limited parking on Titus Canyon Road, and no facilities. Do not count on water at Lostman Spring. Bring your own. Give yourself plenty of time for the 13-mile drive down the rest of Titus Canyon Road before dark. It takes at least an hour.

**Finding the trailhead:** From NV 374, 10.5 miles east of the Hells Gate entrance to Death Valley National Park and 6.5 miles west of Beatty, Nevada, turn northwest onto signed Titus Canyon Road. This is a one-way limited-access gravel jeep road. High-clearance vehicles are recommended; four-wheel drive is also advised. Check with the Furnace Creek Visitor Center for road conditions. It is a slow and careful drive to the parking area, 11.2 miles from the turn. Park at the curve at the second drainage into Titanothere Canyon, before the road climbs to Red Pass. Parking is very limited, with a spot available just beyond where the wash crosses the road, and then two more possible parking sites just ahead where the road curves before the final ascent to the pass. GPS: N36 49.683' / W117 01.323'

## The Hike

Above the parking area, on the north side of Titus Canyon Road, a dramatic collection of hoodoos and spires rises above the rock cliffs. It was in this majestic setting, in 1933, that archaeologists unearthed the fossilized remains of the titanothere, an 8-foot-high rhino-like mammal of the Late Eocene era. Compared to Edgar Titus, a prospector who disappeared looking for a spring and got a road and canyon named for him, the titanotheres ruled the region for thousands of years. From prehistoric horses, to gigantic rodents and beavers, to the massive titanotheres, the open savannah of Eocene times, 30 to 35 million years ago, saw a swirl of creatures, providing us with the enchanting canyon name.

In spite of the dotted line on the Trails Illustrated map, there is no trail down the canyon. Seasonal rains quickly erase all traces of hikers in the stream bottom. The pathway is clear, however: Head downhill, using the sandy bottom as a trail whenever possible.

*Titanothere Canyon closes to a narrow necklike gap just above Lostman Spring.*

At 0.9 mile from the road, the east drainage of Titanothere Canyon comes in on the left. Cairns mark the junction, unless they have been washed away. The east drainage is tighter and more difficult going. Continue downhill in the main canyon. The stream floor widens thereafter.

Thimble Peak rises on your right, its striped ramparts very colorful on the skyline. The floor path winds between the sloping hills, taking sharp turns where it hits a mountain wall, steadily dropping. Your route is unencumbered by challenging dry falls. There is only an intermittent step over a 2- or 3-foot chunk of base rock. Occasionally the boulders in the bottom will encourage you to seek a side route, to the right or left, but then it's back to the sandy bottom.

At 2.5 miles from the road, a large side wash comes in on the left as the main wash makes a sharp turn to the right. Rocks and boulders have been transported to the main drainage over the years, but just below the junction you're back walking on sand.

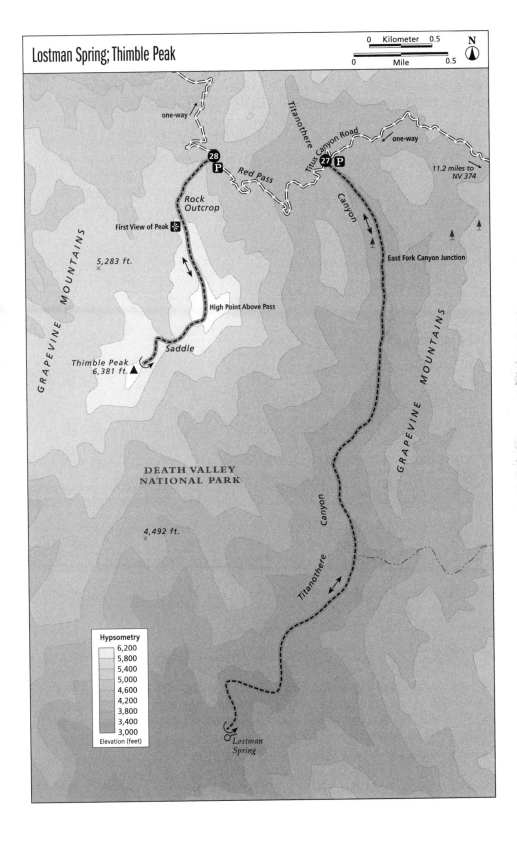

# Lostman Spring; Thimble Peak

0   Kilometer   0.5

0   Mile   0.5

N

one-way

Titanothere

Titus Canyon Road

one-way

28 P

27 P

Red Pass

11.2 miles to NV 374

Rock Outcrop

First View of Peak

Canyon

GRAPEVINE MOUNTAINS

East Fork Canyon Junction

5,283 ft.

High Point Above Pass

Saddle

Thimble Peak
6,381 ft.

GRAPEVINE MOUNTAINS

DEATH VALLEY
NATIONAL PARK

4,492 ft.

Titanothere Canyon

Titanothere

**Hypsometry**

| 6,200 |
| 5,800 |
| 5,400 |
| 5,000 |
| 4,600 |
| 4,200 |
| 3,800 |
| 3,400 |
| 3,000 |

Elevation (feet)

Lostman
Spring

Another drainage comes in on the left at 3.4 miles. The left side of the canyon is rimmed with jagged spires as the geology becomes dramatic. The convoluted canyon walls are compressed. A basalt dike soars above and nearly blocks the wash. At the narrows a 30-foot-wide twisty gorge is the only opening to the valley below, where the spring is visible on the hillside, 0.5 mile below the gap.

At 3,088 feet elevation you've arrived at your destination, 4.3 miles from the parking area. Judging by the size of the cottonwood trees and the large growth of rushes, Lostman Spring used to be a genuine oasis in this otherwise dry drainage. Years of drought have had their impact. What water is left is underground. Even though the foliage is parched from drought, there's still a contrast with the barren hills and peaks that surround the large valley. The spring is upstaged by the geology—dynamic stripes, compressed folds, intricate strata, basalt spires. It's a spectacular spot.

Even without water the spring site provides a soft, peaceful spot for lunch before the uphill hike back to Titus Canyon Road. It also features the only shade you can enjoy on this straight north–south hike. At least going back uphill you will have the sun at your back.

## Miles and Directions

**0.0**  Start at the parking pullout on Titus Canyon Road and head down the canyon.

**0.9**  Arrive at the junction with the east fork of Titanothere Canyon; continue downhill.

**2.5**  Pass a large side wash on the left.

**3.4**  Pass another drainage on the left.

**3.8**  The canyon narrows.

**4.3**  Reach Lostman Spring; turn around here.

**8.6**  Arrive back at the trailhead on Titus Canyon Road.

# 28 Thimble Peak

A short hike to a spectacular peak in the Grapevine Mountains that provides a sweeping view of Death Valley National Park.

**See map on page 117.**
**Start:** At Red Pass, mile 12.5 on Titus Canyon Road
**Distance:** 4.0 miles out and back with 1,700 feet elevation gain/loss
**Hiking time:** 4 to 5 hours
**Difficulty:** Strenuous due to elevation gain/loss and some rock scrambling at the peak
**Trail surface:** Gravel user trail, some rock scrambles
**Best season:** October to April
**Fees and permits:** National park entrance fee

**Maps:** NPS Death Valley Visitors Map; Trails Illustrated Death Valley National Park Map; USGS Thimble Peak-CA
**Trail contact:** Furnace Creek Visitor Center; (760) 786-3200; www.nps.gov/deva
**Special considerations:** Weather and road conditions on Titus Canyon Road can limit access to the hike. Check with the Furnace Creek Visitor Center the day before your outing. Be prepared for wind. The 12-mile drive down the rest of Titus Canyon Road cannot be hurried. Give yourself plenty of time to enjoy the trip—at least an hour.

**Finding the trailhead:** From NV 374, 10.5 miles east of the Hells Gate entrance to Death Valley National Park and 6.5 miles west of Beatty, Nevada, turn northwest onto signed Titus Canyon Road. This is a one-way limited-access gravel jeep road. High-clearance vehicles are recommended; four-wheel drive is also advised. Check with the visitor center for road conditions. It is a slow and careful drive to the parking area at the top of Red Pass, 12.5 miles from the turn. There is room for only 3 vehicles at the pullout at the pass. GPS: N36 49.721' / W117 1.939'

## The Hike

From the pass pick up the footpath just to the west, around the curve at the road summit. The well-traveled pathway zigzags up the ridge 0.2 mile above the parking area to the first rock outcrop. From here, already, a glorious view extends in every direction. The path continues its route upward to the second outcrop, 0.5 mile from the parking area. From there the slope abates somewhat as you continue up the ridge to the hilltop and a view of Thimble rising on your right. This promontory provides a great view of the peak.

After pausing at the basalt outcropping, resume your hike. Take the user trail down the southern flank of the ridge, zigzagging down 400 feet to the saddle below Thimble Peak.

Rising from the saddle on the gravel pathway, you can tackle the summit from the east, or you can wrap around to the north side for a more gentle approach from the western flank. The direct route, from the east, does require a hand-over-hand scramble up a 5-foot slightly tilted ledge. Once past this challenging spot, the route is stable, though steep, to the summit. The alternate route has less exposure.

*The trail drops down the ridge to a saddle before climbing the backside of the towering cliffs of Thimble Peak.*

In either case the view from the top is magnificent, stretching down central Death Valley to south of Badwater, sweeping around to Telescope Peak and the Sierras in the distance. In the foreground Corkscrew Peak rises to the south. And, if you are planning future outings, you can spot Titanothere Canyon below to the east, dropping to Lostman Spring.

Head back to the parking area by the same path you came on. As you pause en route to the parking area and look back, Thimble appears much less daunting than it did on the way up.

## Miles and directions

**0.0**  Start from the parking pullout on Titus Canyon Road; take the footpath to the west.

**0.2**  Reach the first rock outcrop.

**0.5**  Reach the second rock outcrop.

**1.5**  Arrive at the promontory ridge; enjoy the view of Thimble Peak before dropping down to the saddle.

**2.0**  Reach the summit of Thimble Peak (6,381 feet).

**4.0**  Arrive back at the trailhead at Titus Canyon Road.

# 29 Titus Canyon Narrows

This narrow canyon cut deeply into the Grapevine Mountains is dominated by majestic cliffs and arched caverns.

**Start:** About 36 miles north of Furnace Creek
**Distance:** 4.2 miles out and back
**Hiking time:** 2 to 3 hours
**Difficulty:** Easy
**Trail surface:** Rocky four-wheel-drive road
**Best season:** October through April

**Fees and permits:** National park entrance fee
**Maps:** NPS Death Valley Visitors Map; Trails Illustrated Death Valley National Park Map; USGS Fall Canyon-CA
**Trail contact:** Furnace Creek Visitor Center; (760) 786-3200; www.nps.gov/deva

**Finding the trailhead:** The two-way road to the mouth of Titus Canyon is off Scotty's Castle Road, 17.3 miles north of the CA 190 junction. Take the signed dirt road northeast 2.7 miles up the alluvial fan to the mouth of Titus Canyon, where there is a large parking area with a vault toilet. GPS: N36 49.310' / W117 10.458'

## The Hike

Titus Canyon is the longest and one of the grandest canyons in Death Valley. Titus Canyon Road was built in 1926 to serve the town of Leadville, an investor scam that became a ghost town the following year. This 26-mile one-way unpaved jeep road is regularly affected by seasonal floods. Driving the entire length of the canyon requires a four-wheel-drive high-clearance vehicle. If you don't have one, the only way to visit majestic Titus Canyon is by foot.

Titus Canyon is a slot canyon, immediately narrow at its mouth. From the brightness of the desert floor, you are plunged into the cool shadows of the canyon. Cliffs tower hundreds of feet above. Cool breezes rush down through the funnel of the canyon. The display of cliffs continues without intermission for 2 miles as you hike up the primitive canyon road. The variety of colors and textures on the canyon walls is immense and ever changing. The limestone layers are twisted and folded; fault lines run at all angles. In addition to the power of the earth's surface to rise and fall and shift, the power of water is visible throughout the slot canyon. The water-smoothed walls indicate the level of flooding. The curves of the canyon's path reveal the erosive power of the swift floods as they roar down the narrow opening with their load of scouring boulders. Flash floods are a real danger in Titus.

The 2-mile hike through the narrows is overpowering. Like walking down the nave of a European cathedral, hiking up (and later down) Titus is a soaring experience, but also an immensely humbling one. The Titus Canyon Fault, which created the canyon, slices through the heart of the Grapevine Mountains, laying their innards bare for both the geologist and layman to enjoy.

*The canyon walls in lower Titus Canyon dwarf hikers.*

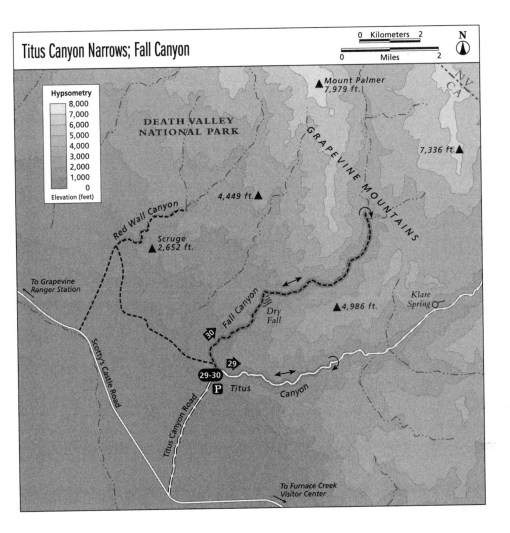

# Titus Canyon Narrows; Fall Canyon

0 Kilometers 2

0 Miles 2

N

**Hypsometry**

Elevation (feet)
- 8,000
- 7,000
- 6,000
- 5,000
- 4,000
- 3,000
- 2,000
- 1,000
- 0

▲ Mount Palmer 7,979 ft.

DEATH VALLEY NATIONAL PARK

7,336 ft. ▲

GRAPEVINE MOUNTAINS

Red Wall Canyon

4,449 ft. ▲

Scruge ▲ 2,652 ft.

To Grapevine Ranger Station

Fall Canyon

Dry Fall

▲ 4,986 ft.

Klare Spring ⚲

30

29

29-30

P  Titus  Canyon

Scotty's Castle Road

Titus Canyon Road

To Furnace Creek Visitor Center

## Miles and Directions

**0.0** Start at the canyon mouth and follow the four-wheel-drive road east into Titus Canyon.

**2.1** The narrow canyon opens into a broader valley. Turn around here and retrace your steps.

**4.2** Arrive back at the parking area.

*Option:* For a longer and more strenuous hike—a total of about 12 miles and 5 to 6 hours—continue up the road another 4 miles to Klare Spring. The canyon floor is considerably broader, after passing from the narrows at 2.1 miles, although quite steep, but the towering peaks of the Grapevines provide a spectacular backdrop for this canyon hike. The spring is on the north side of the road. It is a critical habitat for bighorn sheep, which gather nearby in hot summer months. Some marred petroglyphs are above the spring, a reminder that it is both unlawful and boorish to harm such artifacts. Return the way you came, enjoying your downhill trip.

# 30  Fall Canyon

This twisting, deep canyon in the colorful Grapevine Mountains features one of the most spectacular canyon narrows in the park.

**See map on page 123.**
**Start:** About 32 miles north of Furnace Creek
**Distance:** 16.0 miles out and back
**Hiking time:** 4 to 5 hours
**Difficulty:** Strenuous
**Trail surface:** Sandy path and cross-country on a clear wash

**Best season:** October through April
**Fees and permits:** National park entrance fee
**Maps:** NPS Death Valley visitors Map; Trails Illustrated Death Valley National Park Map; USGS Fall Canyon-CA
**Trail contact:** Furnace Creek Visitor Center; (760) 786-3200; www.nps.gov/deva

**Finding the trailhead:** The trailhead is at the Titus Canyon mouth parking area. The two-way road to the mouth of Titus Canyon is off Scotty's Castle Road, 17.3 miles north of the junction with CA 190. Turn northeast on the signed Titus Canyon dirt road and drive 2.7 miles up the alluvial fan to the mouth of Titus Canyon, where there is a large parking area with a vault toilet. GPS: N36 49.310' / W117 10.458'

## The Hike

Do not attempt this hike if wet weather appears likely. Fall Canyon is highly susceptible to flash flooding. You could easily be trapped in one of the narrow stretches of the canyon by a raging torrent if caught during a mountain storm.

From the parking area at the mouth of Titus Canyon, hike north on an unsigned but easy-to-follow user trail, climbing gradually across several low ridges and gullies. At 0.5 mile the trail enters a side wash and then swings to the right (north) toward Fall Canyon. At 0.8 mile the user trail tops out above Fall Canyon, and drops quickly into the wide graveled wash, and vanishes after another 0.1 mile at the canyon mouth. At first the canyon is wide, up to 150 feet in places. At 1.3 miles the walls steepen and close in; dark shadows fill the bottom, adding to a feeling of intimacy. The canyon quickly opens to a huge amphitheater-alcove, bounded by sheer cliffs on the left, bending tightly to the right. At 1.5 miles a large rock sits in a wide bottom that opens to colorful bands of red, white, and gray on the cliff faces. Continue left up the main wash. The canyon narrows again at 1.8 miles, its sides pocketed with a myriad of ledges and small alcoves, only to open again with the west rim soaring 1,000 feet overhead. At 2 miles a narrow side canyon enters from the left just above a massive boulder that blocks much of the wash. Continue to the right up the main wash next to an isolated rock pinnacle.

Soon the canyon narrows once more with rock overhangs reaching out above. At 2.2 miles colorful folded rock dramatizes the powerful forces that continue to shape this rugged landscape. The canyon squeezes to a gap of only 8 feet at 2.6 miles,

*A hiker sits above a 20-foot-high dry fall 3 miles up Fall Canyon.*

widens, and then narrows again at 2.9 miles. A sheer 20-foot-high dry fall is reached at 3 miles. The fall cannot be safely or easily climbed, so this is a good turnaround point for an exhilarating 6-mile out-and-back exploration of Fall Canyon. To this point the difficulty rating is moderate.

To continue up Fall Canyon, drop back down the wash less than 0.1 mile and look for rock cairns on the left (south) side (right side of the canyon going up). This bypass route around the fall should only be attempted by those with at least moderate rock-climbing skills and experience. Begin by climbing a steep but solid rock pitch to a well-defined user trail that angles above and around the right side of the fall. Exercise caution on the loose gravel directly above the canyon. Immediately above and beyond the fall, the canyon becomes extremely narrow, bounded by sheer cliffs, folded layers of rock, overhangs, and semicircular bends of smooth gray rock. There are a few short rock pitches that can be easily scrambled up.

At 3.2 miles the tight chasm opens to more distant cliffs, but the actual wash remains narrow. At 3.4 miles a massive boulder blocks most of the wash, with the easiest way around being to the left. Here the hardest part about turning around is turning around; every steep-walled bend entices further exploration. The gray-walled canyon, polished smooth by the action of water, is exited at 3.5 miles with the valley opening to reddish rhyolite cliffs and peaks.

At 4.1 miles dramatic cliffs rise above steep slopes punctuated with jagged columns of dark rhyolite. Anywhere in this stretch provides a good turnaround point, but it is possible to continue climbing northward for another 4 miles to the head of the canyon, where the country opens up into low ridges, high plateaus, and open desert. Retrace your route to complete your exploration of this enchanting canyon.

## Miles and Directions

**0.0** Start at the trailhead at the mouth of Titus Canyon, behind the vault toilet. Head north on a user trail.

**0.8** The user trail meets the Fall Canyon wash.

**0.9** Arrive at the mouth of Fall Canyon.

**1.3** The canyon narrows dramatically.

**2.9** Rock cairns mark a faint, scrambling user trail to the right that climbs above the dry fall.

**3.0** Reach a 20-foot dry fall. (**Option:** Turn around here for a shorter hike.)

**3.1** The canyon narrows.

**4.1** The canyon opens up to high peaks and ridges beyond.

**8.0** Reach the head of the canyon. Turn around here and retrace your steps.

**16.0** Arrive back at the trailhead at the parking area.

# 31  Palmer Canyon

Palmer Canyon is a complementary blend of its better-known neighbors to the south and north: Fall and Red Wall Canyons. With colorful badlands, arches, monumental cliff walls, one of the loftiest dry falls in Death Valley, and a reasonable chance to see desert bighorn sheep, Palmer has it all.

**Start:** About 32 miles north of Furnace Creek
**Distance:** 9.6 miles out and back from the Titus Canyon trailhead
**Hiking time:** 6 to 8 hours
**Difficulty:** Strenuous due to distance and elevation gain/loss of nearly 2,000 feet
**Trail surface:** Clear user trail, cobbled wash, gravel, sandy bottom
**Best season:** Late October to mid-April
**Fees and permits:** National park entrance fee

**Maps:** NPS Death Valley Visitors Map; Trails Illustrated Death Valley National Park Map; USGS Fall Canyon-CA
**Trail contact:** Furnace Creek Visitor Center; (760) 786-3200; www.nps.gov/deva
**Special considerations:** This is a long hike, so carry sufficient water. Avoid the canyon during times of inclement weather that may cause flash flooding.

**Finding the trailhead:** The recommended trailhead is at the Titus Canyon mouth parking area. The two-way road to the mouth of Titus Canyon is off Scotty's Castle Road, 17.3 miles north of the junction with CA 90. Turn northeast on the signed Titus Canyon dirt road and drive 2.7 miles up the alluvial fan to the mouth of Titus Canyon, where there is a large parking area with a vault toilet. GPS: N36 49.310'/W 117 10.458'

For the alternative and slightly longer route to Palmer Canyon, continue north on the Scotty's Castle Road for about 3 miles past the Titus Canyon Road and park next to milepost 18. GPS: N36 49.828' / W117 13.144'

## The Hike

An obvious user-created trail leads north from the trailhead at the mouth of Titus Canyon. It reaches the south ridge above the Fall Canyon wash at 0.8 mile. Look for a faint trail that crosses the wash. After crossing the wash, climb the opposite (north) ridge and follow the ridgeline downhill. You'll be hiking in a west–northwest direction facing toward the distant Cottonwood Mountains.

Drop into the first side canyon at mile 1.1 which might be marked with a small rock cairn. At 1.4 miles you'll pass beneath a small, light-colored arch with badlands beyond. The main canyon continues down to the left.

If time permits, a couple of short side hikes in the badlands totaling 0.8 mile round-trip are worthwhile. From the arch turn right to an immediate canyon split. For starters take the left branch, which is bound by conglomerate and mudstone slightly reddened by iron oxide. You'll quickly find yourself in colorful badlands highlighted by overhangs and caprock spires. The other branch to the right (left coming back down) opens up and then quickly dead-ends.

*Hikers arrive at the Palmer Canyon turnaround below towering red cliffs of oxidized iron that frame an 80-foot dry fall.*

Once back at the arch, continue down the main canyon wash. This is actually an uplifted section of an old alluvial fan. After only 0.1 mile turn right (north) up a small gully that might be marked with cairns. A distinct user trail climbs gray slopes above colorful badlands for about 0.6 mile to Palmer Canyon wash. At this point you've covered 2.1 miles, or about 2.9 miles if you've taken the side hikes in the badlands.

The mouth of Palmer Canyon is a blend of conglomerate and mudstone. Behind to the west is the grand sweep of the Cottonwoods, which contain the largest contiguous expanse of wilderness in the park—some half million acres.

The first set of narrows is just above the canyon mouth. They are bound by alcoves, overhangs, and rock tilted at a 60-degree angle. The canyon floor is swept free of vegetation from major flooding that occurred during October 2015. After the narrows the canyon opens to a wide valley. Suddenly a varied scattering of desert plants appear—rock nettle, flagrant arrow leaf, brittlebush (in bloom during winter), endemic Death Valley sage, and conifer-like sprucebush—which isn't a conifer at all—to name only a few.

At 0.8 mile above the mouth, a side canyon joins on the left with the main wash veering to the right. At this point a deep gully that was recently scoured out, perhaps by an intense localized thunderstorm, enters from the right. The canyon bottom contains abundant evidence of bighorn sheep along with one of their favorite snacks—sweet bush. Just above is a huge circular room and the beginning of the second set of narrows. They are entered by way of a moderate climb past a 10-foot-high chokestone. Soon a second room is reached with a moderate pullup, followed by pink-walled narrows. Suddenly the valley opens dramatically with the monumental folding and faulting of Mount Palmer straight ahead.

At 1.5 miles above the canyon mouth, an arch-like window rock appears on the right. The wide canyon narrows somewhat with brown limestone walls. The canyon continues to steadily climb. Striking red wall cliffs force an abrupt turn to the right. Just as quickly a sheer white wall marks a sharp turn to the left. Then comes the signature hallmark of Palmer Canyon—a gigantic red amphitheater bound by majestic red and white limestone walls and a stunning 80-foot dry fall. Stand at the base of the dry fall and look straight up at the neck-craning pour spout. You'll have no doubt that this is the turnaround point for exploring Palmer Canyon. And what an exploration it's been! Turn around at the base of the dry fall, scan the opposite cliff wall, and you just might see an arch on the horizon. If you know your desert plants, look carefully along the cracks and ledges on lower rock walls for species endemic to Death Valley.

During the return hike back down the canyon, 1.7 miles below the dry fall, the 10-foot chokestone you climbed around requires an equally careful descent. Another 0.8 mile gets you to just below the canyon mouth. This is where the user trail leads left (south) for the final 2.1 miles back to the Titus Canyon trailhead.

## Miles and Directions

**0.0**  Start from the parking area/trailhead at the mouth of Titus Canyon. Head north on a user trail.

**0.8**  Reach the Fall Canyon wash.

**1.4**  A small arch marks an area of badlands. (Option: Explore the side canyons, adding 0.8 mile to the hike.)

**2.1**  Arrive at Palmer Canyon wash.

**2.2**  Arrive at Palmer Canyon mouth. GPS: N36 50.491' / W117 10.806'

**3.1**  Climb around 10-foot chokestone.

**4.8**  Reach the 80-foot dry fall; turn around and retrace your steps.

**9.6**  Arrive back at the trailhead.

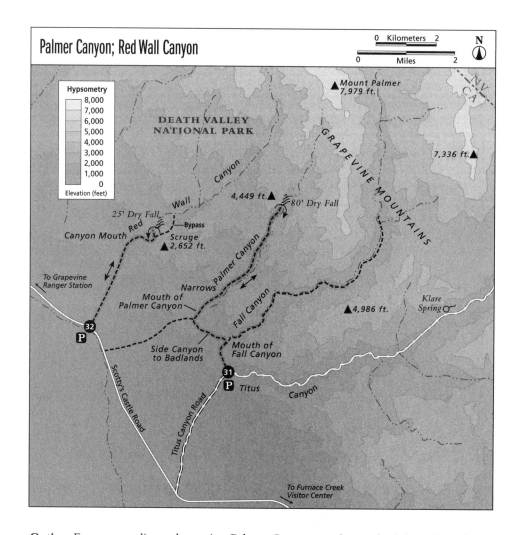

**Option:** For a more direct alternative, Palmer Canyon can be reached from Scotty's Castle Road. This adds 1 mile to the round-trip plus an additional 500 feet of elevation gain/loss, bringing the total up and down to around 2,500 feet. Park parallel to the road at milepost 18, which is about 3 miles north of Titus Canyon Road. From here the route traverses the alluvial fan to the mouth of Palmer Canyon. As much as possible weave your way toward the canyon by using sandy washes and desert pavement to minimize the rougher, rockier stretches. The canyon is northeast of the parking area but isn't readily visible from there, so a bit of route-finding is necessary. The canyon lies between the old lake bed sediment of two yellow hills, colored by iron oxide. Aim directly toward Mount Palmer, which is the high point on the horizon. Stay on the right side of an isolated ridge that divides the wash, entering Palmer Canyon at 2.6 miles. The dry fall/turnaround is another 2.7 miles up the canyon for a total of 5.3 miles one-way, 10.6 miles round-trip.

# 32 Red Wall Canyon

Red Wall Canyon deserves its name. After crossing the open desert floor of Death Valley, this hike takes you into a rugged, brightly colored canyon in the Grapevine Mountains. Its treasures include dramatic red cliff narrows, polished rock, and magnificent dry falls.

**See map on page 130.**
**Start:** About 36 miles north of Furnace Creek
**Distance:** 7.0 miles out and back to a 25-foot dry fall (with optional bypass described below).
**Hiking time:** 3 to 5 hours
**Difficulty:** Moderate
**Trail surface:** Sandy rocky wash, gravel canyon floor

**Best season:** October through April
**Fees and permits:** National park entrance fee
**Maps:** NPS Death Valley Visitors Map; Trails Illustrated Death Valley National Park Map; USGS Fall Canyon-CA
**Trail contact:** Furnace Creek Visitor Center; (760) 786-3200; www.nps.gov/deva

**Finding the trailhead:** The main wash of the alluvial fan is 35.5 miles north of Furnace Creek, 17.4 miles south of Scotty's Castle, and 14.1 miles south of the Grapevine Ranger Station. The hike takes off from Scotty's Castle Road near milepost 19, 3.8 miles north of Titus Canyon Road, and heads northeast across 3 miles of sloping desert alluvial fan to the mouth of Red Wall Canyon. Find a wide spot to park alongside the highway. GPS: N36 50.164' / W117 13.513'

## The Hike

Although advanced rock-climbing skills are needed to climb a dry waterfall 0.5 mile up the canyon, this hike provides delightful vistas in the lower canyon region for the casual hiker. A challenging optional route bypasses the dry fall.

The approach to the canyon via the alluvial fan is not particularly challenging, but it is certainly not easy! The easiest hiking is on the dark desert pavement of the old alluvial fan. The wash route changes directions with its tributaries, so it's necessary to cut from wash to wash to maintain the route to the canyon mouth. Above the wash the sections of smoother varnished desert pavement provide some respite, but these sections are brief, interspersed with sections of cobbled, bouldered, and eroded washbeds.

The canyon mouth opens to the northwest; except for the red and black wall contrast, it is nearly hidden in the cliff faces. The canyon, which looked so narrow or even invisible during the approach, is surprisingly wide, at least 50 yards from wall to wall. At the entrance the north wall is a sheer red cliff face, while the south side is a black slope. The canyon takes a sharp turn to the north 0.2 mile farther, and suddenly the Red Wall towers 400 feet above you on the right. A narrow S-curve brings you to another red wall, now on your left. A short distance farther an even redder wall appears. The red walls, alternating with the black, provide a blast of sharp color on the beige desert palette.

*The entrance to Red Wall Canyon.*

At mile 0.4 in the canyon, water-sculpted narrows enclose an easily climbed low dry fall. Just beyond this obstacle is the 25-foot dry fall with a massive chokestone that blocks the canyon to all but seasoned rock climbers. If a knotted rope is hanging at the dry fall, don't trust it. Using ropes of unknown origin, age, or strength is never a good idea. So for most hikers this is a good turnaround spot. The cool shadows of the deep canyon provide a welcome respite from the desert glare outside.

In Red Wall the variety of canyon architecture lures you onward as the canyon is constantly bending out of sight. Only upon turning around for the hike back are you aware of the elevation gained (800 feet in 0.5 mile). The descent from the dry fall provides numerous vistas of Death Valley in the distance.

The sharp slope of the canyon floor and its heavy gravel surface both indicate that this is a relatively young canyon. There is still a lot of erosive energy in the uplifting Amargosa Range, of which these Grapevine Mountains are a part.

## Miles and Directions

**0.0** Start from the parking pullout on Scotty's Castle Road, aim northwesterly for the Grapevine Mountains. The canyon mouth is where the red and black rock faces meet. The alluvial fan emerging from the canyon forms a distinct triangle. Head up this alluvial fan, cross-country, or via one of the washes.

**3.0** Enter Red Wall Canyon.

**3.5** A 25-foot dry fall blocks the canyon. Return to the trailhead by the same route.

**7.0** Arrive back at the trailhead on Scotty's Castle Road.

*Option:* If a rope of unknown age and origin is present at the dry fall, do not use it for scaling the dry fall. For the seasoned hiker with solid route-finding experience, there is a way around the dry fall that's named for its discoverer, Talus Jack. The Talus Jack Bypass is just below the dry fall on the right (east) side of the canyon. Look for an open southwest-facing slope that is easy at first to climb but becomes more difficult higher up with big boulders that must be climbed over. Angle to the right toward a low saddle to avoid being cliffed out on the other side. The saddle sits about 500 feet above the canyon floor. The northwest-facing gully on the other side is short but steeper and is best descended on its right side. The lower part contains large boulders in a narrow chute. The bypass distance is short but will take about 1 hour. Upon reaching the bottom of Red Wall, drop back down the canyon to the top of the dry fall to see the amazing high walls of the first narrows. Up the canyon another dry fall rises above a second set of narrows with impressive slickenside walls. The dry fall presents moderate difficulty but can be climbed with careful rock work. Beyond lies yet another set of narrows for the intrepid hiker willing to put in a long 12-plus-mile day with some 3,000-plus feet of elevation gain/loss to more fully experience the wonders of Red Wall.

# 33 Moonlight Bridge Canyon

This outing takes you through a winding conglomerate canyon to the loftiest known natural bridge in Death Valley National Park. Vast areas of fresh gravel on the canyon floor indicate the constant dramatic changes in the geology of Death Valley canyons.

**Start:** About 31 miles north of Stovepipe Wells on Scotty's Castle Road
**Distance:** 8.2 miles out and back
**Hiking time:** 5 to 6 hours
**Difficulty:** Moderate, with some hard hiking in the bouldered approach wash and some tough slogging in heavy gravel in the canyon itself
**Trail surface:** Bouldered wash, gravel wash
**Best season:** Mid-October to late March (full sun for first and last 3 miles of the hike)
**Fees and permits:** National park entrance fee

**Maps:** NPS Death Valley Visitors Map; Trails Illustrated Death Valley National Park Map; USGS East of Tin Mountain-CA and Grapevine Peak-CA
**Trail contact:** Furnace Creek Visitor Center; (760) 786-3200; www.nps.gov/deva
**Special considerations:** As usual, be alert for precipitation forecasts for Death Valley and the Grapevine Mountains. Flash flooding is a hazard in Moonlight Canyon, as you will see on your hike.

**Finding the trailhead:** From CA 190, 7 miles east of Stovepipe Wells, turn north on Scotty's Castle Road. The parking area is 24 miles north of the intersection at a decisive curve in the highway where it turns to the northwest. The Trails Illustrated map has a "radiator water" site marked at this curve. Parallel park on the right side of the highway, at the curve. GPS: N36 53.432' / W117 16.424'

## The Hike

The foothills of the Grapevine Mountains have many folds that could lead you astray. From the parking area you will be able to see a sharp conglomerate cliff on Moonlight's southeastern flank. While you can get this visual fix from your vehicle, the preferred pathway to the canyon is not a straight line. Instead, avoid the cobbled ridges and trenches of the alluvial fan and follow the sandy wash at the road's edge. The wash goes almost north and then curves southeast along the edge of the hills, to the canyon mouth, with its telltale conglomerate cliff wall. This circuitous route is much easier. At 0.8 mile you are at the canyon mouth.

Depending upon the precipitation and the season, you may encounter flowers in the canyon wash. Bighorn sheep droppings indicate this is a favorite spot for them. This is no surprise, because at 1.7 miles from the parking area there is a spring on the northwest canyon wall. The saline white wall is visible from a distance. The water seeps rather than flows, so it is nonrecoverable and nonpotable for us humans. The dripping garden on the canyon wall provides stark contrast with the adjacent barren conglomerate surfaces.

*Great mounds of conglomerate form the walls of Moonlight Bridge Canyon above its flood scoured gravel floor.*

Continuing on up the canyon, these conglomerate walls illustrate the geologic history of major flood events over the last million years or so. Some strata are all mud, some are chunky with boulders, some are dense as concrete, others are friable.

The wide-open canyon floor has many meandering washes, interrupted by rocky dams and ridges, so travel is slow. There is no shade. In early spring this is a good flower spot if the fall and winter rains arrived.

False canyons exist on both sides. Continue in the main canyon toward the reddish slope straight ahead. At 3.0 miles from the road, a large ridge hooks into the center canyon wash from the right. This is it! A conglomerate wall with enchanting alcoves is on the south wall here at the canyon mouth. Across the way, on the north side, steep conglomerate walls rise abruptly for the first time in the hike. Watch for them so you know when to turn off to the right. The canyon entrance is framed with conglomerate mud towers at its entrance, and an unnamed pyramidal peak rises on the skyline above the side canyon.

The mouth of the natural bridge canyon exhibits evidence of the tumultuous flooding—boulders have left deep gouges on the canyon floor. The canyon walls of dense conglomerate are narrow at first, then they open up. As the canyon twists to the east there is an enormous deposit of gravel on the canyon floor left from the October

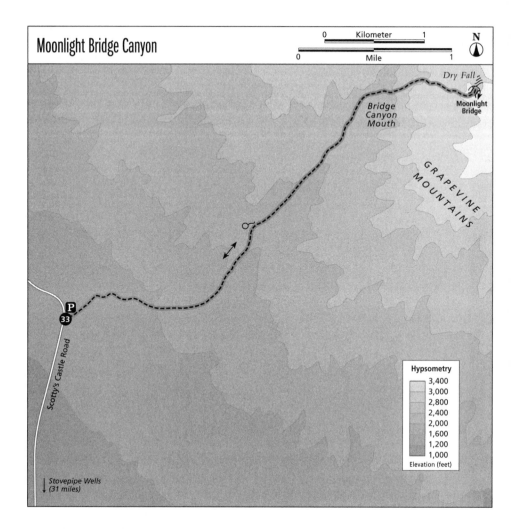

2015 flood. It's like a huge belly-dumper dropped several loads in the canyon, leaving a 0.5-mile stretch 10 feet deep with gravel. All evidence of vegetation is gone. Floods scour canyons, but they also bring fresh deposits. It's a rough uphill slog through this stretch. Slot canyons jut off in both directions, going nowhere.

After the final turns of the deep narrows, a chokestone blocks the pour-off, marking the turnaround spot. And, there, overhead, is the bridge, at 4.1 miles. First reported by a young hiker in 2013, this natural bridge, at 55 feet high, is perhaps the highest one on record.

On your way back down, it's easier to notice the canyon's details. Interesting stones protrude from the walls. Evidence of pack rats and other rodents can be seen in the alcoves, now exposed by the whoosh of the flood. On the skyline precarious boulders hang on the rim, awaiting the next wind or rain event to dislodge them. You might even spot a tarantula making its way across the gravel bottom.

At the mouth of the main canyon, resist the urge to make a beeline for your vehicle. Follow, instead, the wash to the right, retracing your original path. In spite of its name, this is not a hike to take at night. Even with a full moon, the uneven surface would be hazardous. Go in the daytime and get an early start.

## Miles and Directions

**0.0**  Start at the parking pullout on Scotty's Castle Road. Follow the sandy wash along the road.

**0.8**  Reach the mouth of Moonlight Canyon.

**1.7**  Pass a spring on the left canyon wall.

**3.0**  Come to a ridge on the canyon floor.

**3.1**  Reach the mouth of Bridge Canyon on the right.

**4.1**  Arrive at the dry fall/natural bridge. Turn around here and retrace your steps.

**8.2**  Arrive back at the parking pullout.

*At the turnaround for this hike, you'll find what you've come to experience—the highest known natural bridge in Death Valley.*

# Northern Death Valley

## 34  Ubehebe and Little Hebe Craters

These volcanic craters are a fascinating geology lesson on the forces that helped form Death Valley. A short loop hike around the large Ubehebe Crater and the several smaller ones enables you to witness the complex erosion patterns that have occurred since the craters' birth.

**Start:** About 51 miles northwest of Furnace Creek
**Distance:** 1.5-mile double loop
**Hiking time:** 1 to 2 hours
**Difficulty:** Easy (moderate to the bottom of the crater)
**Trail surface:** Volcanic cinder

**Best season:** Late October through April
**Fees and permits:** National park entrance fee
**Maps:** NPS Death Valley Visitors Map; Trails Illustrated Death Valley National Park Map; USGS Ubehebe Crater-CA
**Trail contact:** Furnace Creek Visitor Center; (760) 786-3200; www.nps.gov/deva

**Finding the trailhead:** From the Grapevine Junction of Scotty's Castle Road and Ubehebe Crater Road, 45 miles north of Furnace Creek, take Ubehebe Crater Road northwest. Drive 5.7 miles to the Ubehebe Crater parking area for the Ubehebe Crater/Little Hebe Crater trailhead. The parking area is on the eastern side on the one-way loop of paved road at the end of Ubehebe Crater Road. GPS: N37 0.504' / W117 28.391'

## The Hike

The volcanic region at the north end of the Cottonwood Mountains, near Scotty's Castle, is evidence of recent cataclysmic events in Death Valley, geologically speaking. The huge Ubehebe Crater was created maybe as recently as 300 years ago when magma heated groundwater and the pressure from the resulting steam blew the overlying rock away. This explosion covered 6 square miles of desert with volcanic debris 150 feet deep. Called a maar volcano by geologists, Ubehebe is a crater without a cone. The rim has been eroding ever since the explosion, gradually filling the crater with alluvial fans.

Little Hebe, directly south, is much younger. It is one of the newest dramatic geologic features of Death Valley. Little Hebe's rim is neat and well defined, exhibiting little of the erosion that has reduced Ubehebe's edge.

Pausing at the parking lot to read the information on the board and glancing at these monstrous holes in the earth might seem sufficient, but hiking all the way around this monumental display of volcanic power provides a much better understanding of the dimensions of the Ubehebe complex.

*The sharply defined rim of Little Hebe Crater is evidence of its youth, geologically speaking.*

The first fourth of the hike takes you along the rim of the main crater. The size of the hole is overpowering. It is almost 0.5 mile across from rim to rim. Alluvial fans have formed on the walls as the rains tear down the crater's edges.

In the vicinity of Ubehebe, there are as many as twelve additional craters, all examples of more maar activity. You will see numerous craters in various stages of eroding deterioration. Little Hebe stands out as a jewel of a crater. Neat and trim, this volcanic chasm is only 200 yards across. The younger, fresher rim has barely begun to weather. Volcanic materials are very durable. Clearly visible on the walls of Little Hebe are the layers beneath the earth's surface. Especially noticeable is a thick layer of viscous lava that had oozed from the earth's interior prior to the explosion of Little Hebe.

After the tour around Little Hebe, continue your hike around the main crater, which seems even larger after visiting its younger neighbor. A well-defined trail leads around Ubehebe. At 1.3 miles pass the trail that slopes down into the crater (see the

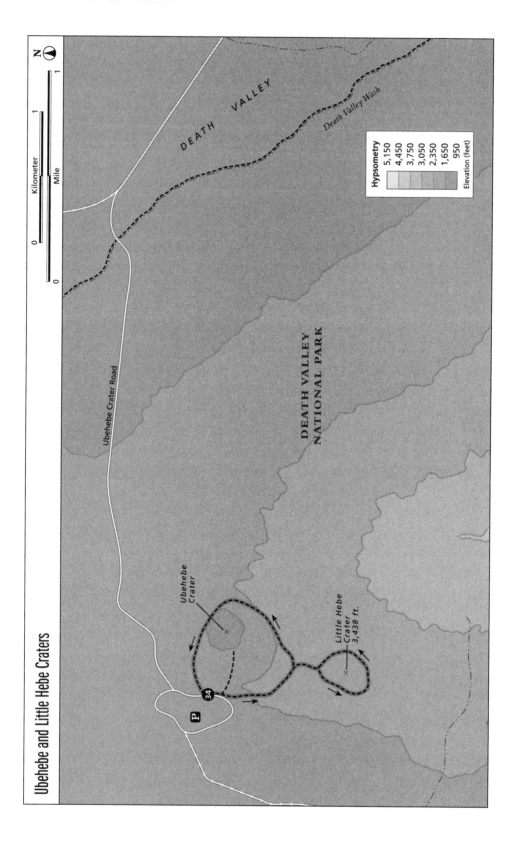

# Ubehebe and Little Hebe Craters

DEATH VALLEY

Death Valley Wash

Ubehebe Crater Road

DEATH VALLEY NATIONAL PARK

Ubehebe Crater

Little Hebe Crater 3,438 ft.

P

34

**Hypsometry**

| | |
|---|---|
| | 5,150 |
| | 4,450 |
| | 3,750 |
| | 3,050 |
| | 2,350 |
| | 1,650 |
| | 950 |

Elevation (feet)

Kilometer

Mile

N

option below). The volcanic cinder trail descends nearly 500 feet to the floor of the crater, where creosote bushes flourish. After major rainstorms the crater also features a small lake. Most of the time it is very dry.

The power of nature to modify the terrain via volcanic action stands in sharp contrast with the more gradual erosive forces that are demonstrated elsewhere in Death Valley. The earth has not finished rearranging its surface here in Death Valley. The forces that created Ubehebe and Little Hebe are merely dormant, not dead.

## Miles and Directions

**0.0**  Start at the trailhead at the parking area. The trail goes south of the information board.

**0.1**  The trail climbs—bear left at the Y. The trail to the right is eroding on both sides and becoming hazardous.

**0.4**  Arrive at a maze of user trails on a small plateau between craters. A sign directs you to Little Hebe, directly south. Follow the trail around Little Hebe.

**0.7**  Back at the intersection, continue to hike around the large Ubehebe Crater.

**1.5**  Arrive back at the trailhead.

*Option:* The 0.6-mile out and back to the bottom of the crater is a breathtaking outing into the earth. At the bottom you can imagine the force that blew off the earth to leave such a hole. The climb back to the parking area requires some exertion due to the skidding quality of the volcanic cinders. The park service runs interesting guided hikes at the craters; check the park website for schedules.

# 35 Eureka Dunes

In a remote desert valley, against the scenic backdrop of the colorful Last Chance Mountains, lie the Eureka Dunes. These are the tallest sand dunes in California and the second highest in all of North America, although their constantly shifting nature would make that tough to measure. Your cross-country walk to their summit will be a soft sandy stroll.

**Start:** About 90 miles north of Furnace Creek
**Distance:** 3.0-mile loop
**Hiking time:** About 2 hours
**Difficulty:** Moderate
**Trail surface:** All-sand cross-country route
**Best season:** October through April

**Fees and permits:** National park entrance fee
**Maps:** NPS Death Valley Visitors Map; Trails Illustrated Death Valley National Park Map; USGS Last Chance Range Southwest-CA
**Trail contact:** Furnace Creek Visitor Center; (760) 786-3200; www.nps.gov/deva

**Finding the trailhead:** From the south, take Scotty's Castle Road to Grapevine Junction and proceed northwest on Ubehebe Crater Road for 2.8 miles to Big Pine Road, which is also known as North Entrance Highway and Death Valley Road. The turnoff is signed Eureka Dunes 45 Miles. Turn north onto the washboarded, graded gravel Big Pine Road and drive 34 miles to South Eureka Valley Road, which is the road to the Eureka Dunes. Turn left (south) onto this road and drive 10 miles to the end-of-the-road picnic/parking area near the base of the dunes. GPS: N37 6.840' / W117 40.051'

From the north, Eureka Dunes can be reached from Big Pine via 28 miles of paved road and 11 miles of graded dirt road to South Eureka Valley Road. Turn right (south) and follow the narrow road for the final 10 miles to the camping and parking areas just north of the dunes.

## The Hike

The Eureka Dunes are a fascinating island of sand in a desert sea, within the northern portion of the park. From a distance this 1- by 3-mile mountain of sand seems to hover over the remote Eureka Valley floor. Although not extensive, these dunes are the tallest in California and the second-tallest in North America after the Great Sand Dunes in Colorado. From the dry lake bed at their western edge, the Eureka Dunes rise abruptly more than 600 feet. Equally impressive is the sheer face of the Last Chance Mountains to the immediate east, with their colorfully striped bands of pink, black, and gray limestone.

If the sand here is completely dry, you may hear one of the most unusual sounds in the desert: singing sand. When the sand cascades down the steepest pitch of the highest dune, a rumbling sound comparable to the bass note of a pipe organ emanates from the sand. No one knows exactly why this happens, but the friction of smooth-textured sand grains sliding against each other probably has something to do with it.

*The multibanded Last Chance Mountains provide a colorful backdrop to the 3,480-foot summit of the Eureka Dunes.*

These dunes receive more moisture than others in the park because they are positioned at the western foot of a high mountain range that intercepts passing storms. The isolation of the Eureka Dunes, far from any other dunes, has resulted in endemic species of animals and plants found nowhere else. For example, there are five species of beetles and three plants that have their entire range limited to these lofty mounds.

The three endemic plant species are shining locoweed—a candidate for endangered species listing—Eureka dune grass, and Eureka evening primrose; the latter two are listed as endangered species under the federal Endangered Species Act. The camping area and trailhead were recently moved off the dunes to protect these species. Shining locoweed is a hummock-forming plant with root nodules that fix nitrogen from the air, a vital plant nutrient not available in the sand. When windblown sand covers the leafy flower shoots of the Eureka evening primrose, a new rosette of leaves forms at the tip. Large, white flowers bloom at night so that moths and other

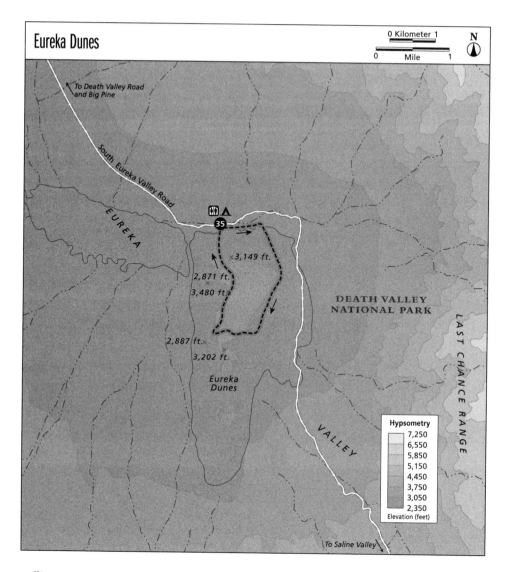

Eureka Dunes

0 Kilometer 1

0 Mile 1

N

To Death Valley Road
and Big Pine

South Eureka Valley Road

E U R E K A

35

×3,149 ft.

2,871 ft.×

3,480 ft.×

2,887 ft.×

×3,202 ft.

Eureka
Dunes

DEATH VALLEY
NATIONAL PARK

LAST CHANCE RANGE

VALLEY

**Hypsometry**
7,250
6,550
5,850
5,150
4,450
3,750
3,050
2,350
Elevation (feet)

To Saline Valley

pollinators can avoid daytime heat. Usually Eureka dune grass is the only plant on the higher slopes of the dunes. Its thick roots hold shifting sand, forming hummocks. Stiff, spiny leaf tips discourage herbivores.

The Eureka Dunes are a small, ecologically unique place requiring our special care. Camp and keep vehicles a good distance from the base of the dunes, which is where most of the endemic plants and animals live. If possible, walk where others have in order to concentrate the impact away from pristine areas.

There are two basic choices for climbing the dunes, which can be hard work at times in the loose, shifting sand. The most direct route for the 600-plus-foot climb to the top is a 1.5-mile straight-up-and-back route by way of a series of knife ridges.

Because of the long driving distance to the trailhead, a somewhat longer 3-mile loop is your better choice, as you'll gain more intimacy with the dunes and their majestic Last Chance Mountains backdrop.

From the parking/camping area, head east cross-country along the base of the dunes toward the color-banded Last Chance Mountains, which rise an impressive 4,000 feet above the Eureka Valley floor. Hiking along the base provides a constantly changing perspective of this unusual landscape as well as a good warm-up for climbing the steep backside of the dunes. A profusion of animal tracks will appear as well as the circular paths of grass tips in the sand from the ever-changing wind.

At 0.8 mile the initial flat stretch becomes laced with up-and-down gullies with volcanic "bombs" (rounded chucks of lava emitted during the volcanic explosion that can make walking difficult) embedded in the sand. At this point begin curving around the base of the dunes to the right (south). This wonderfully wide-open trek stands in startling contrast to the closed-in feeling one gets when exploring the deep canyons of Death Valley.

At around 1.5 miles begin climbing westward up any one of the several narrow knife-edge sand ridges that converge at the apex of the dunes. A vertical gain of about 600 feet to the 3,480-foot high point is spread over about 0.7 mile, with most of the climb during the final 0.2 mile. The dry lake bed, expansive Eureka Valley, colorful Last Chance Range, and the dunes themselves combine to form a stunning 360-degree panorama. To complete the 3-mile loop, continue back down along narrow ridges and steep, scooped-out bowls of sand in a north to northwesterly direction to the trailhead.

## Miles and Directions

**0.0** Start from the trailhead located at the picnic tables/parking area. Head east along the base of the dunes.

**1.5** Begin climbing up the west side of the dunes.

**2.2** Reach the top of the dunes.

**3.0** Complete the loop and arrive back at the trailhead.

# 36 Ubehebe Lead Mine/Corridor Canyon

This exploration of a historic mine site with a tram will appeal to mining and history buffs. The longer leg in Corridor Canyon will enchant those who appreciate excellent vistas of cliffs and mountains.

**Start:** About 79 miles northwest of Furnace Creek
**Distance:** 6.0 miles out and back
**Hiking time:** About 4 hours
**Difficulty:** Moderate
**Trail surface:** Dirt path to mine; clear wash in canyon
**Best season:** October through March

**Fees and permits:** National park entrance fee
**Maps:** NPS Death Valley Visitors Map; Trails Illustrated Death Valley National Park Map; USGS Ubehebe Peak-CA and Teakettle Junction-CA
**Trail contact:** Furnace Creek Visitor Center; (760) 786-3200; www.nps.gov/deva

**Finding the trailhead:** From Grapevine Junction in the northeastern corner of the park, take Ubehebe Crater Road northwest 5.5 miles to the end of the pavement and the sign for Racetrack Valley Road. Turn right onto Racetrack Valley Road. Four-wheel drive is recommended but under normal weather conditions is unnecessary. Racetrack Valley Road is severely washboarded but contains no other obstacles as far as the Racetrack. Go south on Racetrack Valley Road 19.6 miles to Teakettle Junction. Bear right and continue 2.2 miles to the right turn to Ubehebe Lead Mine Road (signed). The dirt road leads 0.7 mile to the parking area at the mine site. GPS: N36 44.712' / W117 34.902'

## The Hike

The Ubehebe Mine has a lengthy history, beginning in 1875 when copper ore was found here. The copper mine was not fully developed until early in the twentieth century, but the profitable ore was soon depleted. In 1908 lead mining began and continued until 1928. Ubehebe Mine had another renaissance in the 1940s as a zinc mine. Mining activity came to an end in 1951.

After all this mining it is not surprising to find a plethora of mining artifacts in the valley and in the hills above. Remember that it may be unwise to enter deserted buildings due to deer mice and the risk of hantavirus.

In the wash above there are other traces of crude dwellings of miners. Stacked stone walls are still in place. The men worked inside rock walls by day and slept in them at night. Rusty debris and small, level tent sites are scattered about. The usual squeaky bedspring (burned and rusted) lies amid the creosote bushes. This is an appropriate place to pause and contemplate the bustle of activity and spirit of optimism that must have prevailed in this mining valley in its various heydays.

Below the housing area sits the ore chute, with rail tracks still leading from a mine opening. The area looks like it had been deserted only a year ago. The sagging old

*The chute at the Ubehebe Lead Mine.*

tram cable still hangs from the tower atop the hill to the valley floor. Unsecured mine openings dot the hillside. The National Park Service emphatically warns visitors not to get close to the mines; the tram should also be given a wide berth.

The hike up the trail to the overlook gives you a magnificent aerial view of the mine encampment and the rolling hills of the Last Chance Range. Mine openings proliferate like rodent burrows. The rust-colored rock and earth in piles at each opening give the mining operations an eerie fresh appearance, as if the work here just stopped yesterday instead of sixty or one hundred years ago. Numerous wooden posts mark the mountainside along the trail to designate claims of long-gone prospectors. Crossing carefully beneath the hilltop tram tower, you arrive at trail's end and a view westward of winding Corridor Canyon. For more information about the history of mining in Death Valley, visit the Borax Museum (free admission) at Furnace Creek Ranch.

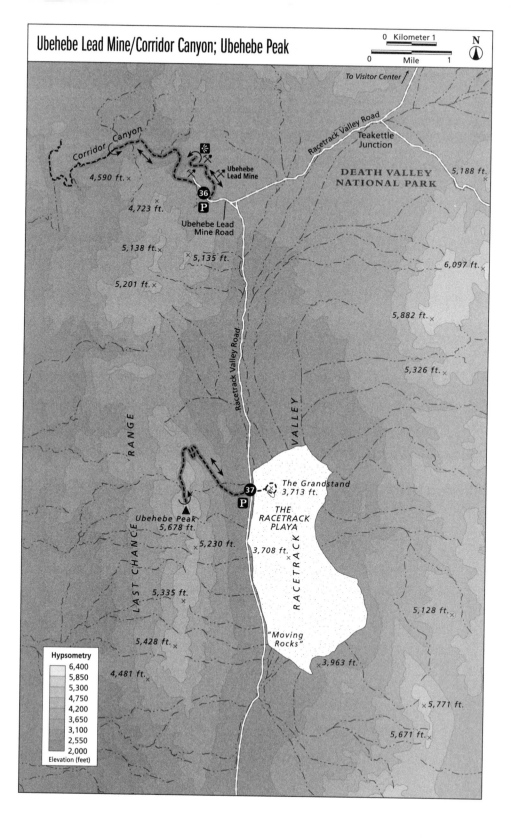

Ubehebe Lead Mine/Corridor Canyon; Ubehebe Peak

0   Kilometer 1

0        Mile        1

N

To Visitor Center

Corridor Canyon

Racetrack Valley Road

Teakettle
Junction

DEATH VALLEY
NATIONAL PARK

5,188 ft.

4,590 ft.

36

Ubehebe
Lead Mine

P

4,723 ft.

Ubehebe Lead
Mine Road

5,138 ft.

× 5,135 ft.

6,097 ft.

5,201 ft.

5,882 ft.

5,326 ft.

Racetrack Valley Road

RANGE

VALLEY

37

The Grandstand
3,713 ft.

P

THE
RACETRACK
PLAYA

Ubehebe Peak
5,678 ft.

5,230 ft.

3,708 ft.

RACETRACK

LAST CHANCE

5,335 ft.

5,128 ft.

5,428 ft.

"Moving
Rocks"

4,481 ft.

3,963 ft.

× 5,771 ft.

Hypsometry

6,400
5,850
5,300
4,750
4,200
3,650
3,100
2,550
2,000

Elevation (feet)

5,671 ft.

For the 5-mile out-and-back leg into Corridor Canyon, start at the mine chute and drop down the wide and graveled wash to the head of the canyon, generally westward. At 0.3 mile a tantalizing, narrow stair-step chute of a canyon enters from the left, inviting exploration—although large boulders may prevent you from getting very far.

At about 1 mile impressive cliff walls soar high to the left, whereas the right side is marked by folded rock layers altered by fault lines. Below, as the canyon turns left, are colorful bands of rock. The cliffs are pockmarked with caverns and other small openings, some of which serve as active dens for animals.

The canyon is unique in that it provides both a closed-in experience as well as far distant vistas of cliffs, overshadowed by even higher cliff layers beyond, opening to expansive views of adjacent and faraway mountains. Hike another 1.5 miles in the wide wash before turning around and retracing your steps.

## Miles and Directions

**Mine:**

- **0.0** Start at the parking area at the mine site.
- **0.1** Back up the road from the miner's shack, on the north side by a low stone wall, the trail leads up the hillside.
- **0.4** Reach the tram cable tower at the hilltop.
- **0.5** Enjoy the view at the overlook, then return to the trailhead by the same route.
- **1.0** Arrive back at the trailhead.

**Canyon:**

- **0.0** Start at the mine chute and head west down the wash.
- **0.3** A chute canyon enters from the left.
- **1.0** View dramatic cliffs to the left, then continue in the canyon until you decide to turn around at one of various turnaround points.
- **2.5** By this point you've seen what makes this canyon special. For more of the same, you could continue as much as 2.5 miles more. Retrace your steps to the trailhead.
- **5.0** Arrive back at the parking area.

# 37 Ubehebe Peak

Ubehebe Peak is one of the few Death Valley peaks largely accessible by trail. The steep out-and-back hike leads to a remote peak in the southern Last Chance Range from which you will enjoy spectacular views of surrounding basin and range country.

**See map on page 148.**
**Start:** About 81 miles northwest of Furnace Creek
**Distance:** 6.2 miles out and back
**Hiking time:** 3 to 5 hours
**Difficulty:** Strenuous
**Trail surface:** Clear rocky trail, changing to good, then to primitive, and finally to no trail for the final 0.4 mile to the summit

**Best season:** October through June
**Fees and permits:** National park entrance fee
**Maps:** NPS Death Valley Visitors Map; Trails Illustrated Death Valley National Park Map; USGS Ubehebe Peak-CA
**Trail contact:** Furnace Creek Visitor Center; (760) 786-3200; www.nps.gov/deva

**Finding the trailhead:** From Grapevine Junction in the northeastern corner of the park, head northwest on the paved Ubehebe Crater Road. The pavement ends after 5.5 miles at the turnoff to Ubehebe Crater. Continue south on the washboarded dirt Racetrack Valley Road 19.6 miles to Teakettle Junction. Here Racetrack Valley Road turns right; continue to follow it another 5.7 miles to the Grandstand parking area, which is opposite the "grandstand" of gray rocks in the dry lake bed east of the road. The trail heads west from the parking area toward the prominent Ubehebe Peak. GPS: N36 41.594' / W117 35.561'

## The Hike

Before climbing Ubehebe Peak, a short 1-mile round-trip hike east to the Grandstand is a worthwhile warm-up and also provides a good perspective on your journey to the top of Ubehebe Peak. From the Grandstand a pre-climb visual orientation involves identifying Ubehebe Peak on the left with your route going up the east face of the north peak, then around the back side into the prominent notch, then left up the skyline to the summit.

Be sure to carry sufficient water for this high, dry desert peak climb. The clear trail, originally an old mining path, begins by ascending gradually to the northwest up an alluvial fan clothed with desert trumpets and creosote bushes. Within 0.5 mile the trail begins a long series of steep switchbacks up the east face of the 5,519-foot north peak. This imposing buttress is made even more impressive with broken cliffs of desert varnish. After climbing nearly 1,200 feet in 1.8 miles, the trail reaches the north ridge of the peak, just after passing an outcropping of limestone where the blue-green copper of malachite rock lines a shallow mine digging. From this point a trail takes off to the right, ending after 0.1 mile at an overlook above an old mine entrance. The

*Ubehebe Peak (right) towers over the playa (dry lake bed) far below.*

summit of Ubehebe Peak can be seen in the distance beyond the north peak, which rises directly above.

Continue up the left-hand trail, which climbs steeply up the ridge through the rocks to 5,160 feet at 2 miles. The trail then wraps around the west side of the mountain, reaching an elevation of 5,440 feet at 2.4 miles. From here on, the trail becomes rougher and more faint, compensated somewhat by stupendous views of the playa to the southeast. The trail then drops for another 0.3 mile to the 5,220-foot saddle between the two peaks. Any resemblance to a trail ends at the saddle, which is a good turnaround point for those not wishing to scramble the steep rocky ridge another 0.4 mile and 460 vertical feet to Ubehebe Peak.

To attain the summit, climb southward straight up the rugged spine of the north ridge. Much of this route is marked by rock cairns. There are no technical sections, but care must be exercised in negotiating narrow chutes around steep rock faces.

The quartz granite top of 5,678-foot Ubehebe Peak contains a summit register and is marked by a wooden triangle. Although narrow, there are lots of ideal sitting spots upon which to relax and soak up the incredible 360-degree vista.

The Saline Valley lies 4,500 feet below to the west. Beyond is the soaring 10,000-foot crest of the Inyo Mountains with the even higher Sierra Nevada looming farther to the west. The crown of Death Valley—lofty Telescope Peak—can be seen to the southeast, along with the vast wooded plateau of Hunter Mountain. Perhaps most impressive is the eagle's-eye view of the gleaming white Racetrack Playa encircling the tiny dark specks of the Grandstand far below. Return to the parking area by the same route.

## Miles and Directions

**0.0** Start from the trailhead at the Grandstand parking area on Racetrack Valley Road.

**1.8** The trail switchbacks to the north ridge of the peak. Where the trail splits, stay left.

**2.4** The trail reaches a ridge on the west side of the mountain, becoming rougher and more faint.

**2.7** The trail drops to a saddle between the two peaks. Begin the route-finding segment to the peak.

**3.1** Reach Ubehebe Peak (5,678 feet). Return by retracing your steps.

**6.2** Arrive back at the trailhead.

# 38 The Grandstand

The Grandstand is a high mound of dark rock contrasting dramatically within the gleaming white Racetrack Playa. A mountainous backdrop, intense isolation, and outstanding scenic views await the visitor.

**Start:** About 82 miles northwest of Furnace Creek
**Distance:** 1.0 mile out and back
**Hiking time:** Less than 1 hour
**Difficulty:** Easy
**Trail surface:** Smooth sand
**Best season:** October through April

**Fees and permits:** National park entrance fee
**Maps:** NPS Death Valley Visitors Map; Trails Illustrated Death Valley National Park Map; USGS Ubehebe Peak-CA
**Trail contact:** Furnace Creek Visitor Center; (760) 786-3200; www.nps.gov/deva

**Finding the trailhead:** From the Grapevine Junction in the northeastern corner of the park, head northwest on the paved Ubehebe Crater Road. The pavement ends after 5.3 miles at the turnoff to Ubehebe Crater. Continue south on the washboarded dirt Racetrack Valley Road for 19.7 miles to Teakettle Junction. Take the right-hand turn for Racetrack Valley Road and drive another 5.7 miles to the Grandstand parking area, which is opposite the "grandstand" of gray rocks in the dry lake bed east of the road. The parking area with an interpretive sign is adjacent to the dirt Racetrack Valley Road. GPS: N36 41.594' / W117 35.561'

## The Hike

The Grandstand is about 0.5 mile directly east of the parking area. It consists of a large, 70-foot-high mound of gray rocks rising in stark contrast to the surrounding white flatness of the Racetrack Playa, a dry lake bed. For added perspective, walk around the Grandstand then scramble up some of the large boulders. The Grandstand can be easily climbed 40 to 50 feet above the playa. Don't expect to see the famous "moving rocks" here, as they are found a couple of miles to the south. The Grandstand provides a superb perspective of formidable 5,678-foot-high Ubehebe Peak, rising 2,000 feet 1.5 miles to the west.

**Option:** To view the magical moving rocks, drive south from the Grandstand another 2 miles. Look for a short user trail heading eastward across the southern end of the 3-square-mile pancake-flat Racetrack Playa. This is where you will find the best view of the strange trails of the moving rocks. The mystery of these mobile rocks was partially solved when researchers actually saw them moving during December 2014. The stones, some of which weigh hundreds of pounds, move slowly by wind-driven ice that forms and then breaks up under very rare conditions. The tracks left by the slowly moving stones have dumbfounded visitors for decades, so this discovery has been a breakthrough!

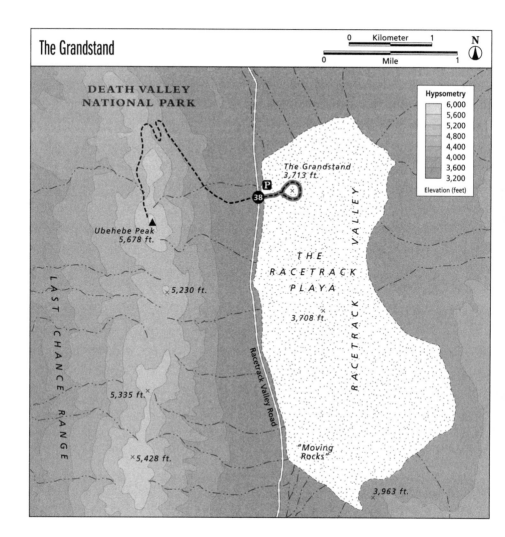

## Miles and Directions

**0.0**  Start from the Grandstand trailhead and head east.

**0.5**  Reach the Grandstand.

**1.0**  Walk west across the playa back to the trailhead.

# Central Death Valley

## 39 Mesquite Flat Sand Dunes

These sand dunes cover more than 14 square miles, the largest area of any of the seven major sand dunes in the park. They are also the most easily accessible from a road and very scenic with a scattered mantle of mesquite trees and a surprising array of nocturnal wildlife. As such, they are the most popular and heavily visited sand dunes in Death Valley National Park. This hike takes you to a more remote corner of the dunes where you'll see a lot more tracks of wildlife than of humans. To see the most animal tracks, before they are obscured by wind and shifting sand, get there early in the morning.

**Start:** About 11 miles northeast of Stovepipe Wells
**Distance:** 2.0- to 4.0-mile lollipop, depending on how large a circle through the dunes one makes
**Hiking time:** 1 to 3 hours
**Difficulty:** Easy
**Trail surface:** Two-track trail, loose to compacted sand
**Best season:** November to April
**Fees and permits:** National park entrance fee
**Maps:** NPS Death Valley Visitors Map; Trails Illustrated Death Valley National Park Map; USGS Stovepipe Wells NE-CA

**Trail contact:** Furnace Creek Visitor Center; (760) 786-3200; www.nps.gov/deva
**Special considerations:** During the hotter months ground temperatures can exceed 180°F. Carry ample water even during short hikes, at least twice what you think you'll need. Do not attempt this hike during the heat of the summer or anytime when temperatures exceed 100°F. Once in the dunes it is easy to become disoriented and lose track of where you started from. From the trailhead carefully mark a key point that you can remember. You'll then be able to visually navigate back toward it and to the trailhead if you get turned around.

**Find the trailhead:** From Stovepipe Wells drive 7.5 miles east on CA 190 to the junction of CA 190 and Scotty's Castle Road. Continue left (north) on Scotty's Castle Road 2.9 miles and turn left (west) onto the historic Stovepipe Well Road. If coming from the north on Scotty's Castle Road, the turnoff is 32.7 miles south of the Grapevine Ranger Station. Follow this dirt road 0.8 mile to the road closure at the wilderness boundary. Here you'll find a large parking area, a monument to Old Stovepipe Wells, and the original Stovepipe Well. GPS: N36 39.543' / W117 04.764'

## The Hike

This leisurely sandy stroll takes you to dunes that are lower than the 100-foot-high dunes near the expanded parking area 2.5 miles east of Stovepipe Wells. The payoff is a far less crowded opportunity to experience the Mesquite Flat Sand Dunes. The interesting Old Stovepipe Wells monument at the parking area is in itself worth the

*The ever-shifting sands of the Mesquite Flat Dunes are highlighted by the rugged beauty of massive Tucki Mountain.*

short drive from Scotty's Castle Road. The monument sits next to the original well head of the only waterhole in the Death Valley sand dunes, at the junction of two Indian trails. When sand began covering up the well head, a length of stovepipe was inserted, hence its distinctive name.

Begin by hiking southward along a two-track trail that was once known as the Sand Dunes Picnic Area Road. This old, closed two-track has been converted to an excellent hiking trail. The two-track nature of the trail is fading in places, thanks to its being closed to vehicular traffic at the wilderness boundary near the trailhead. The boundary is marked by a large wooden wilderness restoration sign. As you walk along the trail, you'll parallel the east-central edge of the extensive Mesquite Flat Sand Dunes with a grand view straight ahead of Tucki Mountain, a massive mound that rises nearly 5,000 feet above the valley floor.

The Mesquite Flat Sand Dunes are formed by north winds that carry sand down Death Valley until backing up against the buttress of Tucki Mountain, causing the sand to amass at its foot. Southerly winds have formed a vast eddy on the leeward side of Tucki, adding yet more sand. The dunes are ever shifting but are trapped in place.

After about 1 mile the trail bends to the right to meet the dunes. This is a good place to leave the trail and venture southwesterly into the dunes. In early spring

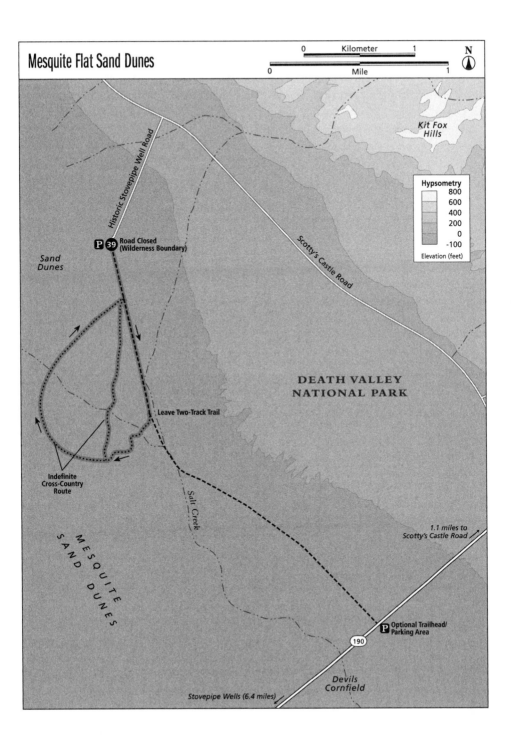

Mesquite Flat Sand Dunes

0    Kilometer    1

0         Mile         1

N

Kit Fox
Hills

Historic Stovepipe Well Road

Scotty's Castle Road

**Hypsometry**
800
600
400
200
0
-100
Elevation (feet)

Sand
Dunes

P 39  Road Closed
(Wilderness Boundary)

DEATH VALLEY
NATIONAL PARK

Leave Two-Track Trail

Indefinite
Cross-Country
Route

Salt Creek

M E S Q U I T E
S A N D   D U N E S

1.1 miles to
Scotty's Castle Road

P  Optional Trailhead/
Parking Area

190

Devils
Cornfield

Stovepipe Wells (6.4 miles)

during a good flower year, you'll see an abundance of wildflowers, especially desert gold and evening primrose. Dense clusters of bright green mesquite crown the tops of small dunes. In canyon bottoms 20-foot-tall mesquite are a short tree, but here, in the harsh environment of the dunes, they are a tall shrub. Yellow catkins cover the plant during late spring, which become long brown bean pods by early fall. These sweet pods are favored by an amazing array of desert denizens. To survive on an average of less than 2 inches of annual precipitation, and in some years no rain at all, mesquite can send a taproot more than 150 feet deep.

One of the great joys of dune trekking is looking for and trying to identify a myriad of animal tracks. The mostly hard-packed sand provides an ideal palette for recording the artistry of prints, at least for a few hours until erased by windblown sand. You'll find evidence of kangaroo rats, lizards, beetles, and several kinds of snakes, including sidewinder rattlesnakes with their distinctive sidewinding imprint.

For your cross-country dune hike, imagine a giant half circle that begins with a southwesterly sweep that gradually angles west, then north, then northeast back to the trail that you started the hike on. Follow it northward to the parking area. Along the way you'll see several types of dunes, with the most obvious being crescent-shaped barchan dunes with arms trailing downwind. You may also find transverse dunes along linear ridges at right angles to the prevailing wind, and perhaps even a localized star dune or two. The graceful curves and varied colors, ripples, and shadows of the dunes will pull you in different directions, which is all the more reason to wander without any particular destination in mind.

If you've marked a point on the southern Grapevine Mountains to navigate toward, you'll have no trouble intersecting the trail just south of the parking area. Good recognizable landmarks to mark include Death Valley Buttes and aptly named Corkscrew Peak.

## Miles and Directions

**0.0** Depart from the Stovepipe Well (northern) parking area. Hike south along an old two-track.

**1.1** Head southwesterly into the dunes from where the trail bends right to meet the dunes. Wander in the dunes by making a giant circle so as to intersect the trail after hiking 1 to 3 miles.

**3.7** After meeting the trail, head north the short distance to the parking area.

**4.0** Arrive back at the trailhead at the parking area.

*Option:* You can start the hike from the south where the two-track trail intersects CA 190, about 1.1 miles southwest of the junction of CA 190 and Scotty's Castle Road. GPS: N36 37.714' / W117 03.113'

The trail angles to the northwest. After about 1.5 miles you'll reach the same edge of the dunes described above from the north. Turn left (west) and wander off-trail into the dunes, making a broad circle in the opposite direction than described above. After circling west to south to southeast, you'll eventually intersect the trail you started on. Turn right (south) to get back to where you parked alongside CA 190.

# 40 Salt Creek Interpretive Trail and Beyond

A nature trail on a boardwalk along Salt Creek features pupfish, pickleweed, and salt grass. Extend the interpretive hike by heading up the creek or high on the nearby ridge.

**Start:** About 14 miles north of Furnace Creek
**Distance:** 4.0 miles out and back or optional lollipop
**Hiking time:** Less than 1 hour; 2 to 3 hours for extended hikes
**Difficulty:** Easy; moderate for extended hikes
**Trail surface:** Boardwalk; sand and clay for extended hikes

**Best season:** November through April
**Fees and permits:** National park entrance fee
**Maps:** NPS Death Valley Visitors Map; Trails Illustrated Death Valley National Park Map; USGS Beatty Junction-CA (Salt Creek Nature Trail), and Grotto Canyon-CA for longer hikes
**Trail contact:** Furnace Creek Visitor Center; (760) 786-3200; www.nps.gov/deva

**Finding the trailhead:** From the park visitor center in Furnace Creek, drive north on CA 190 for 13.8 miles and turn left on the signed Salt Creek Road, 1.2 miles to its end at the Salt Creek Interpretive Trail. There is a picnic area and an information kiosk at the trailhead, as well as a vault toilet. GPS: N36 35.432' / W116 59.439'

## The Hike

Salt Creek Interpretive Trail is a fully accessible, lollipop–shaped boardwalk hike, with trailside signs providing interpretive information. The extended hike continues up Salt Creek beyond the boardwalk. There is a beach-like quality to the short hike, not only due to the boardwalk designed to protect this delicate habitat, but also due to the aroma of saltwater and the salt grass and pickleweed growing in dense clumps on the sandy stream banks.

The Salt Creek pupfish, endemic to Death Valley, are the stars of this hike. In the spring there are hundreds of them in the riffles and pools of the creek. In winter they are dormant, and in summer and fall the stream is reduced to isolated pools.

The boardwalk runs alongside the creek and then crosses it in several spots, so it provides an excellent vantage point to watch the pupfish in the clear shallow water or the deep pools. Pupfish are small (not much longer than an inch) and fast, and enjoy zipping up and down the shallow riffles to bunch up in schools in the deeper terminal pools. As prehistoric Lake Manly dried up and grew saltier, these little fish were able to adapt to the new salty environment. Slimy green and brown algae, caddis flies, beetles, and water boatmen flourish here, too, providing an adequate diet for the pupfish. Their charming name, given to them by Dr. Carl Hubbs, the father of western ichthyology, refers to their zippy playful behavior. Luckily they weren't called "flea fish."

*The vast Salt Creek marshlands are home to an endemic species of pupfish and a surprising array of bird species.*

The walk out along Salt Creek is a startling change from the usual Death Valley desert-floor hike. The sound of the merry running water in the winter and spring, with the flourishing growth of salt grasses, suggests a stroll on the beach. All that's missing are the seagulls. With the interpretive signs along the trail, you can enjoy the fish and birds as well as learn about the dynamic changes of the desert habitat and the ability of some species to adapt to its harsh conditions.

To continue on the longer hikes, take the pathway that leads up Salt Creek from the north side of the bridge over the stream at the far end of the loop. Two wooden steps take you down to the valley floor. The path leads upstream between the golden mustard hills. The well-defined user trail is initially on the flat, skirting around low dunes built up around the tenacious pickleweed bushes. The path goes by marshy areas, as well as large pools, depending on the water level in Salt Creek.

At 0.5 mile from the parking area, the trail begins to seesaw up and down on the mud ridges north of the Salt Creek flats. This rise in elevation allows you to

# Salt Creek Interpretive Trail and Beyond

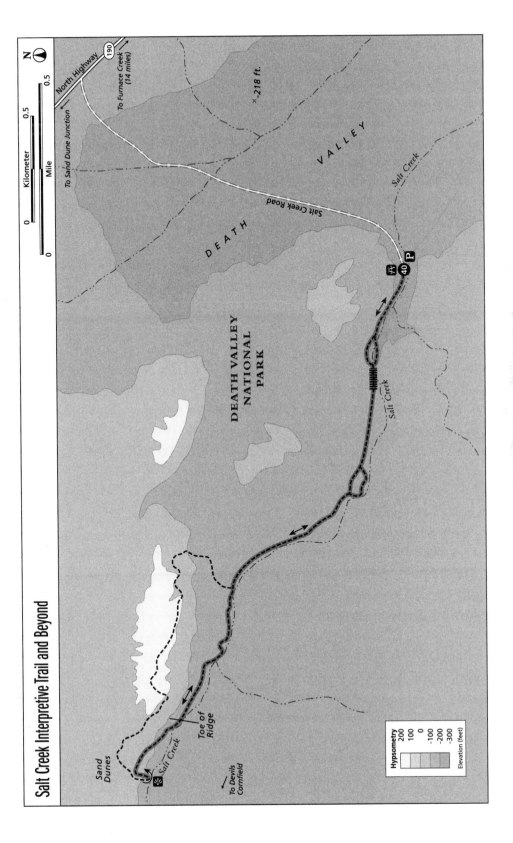

appreciate the large marsh spreading below. With intermittent pools and thick rushes, the marsh looks more like Minnesota than Death Valley. Depending on the season you may see and hear migratory birds and waterfowl, or a great blue heron.

The user trail zigzags up and down the slopes above the stream. At times the pitch is quite steep. Trekking poles can help your traction, especially if it's at all damp.

From the high point of 13 feet below sea level, the trail drops sharply 60 feet to the mouth of a wide wash. The path stays low, providing protection from the eternal Death Valley wind. The path circles around the base of the high conglomerate promontory, 1.3 miles beyond the boardwalk. The broad delta spreads before you to the northwest, where islands of mesquite rise above the swamp. The path continues past the toe of the ridge. Soft sand dunes on your left allow for a gentle perch to enjoy the view before heading back to the boardwalk by the same path.

## Miles and Directions

**0.0**  Start at the boardwalk trailhead at the parking area.

**0.1**  Intersection with loop; go either way.

**0.25**  End of loop. (*Option:* Turn around here for a 0.5-mile hike.) Continue for the longer hike.

**0.5**  Zigzag up and down along the ridge east of Salt Creek.

**2.0**  Reach the sand dune overlook; turn around here and retrace your steps.

**4.0**  Arrive back at the trailhead and parking.

*Option:* For the more adventuresome hiker, the high ridge to the immediate north of Salt Creek offers a lollipop loop back to the boardwalk. From the sand dune perch, 2 miles from the parking area, turn back into the wide valley behind the ridge. In a very short distance (0.1 mile), a visible footpath climbs up a gully to your right. After reaching the head of the gully, climb the pebbly slope to the right to the top of the ridge overlooking the Salt Creek marshlands. The views of Salt Creek and surrounding ranges and desert are wonderful. The south face of the ridge is guarded by sheer cliffs, but you can easily hike eastward along the crest of the ridge. After 0.7 mile a moderate side ridge to the southeast descends to a wash that winds around to the south. Salt Creek and the boardwalk are always in sight, so you won't lose your bearings. At 3.2 miles the mouth of the wash meets the Salt Creek pathway. Turn left and continue on the path back to the boardwalk for a 4.2-mile outing.

# 41 Harmony Borax Works

This short hike on a loop trail leads to a nineteenth-century industrial site on the valley floor. The endless borax flats are an overwhelming sight.

**Start:** About 1.5 miles north of Furnace Creek

**Distance:** 1.0 mile out and back

**Hiking time:** Less than 1 hour

**Difficulty:** Easy

**Trail surface:** Asphalt walkway to Harmony Borax Works (wheelchair accessible); sandy trail to overlook and to borax flats

**Best season:** October through March

**Fees and permits:** National park entrance fee

**Maps:** NPS Death Valley Visitors Map; Trails Illustrated Death Valley National Park Map; USGS West of Furnace Creek-CA and Furnace Creek-CA

**Trail contact:** Furnace Creek Visitor Center; (760) 786-3200; www.nps.gov/deva

**Finding the trailhead:** The trailhead for the Harmony Borax Works Trail is 1.3 miles north of the park visitor center at Furnace Creek via CA 190. The 0.2-mile road on the left is signed. The asphalt walkway leads west of the parking area. GPS: N36 28.812' / W116 52.407'

## The Hike

This desolate site was the scene of frenzied activity from 1883 to 1888, not in the pursuit of gold like so much of the other mining activity, but of borax. Used in ceramics and glass as well as soap and detergent, borax was readily available here in Death Valley. Borax prices were highly mercurial due to soaring supply and moderate demand in the nineteenth century, so the industry was plagued by sharp boom and bust cycles. Here at the Harmony Works, the years of prosperity were typically brief. For more information about the history of mining in Death Valley, visit the Borax Museum (free admission) at Furnace Creek Ranch.

Chinese laborers hauled the borate sludge in from the flats on sledges to the processing plant, remains of which are the focal point of this hike. There the borate was boiled down and hauled 165 miles across the desert to Mojave by the famed twenty-mule teams. One of the wagons that made this journey stands below the borax plant. Although the works were in operation only from October to June, working conditions for man and beast were harsh.

At the end of the loop trail, at 0.2 mile, a 0.5-mile side trip takes you to a low overlook. Follow the asphalt path that intersects with the loop to the hilltop, which gives you an excellent vista of the central valley floor. From here it is easy to imagine the usual workday in operation here at the Harmony Works. To the east of the hilltop is an area that appears to have been a dump for Furnace Creek. A rusty antique car rests on the hillside, surrounded by desert.

Although this is a short hike, be sure to bring water. It's a dehydrating experience.

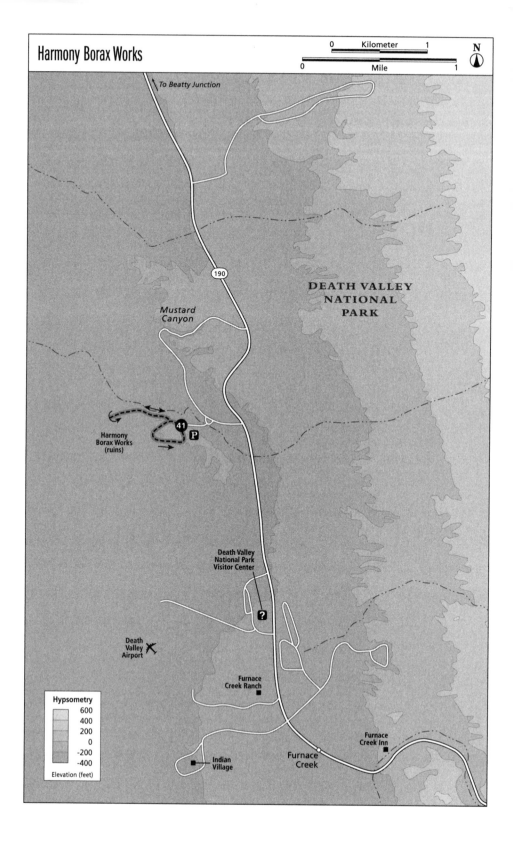

*A twenty-mule team wagon stands at the historic Harmony Borax Works trail.*

## Miles and Directions

**0.0**  Start at the trailhead and follow the asphalt loop trail west of the parking area.

**0.2**  Take the asphalt user trail leading south from the asphalt path to a low overlook on the hilltop.

**0.5**  The loop ends right back where you started. The user trail extends out into the salt flats.

**1.0**  Arrive back at the parking area.

*Options:* For a 5-mile out and back to the flats, the trailhead is located at the far side of Harmony Borax Works, heading west from the loop trail. This hike likewise confirms the arduous conditions of life and work on the valley floor. An unsigned but well-trod path leads west from the end of the paved loop. It travels by a damp slough where groundwater is percolating to the surface, causing borate crystals to form. Farther out on the flats, mounds of borax mud remain where the laborers made piles to validate the works' mining claim more than a hundred years ago.

# 42 Little Bridge Canyon

As its name suggests, this canyon has a natural bridge, as well as an arch. The hike can be done as either a loop or an out and back across a broad alluvial fan.

**Start:** About 3 miles east of Stovepipe Wells Village
**Distance:** 7.0 mile out and back with about 2,000-foot elevation gain/loss
**Hiking time:** 3 to 4 hours
**Difficulty:** Strenuous due to distance and elevation gain/loss
**Trail surface:** Cross-country on rocky alluvial fan, open canyon floor

**Best season:** Mid-October through April
**Fees and permits:** National park entrance fee
**Maps:** NPS Death Valley Visitors Map; Trails Illustrated Death Valley National Park Map; USGS Grotto Canyon-CA
**Trail contact:** Furnace Creek Visitor Center; (760) 786-3200; www.nps.gov/deva

**Finding the trailhead:** The unsigned trailhead/route takes off to the south from CA 190 between Stovepipe Wells and the junction of CA 190 and Scotty's Castle Road. Little Bridge is the first major canyon east of the signed Grotto Canyon Road. The actual starting point/pullout on CA 190 is 3 miles east of Stovepipe Wells. Look for a safe, wide spot off the highway. GPS: N36 36.119' / W117 05.618'

## The Hike

Little Bridge Canyon isn't deep and narrow, but it does contain several hidden points of wonder, making its exploration interesting and enjoyable. Unlike nearby Grotto and Mosaic Canyons, it is lightly visited, primarily because you must hike about 2.5 miles across a graveled alluvial fan just to reach the canyon entrance. One way to add a bit of spice to these first couple of open desert miles is to approach Little Bridge Canyon by way of a southeast-trending gully that parallels the steep mountain slopes on the right (west). By hiking up this gully, then up Little Bridge Canyon, and returning to the trailhead/parking pullout down the alluvial fan, a loop of about 7 miles can be made without increasing the round-trip distance of a less interesting out-and-back route.

Begin the hike by heading south to southeast across desert pavement then up the alluvial fan toward the power line and the Little Bridge Canyon entrance, which cannot be seen from the highway. Soon after passing under the power line at 0.5 mile, you'll enter a deep, graveled wash. At 1 mile the route reaches a high-walled wash where the walking becomes more difficult in loose gravel. Soon a major canyon enters from the right; continue southward up the left-hand wash. At 1.5 miles the wash narrows; climb to the left over a 5-foot dry fall. A 12-foot fall appears around the bend. Backtrack a short distance and take a faint user trail on the right side (going up), which climbs and then drops above the dry fall. Soon the wash narrows to only 3 or 4 feet.

*The Little Bridge of the canyon of the same name, about 1 mile up from the canyon mouth.*

# Little Bridge Canyon; Grotto Canyon; Mosaic Canyon

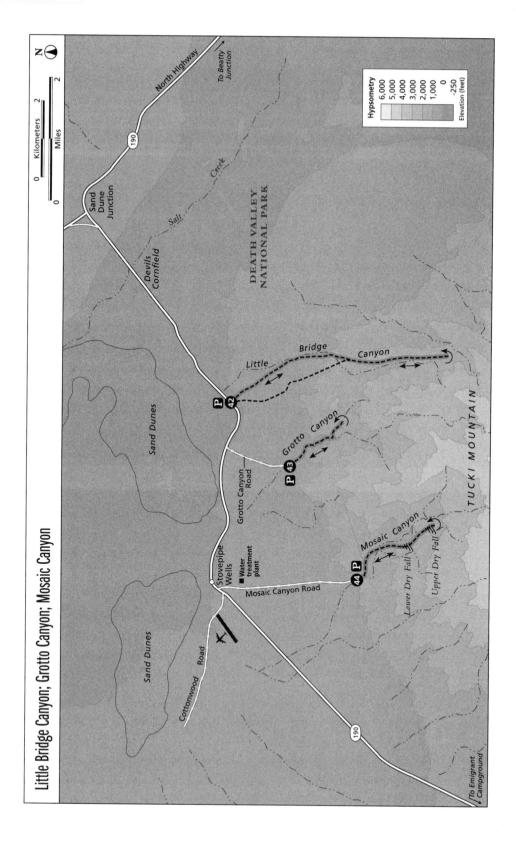

At 1.9 miles large boulders block a narrow gap; climb around to the left with rock walls rising on the right. At 2 miles the wash opens up, with its head being reached at 2.3 miles, just south of Little Bridge Canyon.

The sand dunes of Mesquite Flat can be seen back to the north, with Little Bridge straight ahead and to the right. Drop 20 feet into the wide wash, turn right, and enter the red-walled Little Bridge Canyon entrance at 2.4 miles. At 2.5 miles the canyon narrows a bit, bounded by bright red walls. Compared to most Death Valley canyons, this one runs north–south straight as an arrow. Striking clefts of white quartzite appear on the right at 2.7 miles, contrasting dramatically with adjacent dark rhyolite. Loose gravel makes for tiring walking, but the effort is soon rewarded with a small arch on the right (west) side at 3 miles.

At 3.1 miles a sizable canyon suitable for a side trip enters from the right. At 3.4 miles the main canyon again narrows, with a large cave high on the right side and the namesake natural bridge of Little Bridge Canyon also on the right side. This stunning sweep of white quartzite has a 20-foot-high opening bounded by a 40-foot-high arch. The notch above and to the right of the natural bridge ends quickly at a dry fall but provides a photographic angle for the bridge. With juniper clinging to the cliffs, this is indeed a tranquil and picturesque spot.

Hike up the canyon another 0.1 mile to a white quartzite gap for expansive views of the dunes northward and of great mounds of dark rhyolite rock overhead. The canyon narrows above but can be hiked for several more miles by those with sufficient time, energy, and water. To return, hike back down the canyon past the junction point with the side gully route. Continue to the right down the canyon and gradually angle left across the alluvial fan toward the sand dunes, aiming toward the highway/parking pullout starting point, to complete this adventurous 7-mile round-trip loop.

## Miles and Directions

**0.0**  Start at the parking pullout on CA 190; head southeast up an alluvial fan toward Little Bridge Canyon.

**0.5**  Pass under a power line.

**0.6**  Enter a deep, graveled wash.

**1.0**  At the high-walled gravel wash, continue up the left-hand side.

**1.5**  Where the wash narrows, climb left past a 5-foot dry fall.

**1.6**  At the 12-foot dry fall, climb a faint user trail to the right.

**2.3**  Reach the head of a gully just south of the mouth of Little Bridge Canyon.

**2.4**  Arrive at the mouth of Little Bridge Canyon. GPS: N36 34.599' / W117 04.840'

**3.0**  Reach a small arch on the right (west) side of the wide wash/canyon.

**3.4**  Stop and observe the natural bridge on the right side of the canyon.

**3.5**  The canyon narrows above and can be hiked for several more miles. Turn around here.

**7.0**  Arrive back at the trailhead.

# 43 Grotto Canyon

This out-and-back canyon hike winds through water-carved grottos and narrows of polished rock to a high, dry fall.

**See map on page 168.**
**Start:** About 3.5 miles southeast of Stovepipe Wells Village
**Distance:** 4.0 miles out and back
**Hiking time:** 2 to 3 hours
**Difficulty:** Easy
**Trail surface:** Sandy rocky wash, then open canyon floor

**Best season:** October through April
**Fees and permits:** National park entrance fee
**Maps:** NPS Death Valley Visitors Map; Trails Illustrated Death Valley National Park Map; USGS Grotto Canyon-CA
**Trail contact:** Furnace Creek Visitor Center; (760) 786-3200; www.nps.gov/deva

**Finding the trailhead:** The Grotto Canyon access road heads south from CA 190, 2.4 miles east of Stovepipe Wells Village. The road is signed for Grotto Canyon and four-wheel-drive vehicles. After 1.1 miles the road ends for most vehicles above the wash, which is soft gravel. There's no actual trailhead, but the road/trail continues on up the wash to the canyon. GPS: N36 35.485' / W117 06.632'

## The Hike

With careful driving a passenger vehicle can negotiate the road to the wash on the Grotto Canyon hike. The soft gravel of the wash for the mile to the canyon entrance requires high clearance and four-wheel drive. No signs or markers punctuate the end of the road, but severe washouts end vehicle access just before the first dry fall. Conditions in this canyon change with each flood. At times the gravel is deep and the dry falls are easy to scale, but often floods have scoured the gravel away, making exploring more of a challenge.

Like the other Tucki Mountain canyons, Grotto is a very broad canyon, up to 200 yards wide in many areas. Deeply eroded canyon walls stand like medieval castle ramparts, with short serpentine pathways in their lower reaches. The narrows at 1.8 miles bring welcome shade after the journey up the graveled canyon bottom. A pair of ravens nesting in the aerie alcove above the grotto may provide suitable visual and sound effects for the hiker approaching the almost cave-like section of the canyon. About 0.1 mile back down the canyon, a cairned trail on the eastern side leads you around this barrier to the canyon above. Another dry fall will block your travels there, so this is a good turnaround point.

Even with its proximity to Stovepipe Wells, Grotto Canyon is not heavily visited. Thus the adventuresome hiker can enjoy desert exploration and solitude without a lengthy drive. The high silence above Mesquite Flat rings in your ears—between cries of the ravens.

*The narrows of Grotto Canyon.*

Hiking back to the road, the dunes stretch out below, framed by the Cottonwood and Grapevine Mountains. Grotto Canyon is a desert wonder of a smaller dimension.

## Miles and Directions

**0.0** There's no actual trailhead, so from your car hike up the gravel jeep road in the wash.

**1.8** Arrive at the narrows.

**2.0** Turn around where another dry fall blocks your path.

**4.0** Arrive back at the trailhead.

# 44 Mosaic Canyon

Patterned walls of multicolored rock and water-sculpted formations await you in this picturesque canyon near Stovepipe Wells. If you go here you'll discover why Mosaic is one of the most popular canyons in the park.

**See map on page 168.**
**Start:** About 2 miles south of Stovepipe Wells Village
**Distance:** 3.6 miles out and back (2.8 miles to lower dry fall)
**Hiking time:** 2 to 3 hours
**Difficulty:** Moderate (easy to lower dry fall)
**Trail surface:** Dirt path with rock, then open canyon floor

**Best season:** October through April
**Fees and permits:** National park entrance fee
**Maps:** NPS Death Valley Visitors Map; Trails Illustrated Death Valley National Park Map; USGS Stovepipe Wells-CA
**Trail contact:** Furnace Creek Visitor Center; (760) 786-3200; www.nps.gov/deva

**Finding the trailhead:** From CA 190, 0.1 mile southwest of Stovepipe Wells Village, head south on the rough but passable Mosaic Canyon Road (signed). After 2.3 miles the road ends at the large Mosaic Canyon parking area, and the trail takes off immediately (south). GPS: N36 34.310' / W117 08.657'

## The Hike

The fault in Tucki Mountain that produced Mosaic Canyon consists of mosaic breccia and smooth Noonday Formation dolomite, formed in a seabed 750 to 900 million years ago. After being pressurized and baked at more than 1,000°F, then eroded, the resulting rock has startling contrasts of both texture and color.

Mosaic Canyon drains more than 4 square miles of the Tucki Range, so it is to be avoided, like all canyons, in flash-flood conditions. Rushing water, carrying its load of scouring boulders, has created smooth marbleized waterways out of the otherwise lumpy breccia. Silky surfaces gradually change to ragged lumps from the canyon floor up its walls, reflecting the varying depths of floodwaters.

Like other canyons in Tucki Mountain, Mosaic Canyon is alternately wide and narrow. The wider spots are more numerous, and are broad enough almost to qualify as valleys. Often parties of hikers arrive at these open areas and turn back, figuring that the canyon excitement has ended. With plenty of water and a broad-brimmed hat, you can continue exploring the depths of Mosaic. If it's a hot day, be aware that this is not a deep, shady canyon like the ones in the Grapevine and Funeral Mountains.

The first 0.2 mile of canyon features the smooth marble surfaces that have made Mosaic a favorite destination of Death Valley visitors. After that the canyon opens to a wide, colorful amphitheater, swinging eastward to a broad valley with a 40-foot butte standing in the center. User trails go in all directions, converging at the end of the

*Hikers make their way through the marbleized watercourse of Mosaic Canyon.*

valley where the canyon narrows again. To the right of this butte, a deep wash will eventually become a new branch of Mosaic Canyon.

At 1 mile a small pile of boulders blocks a narrow spot. A well-traveled path to the left provides an easy detour. After another wide spot the canyon narrows again, where an abrupt 40-foot dry fall blocks your passage. It is possible to get around this barrier by way of a well-traveled and cairned trail. Drop 50 yards back from the dry fall to the trail on the sloping canyon wall to the south. This trail takes you to the upper region of Mosaic Canyon where another 0.4 mile of marbleized chutes and narrows awaits you. A steep marble chute, 50 feet high, halts the hike at 1.8 miles. It's a striking spot, with eroding, fragmented Tucki Mountain rising above the silky smooth waterslide.

The hike back down the canyon provides new views of Death Valley and the Cottonwood Mountains in the distance. Sliding down the short water chutes on the return to the trailhead increases the marbleized beauty of these breccia formations; generations of hikers have added to water's erosive force in creating these smooth rocks.

## Miles and Directions

**0.0**  Start at the parking area behind an information sign. Head into the canyon.

**0.2**  The canyon widens into an amphitheater.

**1.4**  A 40-foot dry fall blocks the canyon; 50 yards back, cairns and arrows mark the side trail detour. (**Option:** Turn around here to make a 2.8-mile round-trip hike.)

**1.8**  A 50-foot marble chute blocks the canyon. Turn around here and retrace your steps.

**3.6**  Arrive back at the trailhead from the upper dry fall.

# 45 Marble Canyon

Marble Canyon is a long out-and-back day hike up a deep, narrow canyon in the Cottonwood Mountains. Here you will find colorful rock formations, petroglyphs, and expansive views of remote backcountry.

**Start:** About 14 miles west of Stovepipe Wells Village

**Distance:** 9.6 miles out and back from the road closure 2.6 miles up Marble Canyon Road (if your vehicle is parked at the signed Cottonwood-Marble Canyon junction, add 5.2 miles to the round-trip hiking distance)

**Hiking time:** 4 to 5 hours (7 to 8 hours for the longer outing)

**Difficulty:** Moderate

**Trail surface:** Rocky path for 1.1 miles, sandy wash thereafter

**Best season:** October through May

**Fees and permits:** National park entrance fee

**Maps:** NPS Death Valley Visitors Map; Trails Illustrated Death Valley National Park Map; USGS Cottonwood Creek-CA

**Trail contact:** Furnace Creek Visitor Center; (760) 786-3200; www.nps.gov/deva

**Finding the trailhead:** From Stovepipe Wells Village on CA 190, head west on Cottonwood Road. Cottonwood Road begins on the right near the entrance to the Stovepipe Wells Campground. The two-wheel-drive portion of this slow, rocky road ends after 8.4 miles when the road drops steeply into Cottonwood Wash and turns left up the canyon. High-clearance four-wheel drive is advised beyond this point due to soft gravel and high centers. The junction of Cottonwood and Marble Canyon Roads is 10.7 miles from the Stovepipe Wells Campground. Cottonwood Canyon is to the left. Marble Canyon Road continues to the right another 2.6 miles to the signed vehicle closure at the canyon narrows, but park at the junction if you have any doubts about whether your vehicle can negotiate these final very rough few miles. Junction parking area GPS: N36 37.910' / W117 17.738'; Upper parking area GPS: N36 37.322' / W117 19.814'

## The Hike

The adjacent Cottonwood and Marble Canyons are as different from each other as night and day. Cottonwood is wide and open whereas Marble is a wonderland of intimate narrows and dark alcoves. Marble Canyon is susceptible to flash flooding with a corresponding danger of being caught in one of its steep chutes with no escape. Do not attempt to hike the canyon if wet weather appears imminent.

For the Marble Canyon out-and-back day excursion, the hike might start out of vehicular necessity at the Cottonwood/Marble Canyon Roads junction, but the real adventure begins 2.6 miles up at the canyon gap/road closure. On the way up at mile 2.3, petroglyphs can be seen at the mouth of the canyon. Sadly, some of these irreplaceable cultural links to the past have been senselessly defaced by vandals. There are more pristine petroglyphs farther up Marble Canyon, readily seen going up but more difficult to spot on the way down.

*Marble Canyon contains several sets of petroglyphs—look but don't touch.*

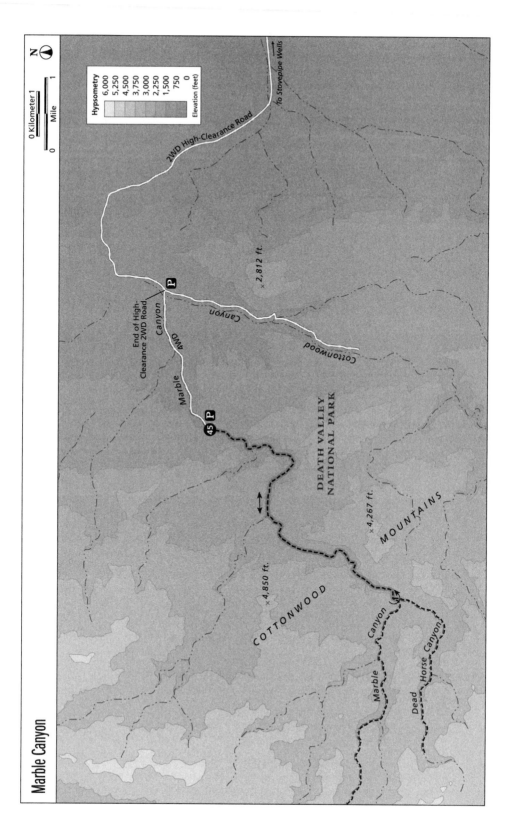

# Marble Canyon

**Hypsometry**

| Elevation (feet) |
|---|
| 6,000 |
| 5,250 |
| 4,500 |
| 3,750 |
| 3,000 |
| 2,250 |
| 1,500 |
| 750 |
| 0 |

0 Kilometer 1

0 Mile 1

N

2WD High-Clearance Road

End of High-Clearance 2WD Road

To Stovepipe Wells

× 2,812 ft.

Marble Canyon

4WD

Cottonwood Canyon

Canyon

P

45 P

DEATH VALLEY NATIONAL PARK

× 4,267 ft.

× 4,850 ft.

COTTONWOOD

MOUNTAINS

Marble Canyon

Dead Horse Canyon

At the trailhead the canyon is only about 6 feet wide, coinciding with the wilderness boundary, which is signed with a closure to vehicular travel. At 0.3 mile a canyon enters from the right, but leads quickly to a 15-foot dry fall. Continue left up the creosote and Mormon tea bottom next to great stair-step beds of tilted gray and red rock. At 1.1 miles a huge boulder blocks the canyon—it can be bypassed on the right by climbing up stepping stones. At 1.3 miles the canyon narrows to sheer, gray cliffs where graffiti mars still more petroglyphs. Here every turn in the twisting canyon brings new variety, with arches being formed from smooth, gently eroded gray cliffs. Overhangs create an almost cave-like effect.

At 1.6 miles the valley opens dramatically only to narrow again at 1.9 miles. Once more the valley widens with brilliant displays of reds, tans, and grays on both sides at 2.3 miles. Here a major canyon enters from the right; stay to the left (west) by entering dark-walled narrows, which soon give way to a long, open stretch. The canyon closes in again at 3.5 miles, marked by a distinctive semicircular alcove on the left. Soon white and gray bands of marble resembling zebra stripes border a wonderland of grottos in the narrow canyon. A second large boulder blocks the wash at 4 miles but can be easily bypassed by climbing a "staircase" rock on the left. A small side canyon, overlooked by buttes and pinnacles, enters on the right at 4.2 miles.

Dead Horse Canyon joins Marble Canyon from the left (south) at 4.8 miles, at an elevation of 3,110 feet. The wide Dead Horse Valley looks deceptively like the main drainage, but Marble Canyon cuts sharply to the right (west). There are several spacious and excellent campsites at this junction, above the wash, for those willing to pack sufficient water for an overnight stay.

Many years ago someone etched "Gold Belt Spring 4 Miles" into the desert varnish of a large rock, with an arrow pointing up Marble Canyon. Another 0.2 mile above the junction, a massive white cliff oversees the left side of Marble Canyon as it climbs steeply toward Goldbelt Spring.

As you return down the canyon to the trailhead, you'll appreciate having had the sun at your back both for the morning ascent and the afternoon descent. This trip is well worth a full day of canyon exploration.

## Miles and Directions

**0.0** Start at the trailhead at the signed vehicle closure 2.6 miles up Marble Canyon Road, where the canyon walls are only 6 or 7 feet apart.

**0.3** Where the canyon (right) leads to a 15-foot dry fall, stay left.

**1.1** A huge boulder blocks the canyon, ending the previously open four-wheel-drive road. Climb up the stepping stones to the right.

**1.4** Overhangs here create a cave-like effect in the canyon.

**2.3** At the major junction, continue left (west) into a narrow, dark-walled canyon.

**3.5** The canyon again narrows, with a semicircular alcove on the left.

**4.0** Another boulder blocks the canyon. Climb the staircase of rocks on the left.

**4.8**  Dead Horse Canyon enters from the south. Turn around here and retrace your steps.

**9.6**  Arrive back at the trailhead.

*Option:* While the recommended trip described here is an out-and-back exploration of scenic Marble Canyon all the way up to its junction with Dead Horse Canyon, a much longer 23-mile backpacking loop through both canyons can be undertaken by those willing to cache water on this dry route and commit a minimum of three days. The loop can start from the Cottonwood/Marble Canyon Road junction. Begin by hiking 8.5 miles up the Cottonwood Canyon road, cross over into Marble Canyon by way of Dead Horse Canyon, and descend 7.4 miles down Marble Canyon from the mouth of Dead Horse Canyon to the point of origin at the road junction. About half of this loop is on open four-wheel-drive roads, with the remainder being canyon washes and an overland cross-country route.

# 46 Black Point Canyon

This highly varied canyon changes dramatically from open desert to colorful narrows with a small arch and interesting formations in between.

**Start:** About 5 miles southwest of Stovepipe Wells Village
**Distance:** 5.6 miles out and back with 1,125 feet elevation gain/loss
**Hiking time:** 3 to 4 hours
**Difficulty:** Moderate
**Trail surface:** Desert pavement, gravel wash, old two-track (closed to vehicles)
**Best season:** November to April
**Fees and permits:** National park entrance fee

**Maps:** NPS Death Valley Visitors Map; Trails Illustrated Death Valley National Park Map; USGS Stovepipe Wells-CA
**Trail contact:** Furnace Creek Visitor Center; (760) 786-3200; www.nps.gov/deva
**Other:** There are no facilities at the unsigned parking area.
**Special considerations:** This mostly open canyon lacks shade and is likely to be dry and very warm. Carry sufficient water for this half-day hike.

**Finding the trailhead:** From Stovepipe Wells Village drive 5 miles southwest on CA 190 and park 0.4 mile past the 1,000-foot elevation sign along a wide pullout on the west side of the highway. The northern edge of Black Point is to the immediate south. GPS: N36 33.151' / W117 12.361'

## The Hike

The wide mouth of Black Point Canyon is directly southeast of the parking area in direct line with the imposing massif of Tucki Mountain. Head toward a small tan mound as well as a line of dark rock on the right side of the wash that will guide you to the correct canyon. The walking is good in the wash but even better on an old roadbed (closed to vehicles) that leads to the historic Stovepipe Wells dump at 0.8 mile.

The canyon gradient is steady but moderate enough to be enjoyable. Creosote and rock nettle bushes dot the wide canyon floor. Tucki Mountain looms ahead and to the right. Soon the wash widens even more as it angles to the right (southeast). Hike toward the right (south) side of the wash, which is bound by a low brown ridge cut with 40-foot-high fluted conglomerate cliffs. You'll pass by several small side gullies. Continue up the main wash toward Tucki Mountain.

At around 2 miles a huge pillar formation with a small arch forms the right side of the canyon. This marks the beginning of a short stretch of narrows bound by low cliffs. Two moderate 6- to 8-foot dry falls can be climbed or easily bypassed on the left side.

Once again the valley opens wide with large block formations containing a small arch that displays a hole in the wall on the uphill side. Desert pavement provides an

*Hikers descend the upper reaches of Black Point Canyon above colorful narrows with the vast sweep of the Panamint Range beyond.*

excellent walking surface. Side slots with low dry falls are cut along the sides of the main wash. The floor of the wash is pocketed with sizable holes made by wildlife—badger, fox, coyote? Look for telltale tracks.

At around miles 2.4 to 2.6, the canyon is defined by colorful narrows—a palette of red, orange, gray, and purple. Compression ledges and layers add form and composition. The upper edge of the colorful narrows is marked by a 6-foot dry fall that can be easily climbed or bypassed.

The narrow canyon floor has sloping sides of polished breccia rock with inclined water funnels that are fun and easy to walk up. At mile 2.8 the canyon is blocked by a 25-foot dry fall composed of slippery rock that would be difficult to climb. The dry fall is an excellent turnaround point for an equally interesting return trip. Let your imagination run wild by naming weird rock formations that you may have missed on the way up. For example, we found a "sleeping ghoul" lying on its side.

## Miles and Directions

**0.0**  Start near the mouth of Black Point Canyon on CA 190. Aim for the right side of the wash.

**0.3**  Enter the mouth of Black Point Canyon.

# Black Point Canyon

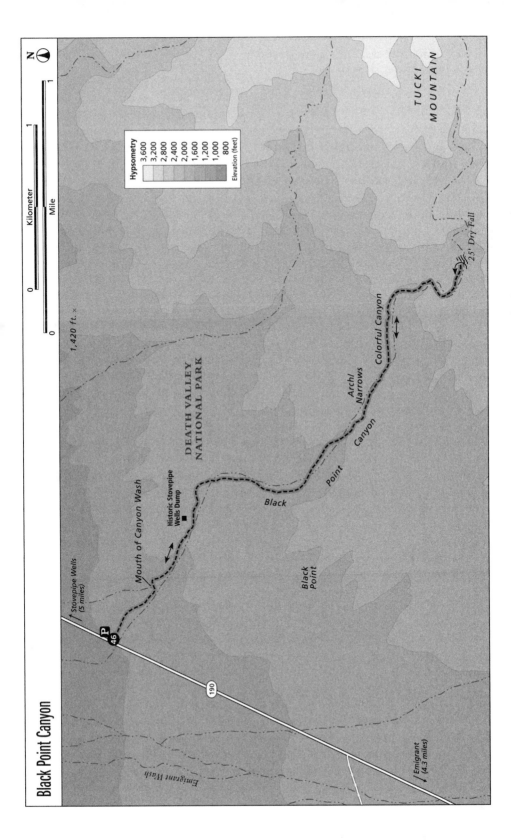

Hypsometry

Elevation (feet)

3,600
3,200
2,800
2,400
2,000
1,600
1,200
1,000
800

DEATH VALLEY
NATIONAL PARK

Stovepipe Wells
(5 miles)

Mouth of Canyon Wash

Historic Stovepipe
Wells Dump

Black
Point

Black

Point

Canyon

Archl.
Narrows

Colorful Canyon

25' Dry Fall

1,420 ft. ×

Emigrant Wash

Emigrant
(4.3 miles)

Black Point
(road marker 190)

Emigrant Wash

N

Kilometer

Mile

TUCKI
MOUNTAIN

**0.8** Arrive at the historic Stovepipe Wells dump.

**2.4** Begin a section of colorful narrows.

**2.8** Reach a 25-foot dry fall; turn around here and retrace your steps.

**5.6** Arrive back at the parking area.

***Option:*** If you still have time and energy after exploring Black Point Canyon consider a romp up Black Point of about 2 miles that will take about 2 hours. Black Point is the distinctive two-mile long north–south ridge that overlooks Emigrant Wash along CA 190. Drive another 0.5 to 1 mile south on CA 190 and park near the orange highway sign. From there you can hike southeasterly up a wash into a box canyon. After entering the canyon climb up fairly stable volcanic rock to the ridgeline. Following an elevation gain of 300 to 400 feet, you'll be treated to spectacular vistas of Death Valley and surrounding mountain ranges. After hiking along the ridge for a ways, look for a safe descent on a rocky slope interspersed with hard-packed pebbles.

*A small arch graces the north side of Black Point Canyon beneath a gigantic anvil-shaped formation.*

# 47 Panamint Dunes

This is a cross-country, open desert hike on relatively inaccessible, high, star-shaped sand dunes in the expanded western region of the park. Spectacular views of the Panamint Valley and surrounding mountain ranges sweep in all directions.

**Start:** About 30 miles southwest of Stovepipe Wells Village
**Distance:** 9.0 miles out and back
**Hiking time:** 3 to 4 hours
**Difficulty:** Moderate
**Trail surface:** Sand, short rocky sections
**Best season:** Mid-October to mid-April

**Fees and permits:** National park entrance fee
**Maps:** NPS Death Valley Visitors Map; Trails Illustrated Death Valley National Park Map; USGS The Dunes-CA
**Trail contact:** Furnace Creek Visitor Center; (760) 786-3200; www.nps.gov/deva

**Finding the trailhead:** From Panamint Springs drive east on CA 190 for 4.4 miles to unsigned Lake Hill Road. Turn left (north) on unsigned Lake Hill Road. This road is easy to miss, so drive slowly and watch carefully just to the east of the dry lake bed. Drive 5.8 miles to where the road begins to deteriorate as it bends toward the mountains to the east. This is the north end of the North Panamint Dry Lake bed. Park at the bend where there is a large, rock-ringed parking area. Begin the hike from here. The access road is rough and graveled but can be negotiated by standard vehicles driven slowly and carefully. GPS: N36 25.278' / W117 24.725'

## The Hike

The Panamint Dunes are clearly visible to the northwest from the trailhead/parking area. Because these extensive dunes rise several hundred feet, they appear deceptively close. In fact, they are 4 miles away across open desert, requiring a steady 1.5- to 2-hour walk just to reach the higher complex of dunes. This relative inaccessibility, compared to most other dunes in the California desert region, accounts for their pristine quality.

These ever-changing mounds of sand are home to several endemic plants, dune grass, vetch, and more. The Panamint Valley is the site of mysterious rock alignments, some of which are called "intaglios." Intaglios are of prehistoric human origin and are huge animal shapes, perhaps hundreds of feet in size. These shapes, one of which is reported to be of a hummingbird, can be discerned from an airplane but not from the dunes. Fortunately, the park's wilderness designation now protects these artifacts from the destructive impact of off-road vehicles.

At first the line-of-sight cross-country route to the dunes crosses a short section of rough, rocky alluvial fan. Don't be discouraged, for soon the open desert floor is made up mostly of well-compacted sand and desert pavement with more solid footing. The ascent is gradual, averaging only about 250 feet per mile. At 2.5 miles and

*Hiking the Panamint Dunes with a view to the northeast—star-shaped dune configurations are visible on the north side of these dunes.*

2,020 feet elevation, you'll reach the lower edge of the dunes, with large creosote bushes dominating the landscape. The going becomes a bit slower in the softer sand.

After another mile and 400-foot ascent, the base of the higher dunes is attained. Dune grass appears in sporadic patches, with the indentations of animal and insect tracks seemingly everywhere. From here pick out a sandy ridge route to the apex of the dunes, reached after another mile, somewhere around 2,700 feet elevation. Depending on angle to the wind and relative moisture, climbing the nearly 300-foot-high dunes can be tiring, but the effort by way of a route of swirling, twisting ridges to the top will be well rewarded.

The star-shaped configuration of these dunes is especially apparent on the northern backside. Here swirls of sand wrap around small circular basins and bowls, forming an intricate maze of shapes and patterns. Some of the sand basins resemble perfectly rounded craters. The view from the knife-ridge apex of the dunes is magnificent.

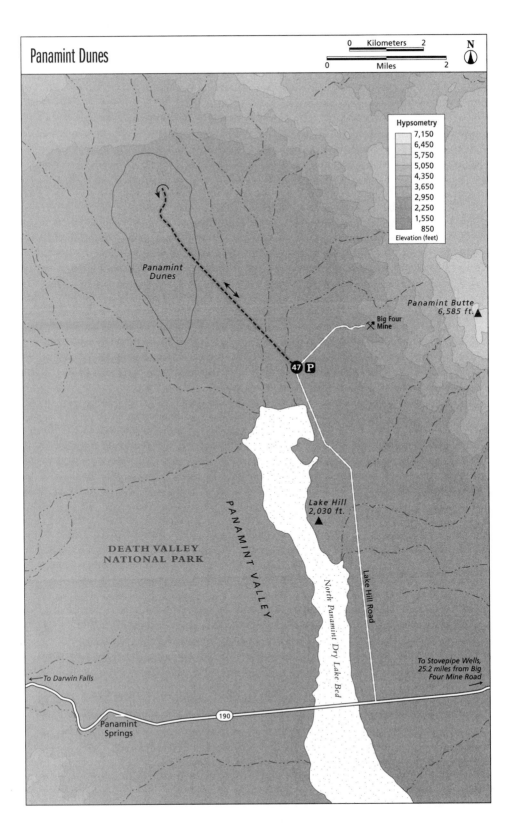

# Panamint Dunes

**Hypsometry**

7,150
6,450
5,750
5,050
4,350
3,650
2,950
2,250
1,550
850
Elevation (feet)

*Panamint Dunes*

*Panamint Butte*
*6,585 ft.* ▲

Big Four
Mine ⚒

**47** Ⓟ

Lake Hill
2,030 ft.
▲

*PANAMINT VALLEY*

**DEATH VALLEY
NATIONAL PARK**

*North Panamint Dry Lake Bed*

*Lake Hill Road*

← *To Darwin Falls*

*To Stovepipe Wells,
25.2 miles from Big
Four Mine Road* →

190

Panamint
Springs

Panamint Springs can be seen far to the southwest. The vast Panamint Valley stretches southward, with the distinctive volcanic remnants of Lake Hill rising from the dry lake bed. Lofty Telescope Peak crowns the Panamint Mountains, with the multicolored bands of Panamint Butte dominating the immediate southeast horizon.

To return, follow a line-of-sight route toward Telescope Peak—by far the highest point to the south—and you'll end up at or very close to the trailhead, thereby completing this varied 9-mile trip to the Panamint Dunes. At first glance you might think that all dunes are somewhat similar, just another "pile of sand" as we heard one casual observer say. Not so. Each of the four dune hikes suggested in this book, and their desert basin and range settings, is so different from the others that they can hardly be compared.

## Miles and Directions

**0.0**   Start at the parking area at the north end of the North Panamint Dry Lake bed. Begin the hike across open, sandy desert.

**2.5**   After a gradual ascent you'll reach the lower edge of the dunes, with creosote bushes dominating.

**3.5**   Reach the base of the higher dunes (2,420 feet).

**4.5**   Reach the high point of the dunes (2,700 feet). Turn around here and retrace your steps.

**9.0**   Arrive back at the trailhead.

# 48 Lake Hill

This hike explores isolated hills surrounded by an ancient lake bed playa with the color-banded Panamint Mountains as a backdrop. This is a perfect complement to Panamint Sand Dunes or to any Panamint Valley visit.

**Start:** About 8 miles northeast of Panamint Springs
**Distance:** 3.2 miles out and back with a loop
**Hiking time:** 2 to 3 hours
**Difficulty:** Moderate due to short distance and modest elevation gain without serious exposure
**Trail surface:** Sandy wash, faint two-track, loose sand and rocky ridge
**Best season:** November to April
**Fees and permits:** National park entrance fee

**Maps:** NPS Death Valley Visitors Map; Trails Illustrated Death Valley National Park Map; USGS The Dunes-CA
**Trail contact:** Furnace Creek Visitor Center; (760) 786-3200; www.nps.gov/deva
**Other:** There are no facilities at or anywhere near the parking area.
**Special considerations:** Off-trail route-finding is needed at the start and along the main Lake Hill ridge. Carry ample water. Expect to see and hear military jet aircraft.

**Finding the trailhead:** From Panamint Springs drive east on CA 190 for 4.4 miles and turn left (north) onto the unsigned Lake Hill Road. This road is easy to miss. It is just west of two large yellow highway signs. The road is suitable for high-clearance two-wheel-drive vehicles, if carefully driven. It is so rough that your speed will average less than 10 mph. Drive north on Lake Hill Road for 4.3 miles and park opposite the gap between the isolated 1,688-foot mound and the main Lake Hill complex of buttes and ridges. Park next to an old dozer cut that is at right angles to the road. Take care to park alongside the road and not in the wide-open flat adjacent to the dozer cut because that would place your vehicle within designated wilderness, which is against both the law and National Park Service regulations. GPS: N36 24.107' / W117 24.081'

## The Hike

From the parking area a dark mound to the south (1,766 feet) marks the northern extremity of Lake Hill to the immediate southwest. Begin by crossing a short stretch of creosote-dotted desert to the base of the mound. The sandy floor is etched by a maze of bird and animal tracks. Angle left (south) and enter a narrow gully at 0.2 mile along the eastern side of the mound.

The top of the short gully, lined by distinctive striped rocks, opens to a high interior flat enclosed by the ridges and buttes of Lake Hill. We call it the "hidden valley." Look for the faint tracks of an old closed road now used mostly by hikers and feral burros.

Continue south into the hidden valley toward a low pass on the far horizon. The pass is on the left side of the dark-colored Lake Hill ridge. At 1 mile you'll walk by an isolated grove of unusually large and dense creosote bushes interspersed with desert

*Climbing Lake Hill above the hidden valley with Panamint Butte looming beyond to the northeast.*

holly. Perched on mini sand dunes, this creosote "forest" is an ecological microcosm that seems almost out of place in the surrounding desert and dark ridges. Upon reaching the gap at the head of the hidden valley, begin climbing to the southwest (right) up the sandy slope to the crest of the ridge. You'll quickly discover that climbing the stable rocks on the right side of the sandy slope provides much better footing than loose sand. The main north ridge of Lake Hill is attained after climbing 300 feet. The V-shaped hidden valley stretches out to the north.

Follow the rocky spine of Lake Hill another 0.2 mile to the south to the hill's 2,030-foot-high apex at 1.4 miles. Two USGS brass reference plaques point toward a benchmark on the very top of the hill. The one on top is labeled "Black" for good reason: These dark hills are literally covered with black rocks of various sizes and shapes. A weather-worn 1992 peak register, fun to read, reveals that Lake Hill is a well-traveled destination. Typical comments extol the "magnificent desolation" while lamenting the roar of Air Force jets buzzing around. One visitor was married in a hot air balloon over the adjacent dry lake bed in 1990! When on top imagine being surrounded by an ancient lake. Was Lake Hill completely underwater at one time? Or was it an island on the eastern edge of a vast lake?

To create a more interesting partial loop for the return while experiencing more of Lake Hill, descend its gently graded north ridge for about 0.6 mile to a low pass.

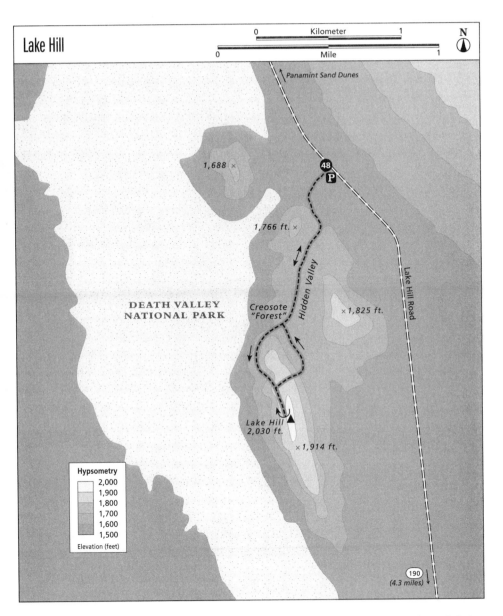

Lake Hill

0    Kilometer    1

N

↑ *Panamint Sand Dunes*

0    Mile    1

1,688 ×

48
P

1,766 ft. ×

*Hidden Valley*

DEATH VALLEY
NATIONAL PARK

Creosote
"Forest"

× 1,825 ft.

*Lake Hill Road*

Lake Hill
2,030 ft. ▲

× 1,914 ft.

**Hypsometry**
2,000
1,900
1,800
1,700
1,600
1,500
Elevation (feet)

190
(4.3 miles) ↓

Look for a sandy trough on the east (right) side of the ridge that provides a delight-ful drop to the creosote grove at 2.2 miles. This is the safest, easiest, and most gradual descent to the hidden valley. Let gravity and the soft sand work their magic.

Upon reaching the valley floor, turn left (north) and retrace the first mile of the route back to the gully that leads to the parking area. After the hike, as you drive south to CA 190, you might conclude that the hardest part of visiting Lake Hill is getting to and from the parking area on the rough Lake Hill Road—a minor inconvenience in exchange for a spectacular hike.

*The peak register atop Lake Hill provides fun and interesting reading.*

## Miles and Directions

**0.0**  Start at the parking area alongside Lake Hill Road. Aim for a dark mound to the southwest.

**0.2**  Enter a narrow gully.

**0.3**  Enter the "hidden valley."

**1.0**  Pass the creosote "forest" and reach the head of the hidden valley. Go right to start the loop.

**1.2**  Reach the Lake Hill summit ridge.

**1.4**  Arrive at the apex of Lake Hill (2,030 feet). This is the turnaround.

**1.6**  Take the right fork to the east-northeast.

**2.0**  Arrive at a low pass after descending the summit's north ridge.

**2.2**  Complete the loop, again coming to the creosote forest.

**3.2**  Arrive back at the parking area.

# 49 Darwin Falls

This is a short hike to a delightful moist microclimate with multitiered waterfalls tucked away in a scenic canyon.

**Start:** About 4 miles southwest of Panamint Springs
**Distance:** 2.0 miles out and back
**Hiking time:** 1 to 2 hours
**Difficulty:** Easy
**Trail surface:** Dirt path
**Best season:** October through June
**Fees and permits:** National park entrance fee

**Maps:** NPS Death Valley Visitor Map; Trails Illustrated Death Valley National Park Map; USGS Darwin-CA
**Trail contact:** Furnace Creek Visitor Center; (760) 786-3200; www.nps.gov/deva
**Special considerations:** This is a day-use-only area. This is the water source for the village of Panamint Springs, so bathing and wading are forbidden.

**Finding the trailhead:** From Panamint Springs, 29.6 miles southwest of Stovepipe Wells on CA 190, drive west 1 mile to the first dirt road on the left. Turn left (west) on the dirt road and drive 2.4 miles to the signed side road on the right for the Darwin Falls parking area. You will notice a pipeline running along the road. The road is rough but passable for a standard passenger vehicle. GPS: N36 19.661' / W117 30.880'

## The Hike

Darwin Stream is the only permanent water in this area of the park. Flowing from the China Garden Spring, Darwin supplies the town of Panamint Springs with water via a pipeline, which is visible on both the drive and the hike to the falls. This year-round water source sustains dense willow and cottonwood thickets in the valley and canyon as well as a thriving population of birds. Swifts and red-tailed hawks soar overhead. Brazen chuckwalla lizards stare at intruders from their rocky lairs.

This hike is a radical change from the usual Death Valley outing. Right from the parking area, a streak of greenery and a glistening brook lead up the gently sloping gravel and sand valley floor. A well-used sandy footpath stays on the right side of the stream. The Darwin Mountains of black rhyolite tower above the bright green grass, the willow saplings, the horsetails and cattails.

When the canyon narrows, many pathways lead through the boulders and trees up to the spring. Some are routes used by agile children who love to scramble over boulders and are not daunted by their slippery surfaces or by splashing through the stream; there are other pathways for the more wary hiker. Pick the trail that suits you. On the right-hand bank is an old roadbed that the town of Panamint Springs uses periodically to maintain its aqueduct. This delicate lush valley experiences periodic flood damage from rainstorms in the Panamints. Major remodeling is a constant factor, except for the falls, which remain spectacular.

*The lush, tranquil setting of Darwin Falls is both the highlight and turnaround for the hike.*

The narrow canyon twists and turns. With steep canyon walls and willow and cottonwood thickets, this is a shady hike, an excellent outing for a hot sunny day!

At 1 mile, after hearing them in the distance, you reach the falls. The forked falls cascade over a 25-foot drop-off, surrounded by large old cottonwoods. Sword ferns, watercress, and cattails flourish in the pool below the falls. This is the turnaround point for the hike. Going farther is highly hazardous, given the slick rocks. Moreover, desert wildlife prefers solitude around their scarce water supplies.

Emerging from Darwin Canyon is an Alice-in-Wonderland experience. After being surrounded by humidity and greenery, the beige world of the desert looks one-dimensional. The valley below the canyon is a striking transition zone, with the soft greenery of the stream ecosystem juxtaposed against the jagged dark rhyolite cliffs of the mountains to the south. The hike to Darwin Falls is a carnival of sensory perceptions. The smells, sounds, feel, and sight of this watery world make this an exceptional experience.

## Miles and Directions

**0.0**  Start at the parking area for Darwin Falls. Head up the footpath along Darwin Stream.

**1.0**  Arrive at the falls. Turn around here and retrace your steps.

**2.0**  Arrive back at the parking area.

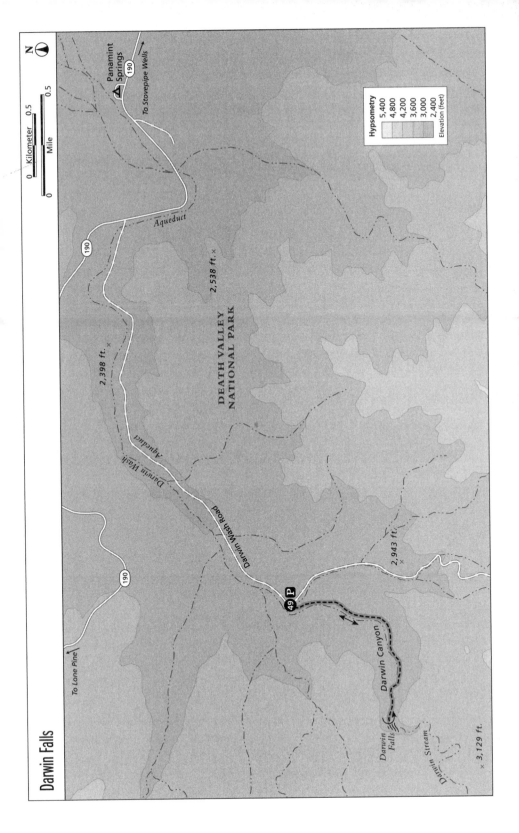

Darwin Falls

# Southern Panamint Range

## 50 Aguereberry Point and Eureka Mine

Two short hikes feature spectacular views from high on the edge of the Panamint Range overlooking Death Valley. Eureka Mine provides a view of a miner's life in the last century.

**Start:** About 26 miles southwest of Stovepipe Wells Village

**Distance:** 0.4 mile out and back to overlook; 1.6 miles out and back to promontory

**Hiking time:** About 20 minutes to overlook; about 1 hour to promontory

**Difficulty:** Easy to overlook; moderate to promontory

**Trail surface:** Dirt, gravel, some rocks

**Best season:** October to April (always check weather reports)

**Fees and permits:** National park entrance fee

**Maps:** NPS Death Valley Visitors Map; Trails Illustrated Death Valley National Park Map; USGS Wildrose Peak-CA

**Trail contact:** Furnace Creek Visitor Center; (760) 786-3200; www.nps.gov/deva

**Special considerations:** At 6,433 feet, with no protection, this is not a place you want to be in stormy or windy conditions.

**Finding the trailhead:** From Stovepipe Wells drive southwest on CA 190 for 8 miles. Turn left (south) on the Emigrant Pass Road. Drive south up the Panamint Valley 11.6 miles and turn left on Aguereberry Point Road. This is a slow, very twisty gravel road. At 2.3 miles you will pass the Harrisburg site and then the remnants of Aguereberry's Eureka Mine. The road winds through shrubby foothills to arrive abruptly at the jaw-dropping overlook at a T intersection 6.2 miles from Emigrant Pass Road. Turn left and continue 0.2 mile to the parking area at the summit. There's an information sign but no facilities at the parking area. GPS: N36 21.474' /W117 02.882'

## The Hikes

*Overlook*

At the parking area, you have arrived at a spectacular spot in the Panamint Range, looking out at Death Valley. An information sign at the trailhead provides the history of the Basque miner who developed the Eureka mine and created this road to share the view. After your trip through the rolling foothills, this perch is breathtaking.

Follow the suggestion on the sign and follow the user trail around the north side of the ridge. It goes out to a point beyond the jutting rocks. Although there are no dangerous places on the hike, this is not a hike for anyone with vertigo or fear of heights. At the overlook there are convenient sitting rocks where you can enjoy the peaceful view, if there is no wind.

The naked geology of the Panamints and Death Valley is laid out before you. Massive alluvial fans pour out of the Panamint canyons and ravines onto the valley floor.

*The adits at the Eureka Mine have been fitted with safety bat gates, which keep people out but allow bats to go come and go.*

The great faulted mountains cut the sloping strata as they dive into the valley below. Tetracoccus Ridge, right in front of you, blocks your view of the Furnace Creek settlement, but all of Death Valley's grandeur is right there at your feet.

This is a mountaintop experience without the climbing, as well as the shortest hike with the biggest punchline.

## Miles and Directions

**0.0**   Start at the parking area and follow the trail north around the ridge.

**0.2**   Reach the end of the path; turn around and retrace your steps.

**0.4**   Arrive back at the parking area.

*Promontory*

Drive back 0.2 mile to the T intersection and park there (or hike from the overlook parking area). The hike starts out on a former jeep track, heading southwest. The track is now barricaded and is being rehabilitated to its original condition. After the long drive to Aguereberry Point, this is a lively leg stretcher, with incredible vistas.

The faint gravel two-track fades in the first saddle, demonstrating that the restoration program is effective. Stay on the ridgetop 0.4 mile to a mound, where your route

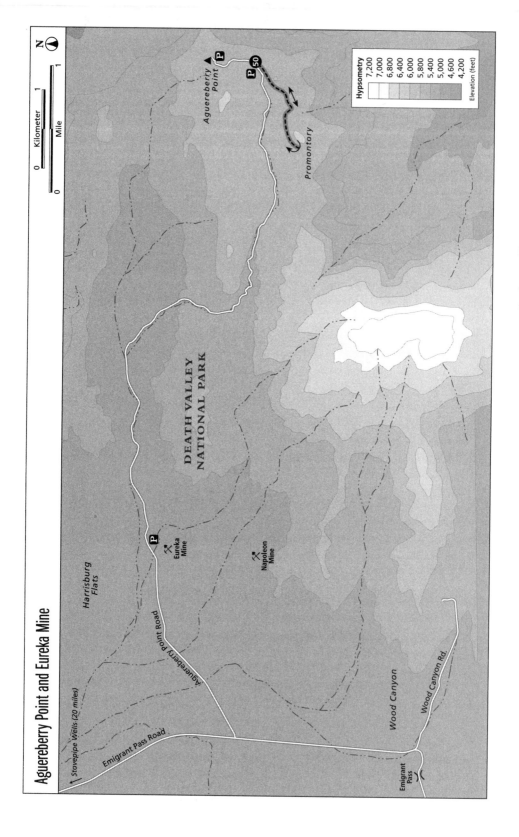

# Aguereberry Point and Eureka Mine

Hypsometry

| Elevation (feet) |
|---|
| 7,200 |
| 7,000 |
| 6,800 |
| 6,400 |
| 6,000 |
| 5,800 |
| 5,400 |
| 5,000 |
| 4,600 |
| 4,200 |

N

0    Kilometer    1

0    Mile    1

Aguereberry Point

Promontory

50

DEATH VALLEY
NATIONAL PARK

Eureka
Mine

Napoleon
Mine

Harrisburg
Flats

Stovepipe Wells (20 miles)

Aguereberry Point Road

Emigrant Pass Road

Wood Canyon

Wood Canyon Rd

Emigrant
Pass

bends westward. Stay always on the ridgeline, heading for the nameless promontory to the west. Now out of sight of your vehicle, the route continues across another soft ridge and then up to the hilltop another 0.4 mile ahead. No jeep trail exists here. Do-si-do through the brittlebush, going around rock outcroppings, to the 6,444-foot point on the topo map.

There are plentiful coyote droppings as well as old traces of burros along the way. The clusters of rodent burrows mimic the miners' adits wherever the dirt is soft enough, with gigantic slag heaps outside their holes. They've been very busy.

From the summit an incredible mining road is visible far below to the south, winding in the valley to a mining camp tucked in a remote ravine. In the far distance, piñon pines dot the slopes of the Panamint Range to the south, while the striped strata dive into Badwater far below.

After enjoying the magnificent view, retrace your steps to the parking area.

## Miles and Directions

**0.0** Start at the T intersection and head southwest on an old jeep track.

**0.3** Reach the first saddle.

**0.4** Reach the top of a mound.

**0.8** Arrive at the top of hill; turn around and retrace your steps.

**1.6** Arrive back at the parking area.

# Eureka Mine

**Start:** About 22 miles southwest of Stovepipe Wells Village

**Distance:** 1.0 mile, depending on your route

**Hiking time:** 1 to 2 hours

**Difficulty:** Moderate, with steep pitches

**Trail surface:** Miner pathways, crumbly gravel

**Best season:** October to April

**Fees and permits:** National park entrance fee

**Maps:** UPS Death Valley Visitor Map; Trails Illustrated Death Valley National Park Map; USGS Wildrose Peak-CA

**Trail contact:** Furnace Creek Visitor Center; (760) 786-3200; www.nps.gov/deva

**Special considerations:** Use extreme caution around mining sites. The park service has fenced off adits and shafts, but these industrial sites remain dangerous, with unanticipated hazards. Keep a watchful eye on your companions.

**Finding the trailhead:** From Stovepipe Wells drive 8 miles southwest on CA 190 and turn left on Emigrant Pass Road. Drive south 11.6 miles and turn left on Aguereberry Point Road. Drive 2.8 miles to the Eureka Mine turnoff on the right. Follow the graded two-track 0.2 mile to the turnaround and parking area at Providence Ridge. GPS: N36 21.743' / W117 06.421'

If coming from Aguereberry Point, go back down the road 3.4 miles to the turnoff to the mine on the left. You can see the ruins of the mill on the slopes of Providence Ridge as you approach the site. Drive 0.2 mile to the turnaround and parking area.

## The Hike

The Eureka mine site is an interesting outing on many levels. Geology, as always, is intriguing, especially when pursuing gold. Here the human history provides another great tale. Pete Aguereberry worked this mine from 1905 to 1945, first as a partner with Shorty Harris and then on his own. Providence Ridge, an unassuming rise sitting apart from the massive Panamints, is a surprising location for Pete's pot of gold, but it is estimated that he did relatively well here in his four decades of work.

The information sign at the parking area provides the mining history as well as information on the endangered Townsend big-eared bat, which uses the mine as a winter home. The adits have bat gates welded in place. These have horizontal bars so the bats can come and go, but humans can't.

From the parking area, wander up the ridge along any of the numerous pathways created by Pete. The ridge is pockmarked with adits and shafts. The park service has fenced off many of the dangerous shafts that dive downward into darkness, but watch your step. Holes are everywhere, and footing is sketchy on the crumbly gravel.

Around the ridge, rusted mine litter is everywhere. As a visitor you may admire these artifacts, but remove nothing. Track, pipes, barrels, stoves, a truck, a 1940s car—it's all slowly rusting away.

Following the pathway west along the valley floor below the ridge, you come upon Aguereberry's camp. Here Shorty and Pete lived modestly, although their accommodations were superior to those in the now nonexistent tent city of Harrisburg, which spread out to the east of the ridge in the 1910s. Hundreds of optimists used to live here.

Some of Pete's buildings are still standing. Again, be careful when investigating these historical structures. A park service sign explains the history of the enterprise.

From the camp head up the ridge on the pathway behind Pete's house. This was his route to and from work for forty years. Dropping back to the parking area near the Cashier Mill, you can admire the work involved in a successful gold mine. This was not an easy way to make a living.

For more information about the history of mining in Death Valley, visit the Borax Museum (free admission) at Furnace Creek Ranch.

## Miles and Directions

**0.0** Start at the parking area at Providence Ridge.

**0.3** Reach the top of Providence Ridge.

**0.6** Arrive at Aguereberry's camp.

**0.9** Reach the Cashier Mill.

**1.0** Arrive back at the parking area.

# 51 Nemo Canyon

The Nemo Canyon hike takes you on a gentle downhill traverse hike through open desert and down a wide graveled wash, bounded by low ridges and multicolored badlands, providing a pleasing contrast to nearby mountain climbs.

**Start:** About 27 miles south of Stovepipe Wells Village
**Distance:** 3.6 miles one way
**Hiking time:** 3 to 4 hours
**Difficulty:** Moderate
**Trail surface:** Cross-country, open graveled wash

**Best season:** October through May
**Fees and permits:** National park entrance fee
**Maps:** NPS Death Valley Visitors Map; Trails Illustrated Death Valley National Park Map; USGS Emigrant Pass-CA
**Trail contact:** Furnace Creek Visitor Center; (760) 786-3200; www.nps.gov/deva

**Finding the trailhead:** From Wildrose Junction (0.2 mile west of Wildrose Campground and Ranger Station), drive 2.2 miles north on the paved Emigrant Canyon Road and turn left (northwest) onto an unsigned gravel road that takes off from the paved road as it veers right (northeast). Drive 0.7 mile to the end of the road at a paved T next to a gravel pit. A USGS benchmark is adjacent to this spot, which is the trailhead/jumping-off point for the hike. GPS: N36 17.547' / W117 11.594'
The end point is the broad mouth of Nemo Canyon on Wildrose Canyon Road, down the canyon 3 miles southwest of Wildrose Junction and 1 mile southwest of the picnic area.

## The Hike

This moderate point-to-point down-canyon traverse begins in open desert country dotted with creosote bushes and Mormon tea. Nemo Canyon drops moderately to the southwest. To avoid walking toward the sun and into a stiff afternoon wind, make this a morning excursion if at all possible.

The canyon is wide open with low-lying hills and ridges. Soon a few scattered yuccas begin to appear. At first the wash is braided and graveled, but it becomes better defined with a sandy bottom after about 1 mile. At 1.5 miles the valley narrows a bit. In another 0.2 mile red rhyolite bluffs rise on the left side. Around the corner the valley opens in a semicircle with several side canyons entering from the right. The white saline seep of Mud Spring is also to the right at 4,020 feet. At 2 miles 100-foot-high cliffs rise on the left as the canyon narrows slightly. After another 0.2 mile the wash parallels brightly colored badlands—red, white, black, gray, pink, and tan—with steep bluffs rising several hundred feet on the left. At 2.4 miles a huge valley enters from the right. At 3 miles and 3,550 feet, the canyon is marked by brown, deeply eroded conglomerate cliffs and spires. Soon large granite boulders appear, resting precariously atop spires of brown conglomerate. At times loose gravel impedes walking, but the steady downhill grade helps. At 3.5 miles the canyon opens to the wide Wildrose

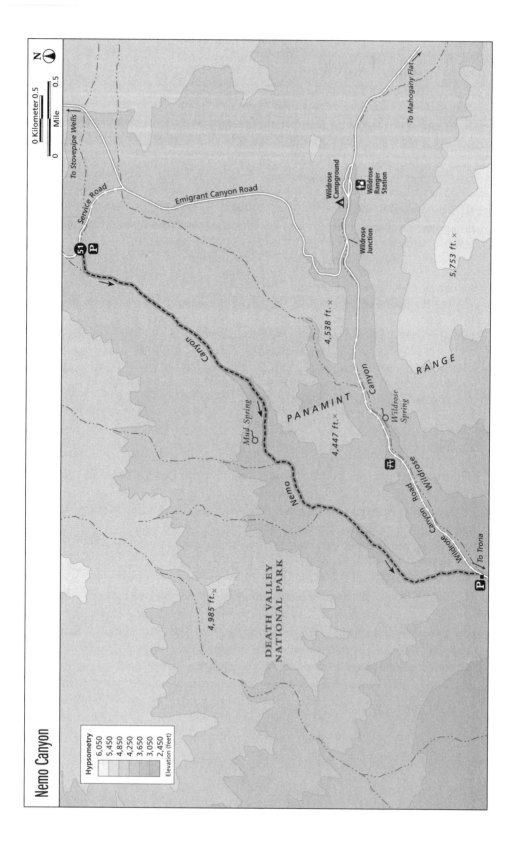

# Nemo Canyon

*Conglomerate mounds and spires are found in lower Nemo Canyon.*

Valley. In just another 0.1 mile, Nemo Canyon meets the rough Wildrose Canyon Road at 3,200 feet, thereby completing this point-to-point downhill traverse.

## Miles and Directions

**0.0**  Start at the trailhead in the Nemo Canyon wash and head southwest.

**1.8**  Arrive at Mud Spring.

**3.6**  Finish the hike at Wildrose Canyon Road.

# 52 Wildrose Peak

The Wildrose Trail takes you to a high Panamint summit from which the highest (Mount Whitney) and lowest (Badwater) land in the lower forty-eight states can be seen.

**Start:** About 36 miles south of Stovepipe Wells Village
**Distance:** 8.4 miles out and back
**Hiking time:** 4 to 6 hours
**Difficulty:** Strenuous
**Trail surface:** Dirt path
**Best season:** September to mid-November and March through June (depending on snow level)

**Fees and permits:** National park entrance fee
**Maps:** NPS Death Valley Visitors Map; Trails Illustrated Death Valley National Park Map; USGS Wildrose Peak-CA and Telescope Peak-CA
**Trail contact:** Furnace Creek Visitor Center; (760) 786-3200; www.nps.gov/deva

**Finding the trailhead:** From CA 190 at Emigrant Junction, drive south on Emigrant Canyon Road 20.9 miles to Wildrose Junction; continue east on Mahogany Flat Road (paved for 4.5 miles) and drive 7.1 miles to the Wildrose Charcoal Kilns parking area. In winter this road may be impassable; check with park authorities for weather and road conditions. The signed trail to Wildrose Peak begins at the west end of the kilns. GPS: N36 14.766' / W117 4.528'

## The Hike

Wildrose Peak provides panoramic views of Death Valley and the surrounding mountain ranges. This official park trail to Wildrose travels through classic piñon-juniper forest to a high saddle, then zigzags to the broad, open summit of this central peak in the Panamint Range. The meadow-like mountaintop is nearly always windy; appropriate clothing is a requirement, as are binoculars to enjoy the sweeping 360-degree view. Summer hikers will appreciate bug dope to combat flies and gnats.

In spite of its rather impressive elevation gain, the Wildrose Trail begins modestly. From the kilns at the trailhead, the trail charges 50 yards uphill to the northwest, achieving a 60-foot gain, but then follows the contour of the hillside for nearly the next mile. This section is a gentle warm-up for the hike ahead. Along the route, rock outcroppings extend to the west, hovering over Wildrose Canyon below. This is classic mountain lion country.

Climbing only slightly the trail joins another trail coming up from the canyon. Numerous pine stumps are a reminder of the logging done over a century ago to supply the charcoal kilns during their brief use in the 1870s. At the head of the canyon, the trail begins its climb. At 1.2 miles the trail bends north and steepens sharply, gaining over 600 feet in less than a mile. Rising to the first saddle, you will enjoy a magnificent view of Death Valley below through the evergreens.

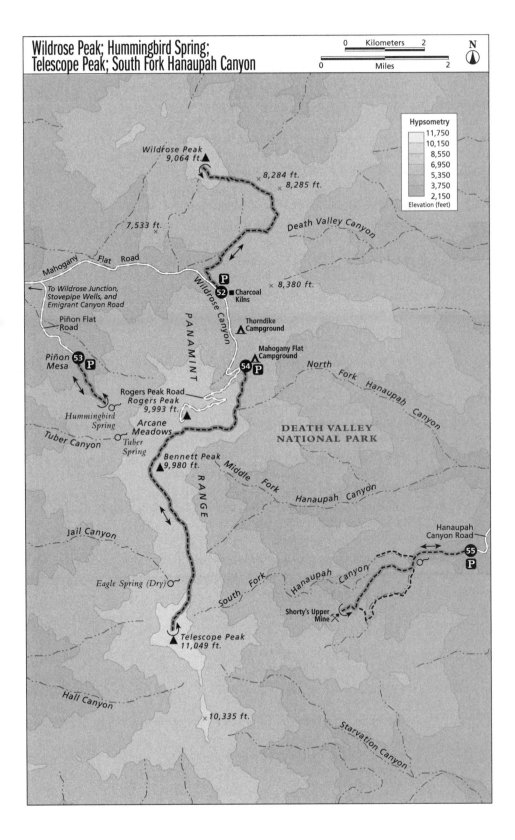

# Wildrose Peak; Hummingbird Spring; Telescope Peak; South Fork Hanaupah Canyon

**Hypsometry**
11,750
10,150
8,550
6,950
5,350
3,750
2,150
Elevation (feet)

Wildrose Peak
9,064 ft. ▲

× 8,284 ft.
× 8,285 ft.

Death Valley Canyon

7,533 ft.
×

Mahogany   Flat   Road

P
**52**  ■ Charcoal
Kilns

× 8,380 ft.

← To Wildrose Junction,
Stovepipe Wells, and
Emigrant Canyon Road

PANAMINT

Wildrose Canyon

Piñon Flat
Road

Thorndike
△ Campground

Piñon
**53** P
Mesa

Mahogany Flat
△ Campground

**54** P

North   Fork   Hanaupah   Canyon

Rogers Peak Road
Rogers Peak
9,993 ft.
▲

Hummingbird
Spring ⚬

Arcane
Meadows

DEATH VALLEY
NATIONAL PARK

Tuber Canyon ⚬ Tuber
Spring

Bennett Peak
9,980 ft. ▲

RANGE

Middle   Fork   Hanaupah   Canyon

Jail Canyon

Hanaupah
Canyon Road

Eagle Spring (Dry) ⚬

**55**
P

South   Fork   Hanaupah   Canyon

Shorty's Upper
Mine ✕

▲ Telescope Peak
11,049 ft.

Hall Canyon

× 10,335 ft.

Starvation   Canyon

0   Kilometers   2
0   Miles   2

N

The trail climbs around three small rises before emerging on a ridge above the saddle below the peak. Here, at 3.1 miles and 8,230 feet, you can pause and view the length of Death Valley. From here a mile of switchbacks leads to the summit. The trail snakes north, then south, then north, and so on, up the 800-foot climb. The changing direction enables you to enjoy a variety of vistas as you ascend the mountain, particularly as you near the windswept summit, which is clear of major vegetation.

A small rock wall on the peak was designed to give some protection from the wind. Or you can drop just a couple of feet down on the leeward side of the mountain to enjoy your stay and write a note for the peak registry. From Wildrose you can see the vast area of mining activity in the north end of the Panamint Range. Just to the northeast in the canyon below, there is a massive mining camp. Farther along Emigrant Canyon Road, the mountainsides are crisscrossed with mining roads. Rogers (with the microwave station) and Telescope Peaks loom above to the south. To the west is the mighty wall of the Sierras. To the east, across the valley, are the Funeral and Black Mountains. This is an eagle's view of the Death Valley world.

The hike back down the mountain allows you to relax and focus on a new view of the scenery. Death Valley Canyon, extending eastward below the high saddle, is just one of the dramatic sights you may notice on the downward trip. Although this is a heavily used trail, its bending pathway preserves the sense of solitude for the hiker.

## Miles and Directions

**0.0** Start at the trailhead at the west end of the Wildrose Charcoal Kilns. The trail climbs, then levels as it follows the contour of a hill.

**0.9** Arrive at the head of Wildrose Canyon.

**1.8** Arrive at a saddle, with views of Death Valley and Badwater to the east. The trail turns north and climbs to a second saddle.

**2.9** Arrive at the second saddle, which offers more panoramas. The trail drops slightly, then switchbacks up the eastern side of Wildrose.

**4.1** Reach the south peak, the false summit.

**4.2** Reach the north peak, the genuine summit, where a register is in an ammo box. Return to the trailhead by the same route.

**8.4** Arrive back at the trailhead at the charcoal kilns.

# 53 Hummingbird Spring

An exploratory hike into a piñon-juniper canyon below Panamint Mountain cliffs takes you into a remote canyon within bighorn sheep habitat, ending at a small spring.

**See map on page 205.**
**Start:** About 35 miles south of Stovepipe Wells Village
**Distance:** 3.0 miles out and back
**Hiking time:** 1 to 2 hours
**Difficulty:** Moderate
**Trail surface:** Rocky path, rocky wash

**Best season:** October to mid-November and March through June
**Fees and permits:** National park entrance fee
**Maps:** NPS Death Valley Visitors Map; Trails Illustrated Death Valley National Park Map; USGS Jail Canyon-CA and Telescope Peak-CA
**Trail contact:** Furnace Creek Visitor Center; (760) 786-3200; www.nps.gov/deva

**Finding the trailhead:** From CA 190 take Emigrant Canyon Road 20.9 miles southward to the junction with Wildrose Canyon Road. Turn left and continue east on Mahogany Flat Road, passing the Wildrose Campground on the way up Wildrose Canyon. Four miles east of the campground, turn right (south) on Piñon Flat Road; there are "jeep" (i.e., four-wheel drive recommended) and "no fires" signs on a post. The gravel road becomes too rough for all but high-clearance four-wheel-drive vehicles at 1.5 miles. Park along the road and hike up the road 0.2 mile to where it bends sharply northeast and rises to the Piñon Mesa picnic area. To prevent vehicular use, stones block the old road that continues straight south. This is the trailhead. GPS: N36 13.921' / W117 06.929'

## The Hike

This hike provides exploratory opportunities for history buffs or anyone who might enjoy a destination-less ramble in a lovely remote canyon high above Death Valley. Although the spring is usually a mere trickle, the area contains dense piñon-juniper vegetation thanks to its mountainside setting. The elevation makes the hike suitable for a summertime outing in the Wildrose region of the park. Also, when the wind is intense on the ridges of the Panamints, the Hummingbird Spring valley offers some protection.

From the trailhead the former road quickly deteriorates to a rocky trail. The area is a favorite of the resident feral burro population. Their tracks and droppings are everywhere. Avoid confrontations with these wild animals. It is unlikely that your paths would cross, since they are not interested in human contact. Whatever trail maintenance has been done in the last sixty years has been done by the burro pack that uses these pathways. The burros compete with bighorn sheep. As such, the park service tries to remove many of the burros from wild-sheep range.

As you climb the road/wash/burro path, you will spot remnants of prior human habitation: rusty cans, barrel hoops, lumber. Several pieces of galvanized pipe can be seen in the underbrush. Watch, too, for ax cuts on the pine stumps. This is a visual

*From the top of Wildrose Peak, a hiker looks northeasterly down the South Fork Canyon and onto Death Valley far below.*

treasure hunt for the history detective. The actual sites of the spring and buildings have vanished, but enough clues remain to suggest their whereabouts. Following the wash will bring you to a high junction of washes directly below a prominent 8,100-foot cliff face of the Panamints.

The immense value of water in the mining era in Death Valley is evident from the Skidoo Pipeline, which crosses Mahogany Flat Road just before the Piñon Flat turnoff. This 1907 pipeline carried water from Birch Spring in Jail Canyon, to the south of Telescope Peak, to the town of Skidoo, 23 miles north. This project cost $250,000 (in 1907 dollars). Even a small spring like Hummingbird was important to the residents of the valley.

Exploring the various small washes and ridges that extend down from the towering cliffs of the Panamint Range behind Hummingbird Spring expands the hike and turns it into a rambling adventure. When you turn for the descent to your car, you will also enjoy vistas of Wildrose Peak and Canyon.

## Miles and Directions

**0.0**  Start at the trailhead where the old road is blocked off by stones and head south up the eroded trail.

**0.7**  The trail and wash divide. Follow the one to the right.

**1.5**  The trail ends at a junction of three small gullies; turn around here and retrace your steps.

**3.0**  Arrive back at the trailhead.

# 54 Telescope Peak

The trek to Telescope Peak is a strenuous all-day hike to the highest point in the park. From here you have spectacular vistas made even more impressive given the astounding elevation difference of 11,300 feet from the valley below.

**See map on page 205.**
**Start:** About 40 miles south of Stovepipe Wells Village
**Distance:** 14.0 miles out and back with 3,500 feet elevation gain/loss
**Hiking time:** 7 to 10 hours
**Difficulty:** Strenuous due to distance and elevation gain/loss
**Trail surface:** Dirt path with some rocky areas

**Best season:** Mid-May to mid-November (check at ranger station for weather information affecting Wildrose Canyon Road)
**Fees and permits:** National park entrance fee
**Maps:** NPS Death Valley Visitors Map; Trails Illustrated Death Valley National Park Map; USGS Telescope Peak-CA
**Trail contact:** Furnace Creek Visitor Center; (760) 786-3200; www.nps.gov/deva

**Finding the trailhead:** The trail begins at the south end of the Mahogany Flat Campground at the end of upper Mahogany Flat Road, 8.7 miles east of Wildrose Junction. To reach the trailhead, take Emigrant Canyon Road 20.9 miles south of CA 190 to Wildrose Junction. Turn left and continue on Mahogany Flat Road. The upper section of the road is rough and steep for the final 1.6 miles after the charcoal kilns.

During winter Mahogany Flat Road above the charcoal kilns is often blocked by snow, adding 3.2 miles to the already long round-trip distance to Telescope Peak. If you are unable to drive all the way to the campground, start the hike from the Thorndike Campground (7.8 miles east of Wildrose Junction) or from the Wildrose Charcoal Kilns parking area (7.1 miles east of Wildrose Junction). This will add 0.9 mile or 1.6 miles, respectively, to the hike each way, making an early start imperative. GPS: N36 14.172' / W117 04.292'

## The Hike

The 7-mile trail to the top of Telescope Peak is one of only two constructed backcountry trails in all of Death Valley National Park. Although no rock cairns or tree blazes mark the way, the clear trail is easy to follow throughout its length. After the snow melts by mid- to late spring, there is no water anywhere along the high, dry ridge route, so be sure to carry an ample supply.

An average 8 percent grade is maintained, but there are long stretches where no significant elevation is gained or lost as well as several very steep switchback pitches to the summit. This high-ridge trail hike is especially enjoyable during summer when temperatures are usually unbearable in the valleys on both sides of Telescope Peak—11,000 feet below. This lofty stretch of the Panamint Mountains catches and holds a lot of snow during winter, but the peak can sometimes be climbed without difficulty as early as mid-March with only a mile or so of deep ridgeline snow to "posthole"

*The 11,049-foot Telescope Peak rises to the south.*

up just before reaching the summit. During winter it may be easier and safer to avoid the first 2 miles of steep sidehill trail by hiking the gated service road to Rogers Peak. Winter climbers should carry and know how to use ice axes and crampons, and be equipped with adequate winter clothing.

Backcountry camping is allowed 1 mile beyond the trailhead, but the first level and somewhat protected tent site is 2.6 miles in, along the edge of Arcane Meadows.

From the signed trailhead the trail starts in a forest of large, old piñon and limber pines, thinning gradually as the elevation increases. A trail register is positioned at 0.2 mile. The trail climbs moderately for 2 miles with spectacular views into the rugged North Fork Hanaupah Canyon, which drains eastward to Death Valley. At 2.6 miles the broad plateau of Arcane Meadows is reached at an elevation of 9,620 feet. This high sagebrush saddle is on the north summit ridge of Telescope Peak, directly below and southwest of the communications facility on Rogers Peak. Twisted tree trunks add a distinctive foreground to the sweep of the high Sierras far to the west, with the wide Tuber Canyon dropping steeply at first and then more gradually into a broad valley.

At 2.7 miles the trail leaves Arcane Meadows as it wraps around the west- to northwest-facing slopes of 9,980-foot Bennett Peak. Expect that about 0.5 mile of this stretch of trail will be snow-covered into early May.

At 4.3 miles the trail reaches the 9,500-foot saddle south of Bennett Peak. In another 0.2 mile the nearly level trail intersects an unsigned side trail that takes off to the right, climbing first then dropping 1 mile to dry Eagle Spring. Talus rock mixed with matted low-lying vegetation and prickly pear cacti add an unusual alpine tundra/high desert flavor. At the junction follow the trail to the left around the east side of the mountain and then back up to the summit ridge at 5 miles.

After another 0.5 mile the trail reaches the south upper end of the rugged cliffs of Jail Canyon at 9,970 feet. Huge bristlecone pine snags provide irresistible photo opportunities. The trail begins a series of steep switchbacks just right (east) of the sharp summit ridge, attaining an elevation of 10,400 feet at 6.2 miles. Gigantic gnarled bristlecone pines adorn these higher slopes. Some of these ancient trees have been bored and are around 3,000 years old. Members of the same species in the nearby White Mountains are among the oldest living creatures on earth at some 4,600 years!

The 11,000-foot mark is finally achieved at 6.8 miles. From here the trail climbs three mounds along the ridge before reaching the one farthest south at 7 miles—this is 11,049-foot Telescope Peak. The summit consists of a long rocky point, dropping off steeply to the south, west, and east. Mercifully, the actual peak is often less windy than the exposed ridge going up, so if conditions are tolerable, spend some time reading and signing the peak register.

The vertical relief is amazing, almost impossible to comprehend unless you make it to the top and look down on the salt flats of Badwater—the lowest point in the Western Hemisphere—more than 11,300 feet directly below. This monumental elevation difference is exceeded in the United States by only three other mountains: Mount Rainier in Washington and Mounts McKinley and Fairweather in Alaska. Telescope also affords a grand distant view of the highest point in the continental United States—14,494-foot Mount Whitney.

The vast desert basins of Panamint and Death Valley surround jagged canyons that emanate from Telescope Peak like spokes on a wheel. The remarkable contrast of basins and ranges that seem to stretch to infinity on a 360-degree arc is made even more dramatic when snow mantles the summit and higher ridges. Retrace your route to conclude a long, invigorating day on Death Valley's rooftop.

## Miles and Directions

**0.0**  Start at the trailhead at Mahogany Flat Campground.

**2.6**  Arrive at Arcane Meadows.

**4.3**  Arrive at the saddle before the summit ridge to the peak.

**7.0**  Reach the summit of Telescope Peak. Retrace your steps for the return route.

**14.0**  Arrive back at the trailhead.

*Option:* For an enjoyable 4-mile loop, hike to the end of the gated Rogers Peak Road, then up the ridge to intersect the Telescope Peak Trail, then north on the trail back to the Mahogany Flat trailhead.

# 55 South Fork Hanaupah Canyon

This vigorous hike on the eastern slopes of the Panamint Range includes a diverse canyon with springs, waterfalls, and a permanent stream, along with some of the most spectacular vistas in Death Valley. Other attractions include old mining artifacts and a chance to see wildlife.

**See map on page 205.**
**Start:** About 27 miles southwest of Furnace Creek
**Distance:** 6.0 miles out and back from upper trailhead with about 2,700 feet of elevation gain/loss to the upper mine (add 6 or 7 miles if driving a 2-wheel-drive vehicle)
**Hiking time:** 3 to 4 hours
**Difficulty:** Moderate
**Trail surface:** Old rocky mining road with rough sections of rock talus
**Best season:** Mid-September to mid-May
**Fees and permits:** National park entrance fee

**Maps:** NPS Death Valley Visitors Map; Trails Illustrated Death Valley National Park Map; USGS Hanaupah Canyon-CA and Telescope Peak-CA
**Trail contact:** Furnace Creek Visitor Center; (760) 786-3200; www.nps.gov/deva
**Special considerations:** The access road and parking area are in the bottom of the wash, so this hike should not be attempted during times of inclement weather due to the danger of flash flooding. For road conditions, check with the Furnace Creek Visitor Center before departing on your hike.

**Finding the trailhead:** From CA 190 drive 7.1 miles south on Badwater Road, then take West Side Road and drive 10.7 miles south to the rough Hanaupah Canyon Road. (Hanaupah Canyon Road is also 25 miles north of the southern Badwater Road/West Side Road junction.) Like all of the canyon roads on the east side of the Panamints, this road climbs up a rocky alluvial fan. The first 4.8 miles of this 8.3-mile-long road can be driven with a high-clearance two-wheel-drive vehicle. Then the road drops into the canyon and becomes four-wheel drive to the end. Once there, find a wide spot to park at the unsigned trailhead. GPS: N36 11.252' / W117 00.079'

## The Hike

Begin by hiking up the brushy bottom of the South Fork of Hanaupah Canyon. Hug the left side of the canyon wall to pick up a user trail next to the stream. The springs that feed Hanaupah Canyon discharge an amazing 250-plus gallons per minute, nurturing a diverse riparian corridor that attracts a wide array of wildlife. The old mines and cabin of "Shorty" Borden are on the hillsides above the springs. The trail cuts through an eroded alluvial fan and reaches permanent water at 0.6 mile, as evidenced by willow thickets. This is also the junction of an old mining road that leads to the upper mine. From here it's about 0.3 mile up the brushy bottom to a waterfall. Many of the granite boulders along the streambed are embedded with feldspar crystals, the same Little Chief granite found on Telescope Peak.

*Bouldering down a side canyon south of the South Fork of Hanaupah Canyon.*

To continue the longer hike to the upper mine, head up the old mining road to the left. The next mile gains 1,000 feet, with breathtaking views of a side canyon waterfall to the west and of Death Valley. The two-track is rough but provides a good hiking trail. It continues climbing up a center ridge between the South Fork of Hanaupah Canyon and an unnamed tributary to the south.

Usually by March the road cuts are ablaze with cliffrose and Indian paintbrush. The trail keeps climbing with some very steep pitches, gaining more than 1,300 feet over the next 1.4 miles to the upper mine perched on an open ledge and strewn with old timbers and debris. The adit has an iron door leading to an ore cart on tracks. The adit is unstable and dangerous, so keep a safe distance.

Retrace your route to complete this scenic 6-mile round-trip in the eastern slopes and canyons of Telescope Peak.

## Miles and Directions

**0.0**   Start at the upper trailhead/parking area 8.3 miles up Hanaupah Canyon Road.

**0.6**   At the springs and a mining road junction, climb to the left.

**1.4**   View the waterfall vista in the side canyon.

**3.0**   Arrive at the upper mine/adit. After exploring, retrace your steps to the trailhead.

**6.0**   Arrive back at the trailhead. (This doesn't include the extra distance required if you're using a two-wheel-drive vehicle.)

*Options:* To turn this out-and-back hike into a diverse but strenuous loop, drop into the unnamed tributary canyon immediately south and east of the upper mine. Plan on 3 to 5 hours to descend this rugged and challenging canyon. It is so rugged that if you were going up, you'd quickly turn around. But with a down-canyon route, you have little choice but to keep going. You begin with a steep 500-foot drop to the canyon floor. Every twist and turn brings new surprises: sheer cliffs, formations, dry falls, and boulders that can be bypassed by climbing up, around, and back down. The midsection contains springs with pools of water in scoured rocks harboring frogs, long-eared owls, and other unlikely desert denizens. A 50-foot dry fall in the lower end forces a climb high on the left shoulder. Then more dry falls force more steep sidehilling. The canyon mouth intersects the trail below the upper mine and about 0.6 mile above the upper trailhead.

With its abundant water the South Fork of Hanaupah Canyon could be used as a base camp for an extremely arduous cross-country climb of Telescope Peak (11,049 feet). The route for the gain of nearly 7,500 feet would be up the middle ridge between the South and Middle Forks of Hanaupah Canyon, intersecting the trail about 1 mile north of the peak.

# 56 Surprise Canyon to Panamint City

The hike to the ghost town of Panamint City follows a year-round canyon stream through a lengthy, dramatic canyon. Contemporary mining activity mingles with the historic in this remote Panamint Mountain location.

**Start:** About 65 miles south of Stovepipe Wells Village

**Distance:** 13.0 miles out and back

**Hiking time:** 4 to 7 hours

**Difficulty:** Strenuous

**Trail surface:** Rocky path

**Best season:** September through May

**Fees and permits:** National park entrance fee

**Maps:** NPS Death Valley Visitors Map; Trails Illustrated Death Valley National Park Map; USGS Ballarat-CA and Panamint-CA

**Trail contact:** Furnace Creek Visitor Center; (760) 786-3200; www.nps.gov/deva

**Finding the trailhead:** From CA 190, 34.5 miles southwest of Stovepipe Wells and 2.6 miles east of Panamint Springs, go south on Panamint Valley Road for 13.9 miles to the junction with Trona-Wildrose Road. Turn right (south) and drive 9.5 miles to Ballarat Road (signed) on your left. Turn left and go 3.6 miles to the tiny town of Ballarat. Turn left at the general store, which is a good stop for ice, cold sodas, and lively conversation with the proprietor. From the store drive north on Indian Ranch Road 1.9 miles to Surprise Canyon Road on your right, which is marked by a signpost and a large white boulder with a red S7 on it. Turn right and drive 4.1 miles to the road's end at the Chris Wicht Camp. The former occupants accidentally burned down the structure. There is now a primitive campsite at the trailhead. GPS: N36 06.756' / W117 10.510'

## The Hike

The Surprise Canyon hike is located on the very western edge of the expansion area of Death Valley National Park above the Panamint Valley. The BLM Surprise Canyon Wilderness Area lies on both sides of Surprise Canyon Road off Indian Canyon Road. Here the BLM's open desert camping regulations are in effect; there are plentiful campsites along the first 2 miles of Surprise Canyon Road before it climbs the alluvial fan.

The Wicht Camp on the topo map straddles the end of the drivable road.

A practical piece of advice is to waterproof your boots before hiking here—especially if the springs are running at full capacity. The trail/river combination makes for very damp hiking in the lower 3.5 miles of the canyon. This is a minor inconvenience in this adventuresome climb to Panamint City.

The vegetation and wildlife of Surprise Canyon is varied and plentiful, due to the presence of water and the elevation change. Birds and burros frequent the lower canyon. The hike will travel through several vegetative zones as it climbs, from riparian willow groves to creosote scrub community to piñon-juniper forest. From your

*A mine mill site in Surprise Canyon just above the trailhead.*

destination in Panamint City, the lofty cliffs of the mountain range soar above forested slopes.

Right from the start the hike up Surprise Canyon is a startling change from the drive through Panamint Valley. Even the bumpy ride up the road to the parking area does not hint at the water and greenery that greet you at Wicht Camp. The first 0.5 mile from the camp involves repeated zigzags along the shallow stream to dry sections of the largely washed-out trail. To enjoy the views of the rugged canyon walls, it is necessary to pause between stream leaps.

At 1 mile, hand and foot scrambling is necessary to get up the sloping gorge, where wet rocks are quite slippery. Another more challenging gorge lies 0.2 mile beyond, leading up to a broader valley. An amusing sight above the gorge is the deserted mine vehicle perched in the eroded trail. More vehicles lie in the brush, probably brought down the valley by the 1984 flood. During this lower third of the hike to Panamint City, the watery trail periodically becomes dry, but the flow from Limekiln and Brewery Springs along the canyon revives the creek.

At 3.4 miles the damp trail bisects an arched willow grove and cuts by a rocky grotto. This is the last contact with the stream until the return trip. The next 1.5 miles of the hike climbs 1,000 feet, with rugged canyon walls of contrasting colors on both sides. Juniper, Mormon tea, and barrel cacti crowd the lower slopes, with barren cliffs bursting above.

By 5 miles you'll begin to spot remains of Panamint City's vast mining activities. Up to 2,000 people lived in the narrow city during its brief heyday in the mid-1870 silver boom. Even today validated mining claims exist here.

At 6.2 miles you'll arrive at the central city site, where it is evident that mining and residential activities have occurred recently. Several cabins are located in the valley above the smelter ruins. Respect private property during your visit. The interface of old and modern mining is also in evidence. Aluminum and plastic debris from the 1950s is mixed with the more traditional rusty tin cans and barrel hoops of ghost towns. Amazingly, much industrial equipment is located in this hard-to-reach spot: a 20-foot propane tank, two trailers, various trucks, and other heavy machinery. Some 1950s-vintage buildings are interspersed with remains of the last century's occupation.

The narrow valley floor below the modern mining outpost is overgrown with creosote and catclaw. Amid the shrubbery are the stone walls and foundations of the nineteenth-century dwellers. Near one of the larger building sites, a garden of iris continues to spring merrily into life, a living artifact of Panamint City's brief but optimistic history. A large stone-walled livestock paddock remains on the north side of the trail; it is apparent that the wild burros of the canyon still like to hang out here.

Binoculars will enable you to explore the canyon visually without plowing through the dense, vicious shrubs. Several other canyons branch out at the eastern end of Surprise Canyon. With topo map in hand, you can explore Frenchmans Canyon to the southeast toward Panamint Pass, or Water Canyon to the northeast. Thompson Camp, in the latter, is 0.5 mile beyond the upper end of Panamint City by way of an

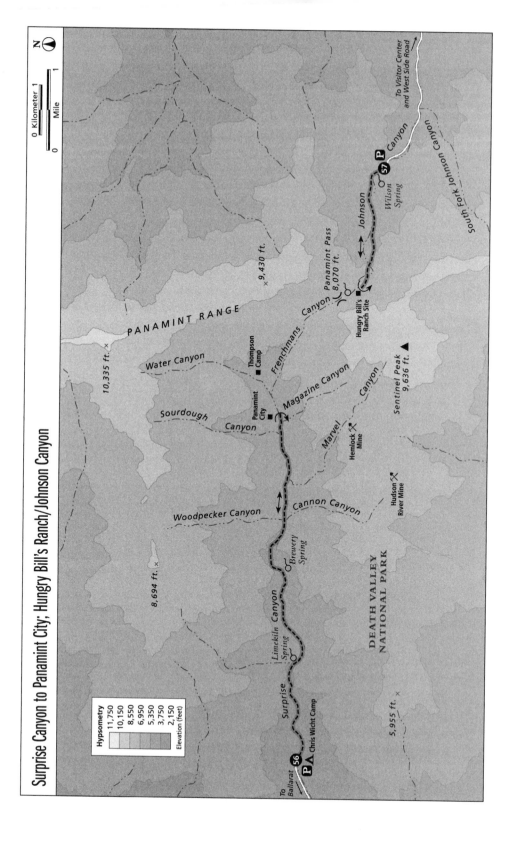

# Surprise Canyon to Panamint City; Hungry Bill's Ranch/Johnson Canyon

Hypsometry

| Elevation (feet) |
| --- |
| 11,750 |
| 10,150 |
| 8,550 |
| 6,950 |
| 5,350 |
| 3,750 |
| 2,150 |

N

0 Kilometer 1

0 Mile 1

PANAMINT RANGE

× 10,335 ft.

× 9,430 ft.

Water Canyon

Thompson Camp

Frenchmans Canyon

Panamint Pass 8,070 ft.

Panamint City

Magazine Canyon

Sourdough

Canyon

Marvel Canyon

Hemlock Mine

Sentinel Peak 9,636 ft.

Johnson Canyon

Wilson Spring

57 P

To Visitor Center and West Side Road

South Fork Johnson Canyon

Hungry Bill's Ranch Site

Hudson River Mine

Cannon Canyon

Woodpecker Canyon

Brewery Spring

Limekiln Spring

Surprise Canyon

Chris Wicht Camp

56 P

To Ballarat

× 8,694 ft.

× 5,955 ft.

DEATH VALLEY NATIONAL PARK

aqueduct trail. A couple of wooden-shell buildings and a water tank mark its 6,500-foot location. There is also a lush spring (Thompson Spring), with a large wooden cask cistern that used to supply the mining community. It is an excellent source of water even today.

Above the industrial city rise the peaks of the Panamints. The towering wall of the divide rises sharply 3,000 feet above the town, dwarfing the 100-foot chimney of the deteriorating smelter. The miners have come and gone, but the majesty of this desert mountain range persists.

For more information about the history of mining in Death Valley, visit the Borax Museum (free admission) at Furnace Creek Ranch.

## Miles and Directions

**0.0** Start at the trailhead at Wicht Camp and head up the former road by Novak Mill.

**0.1** Over the next 0.4 mile the trail and river share the same bed, necessitating much stream-hopping.

**2.8** At the junction with the canyon from the south, continue on the trail (left) up the main canyon.

**3.5** This is the last willow grove—your feet will stay dry from here on.

**4.9** Arrive at a mine opening on the right.

**5.0** At this major canyon junction, Woodpecker enters from the north, Cannon from the south; continue straight up the main Surprise Canyon.

**5.4** Marvel Canyon joins from the south at the trail junction. There's a low rock wall on the left. The chimney of the Panamint City smelter is visible a mile ahead.

**6.2** Arrive at the junction with Sourdough Canyon from the north.

**6.5** View the smelter ruins. The roads branch off to various other mine sites in Magazine, Water, and Frenchmans Canyons. This is the turnaround point for the hike back to the trailhead.

**13.0** Arrive back at the trailhead.

# 57 Hungry Bill's Ranch/Johnson Canyon

This out-and-back hike follows a scenic stream up a canyon to the historic ruins of Hungry Bill's 1870s ranch deep in the Panamint Mountains.

**See map on page 218.**
**Start:** About 37 miles southwest of Furnace Creek
**Distance:** 3.8 miles out and back
**Hiking time:** 3 to 4 hours
**Difficulty:** Strenuous
**Trail surface:** Primitive user trail

**Best season:** October through May
**Fees and permits:** National park entrance fee
**Maps:** NPS Death Valley Visitors Map; Trails Illustrated Death Valley National Park Map; USGS Panamint-CA
**Trail contact:** Furnace Creek Visitor Center; (760) 786-3200; www.nps.gov/deva

**Finding the trailhead:** From CA 190 at the Furnace Creek Inn, drive south on Badwater Road for 7.1 miles, then turn to the southwest on the washboard/gravel West Side Road (closed during summer) and continue south for another 21.7 miles to Johnson Canyon Road. Turn right (west) and drive 10.6 miles to a point about 0.1 mile before the end of the road at Wilson Spring. It is best to park about 0.1 mile below Wilson Spring to avoid driving through the riparian area and thick brush. The final 3.4 miles to the trailhead require a high-clearance four-wheel-drive vehicle. GPS: N36 05.375' / W117 00.448'

Those with standard two-wheel-drive vehicles should park before the rough road drops steeply into the canyon. This will add about 7 miles round-trip distance to the hike. GPS: N36 05.143' / W116 57.317'

The primitive-use trail begins at Wilson Spring, following the stream drainage 1.8 miles to the upper ranch site.

## The Hike

The original Hungry Bill's Ranch in upper Johnson Canyon was first developed in the 1870s by Swiss farmers who sought to grow fruits and vegetables to sell to the residents of Panamint City, over rugged Panamint Pass in Surprise Canyon. The mining camp had its brief heyday from 1874 to 1877. By the time the Swiss farmers were ready to sell their produce, bust had followed boom and the market had vanished! Later the ranch was occupied for many years by a Shoshone Indian named Hungry Bill, whose huge appetite matched his great girth. Today all that remains are fruit trees and extensive stone walls.

The road up Johnson Canyon is very rough, requiring high-clearance four-wheel drive to reach the road's-end trailhead at Wilson Spring. Wilson Spring is a lush and lovely spot with water pouring from a pipe, huge willow and cottonwood trees, and an informal campsite—a true desert oasis. In the absence of four-wheel drive, plan on parking at the burro pen about 3.5 miles short of Wilson Spring, thereby adding 7 miles round-trip to the hike.

*A bubbling brook flows down Johnson Canyon at 1 mile.*

The South Fork of Johnson Canyon enters from the left 1 mile before reaching Wilson Spring. This canyon is wide and graveled and can be hiked up toward the crest of the Panamint Mountains as a side trip.

To reach Hungry Bill's Ranch from just below Wilson Spring, look for the user trail that heads up the canyon on the left side from the road's end. Within 0.2 mile the trail passes the circular stone remnants of an arrastra used by miners for crushing ore. At 0.3 mile the trail fades out. Cross the canyon wash to the right side and look carefully for the continuation of the trail.

At 0.4 mile the canyon narrows, bounded by high rugged cliffs of volcanic rhyolite rock. The primitive trail crosses back and forth through the wash. The canyon again narrows at 0.6 mile; cross and climb around rock spires to the left. At 0.7 mile the trail climbs past hand-built rock walls and then loses 100 feet as it drops to the stream bottom. With a profusion of birds, frogs, lush vegetation, and water, this delightful stretch of Johnson Canyon is a refreshing celebration of life!

At 1 mile the trail reaches an overlook after contouring up and down along the steep rocky slopes. The trail then drops another 50 feet to the stream, crosses to the right, then the left, and continues up-canyon to the lower ranch site on the right (north) side at 1.6 miles. Each stream crossing features well-placed stepping stones, so you are guaranteed a dry journey. At the lower ranch the rock walls, fruit trees, and gurgling rivulet are overseen by massive cliffs toward Panamint Pass.

Cross to the left side and follow the primitive trail another 0.1 mile, where the stream has disappeared beneath the ground—a completely different and drier world. At 1.9 miles the stream resurfaces at the main Hungry Bill's Ranch—a huge open area on the left (south) side of the canyon. The site includes fruit trees surrounded by extensive rock walls. A rock-walled roofless house protected by a stone wall windbreak sits on a hill above the ranch. Hungry Bill certainly had a stunning view of an incredibly rugged cliff face and down across Death Valley to the Black Mountains. It is interesting to reflect on the life he must have led.

You'll probably have an easier time following the user trail back down to Wilson Spring than you did on the way up. With the scenic canyon, rough trail, and ample exploration opportunities at the ranch, there is no need to hurry.

## Miles and Directions

**0.0** Start at the trailhead, located 0.1 mile below Wilson Spring. Head up the canyon on a user trail to the left.

**0.3** Where the user trail fades, cross the canyon to the right side.

**0.6** The canyon narrows. Cross and climb around the rock spires to the left.

**1.6** Arrive at Hungry Bill's lower ranch.

**1.9** Arrive at Hungry Bill's Ranch. After exploring, return by the same route.

**3.8** Arrive back at the trailhead.

# Afterword

As seasoned hikers accustomed to the high snowy mountains of the Northern Rockies, we were excited when the idea of exploring some of the California desert was first presented to us more than twenty years ago. It would be hard to find two more disparate regions—the California desert and the Northern Rockies—within the lower forty-eight states. We viewed the opportunity to learn more about such a different ecosystem as a tremendous challenge. And we foresaw many interim tests along the way, such as truly getting to know this splendid country and its hidden treasures beyond the roads. There would be the trials of climbing rugged peaks, of safely traversing vast expanses of open desert, of navigating across alluvial fans to secluded canyons, of learning enough about the interconnected web of desert geology, flora, and fauna to be able to interpret some of its wonders for others to appreciate. These beckoned to us from blank spots on the park map.

But each of us faces a far greater challenge: wilderness stewardship, which must be shared by all who venture into the wilderness of Death Valley.

Wilderness stewardship can take many forms, from political advocacy to a zero-impact hiking and camping ethic to quietly setting the example of respect for wild country for others to follow. The wilderness and park lines that have been drawn in Death Valley National Park represent a tremendous step forward in the ongoing battle to save what remains of our irreplaceable wilderness heritage.

But drawing lines is only the first step. Now the great challenge is to take care of what we have. We can each demonstrate this care every time we set out on a hike. It comes down to respect for the untamed but fragile desert, for those wild creatures who have no place else to live, for other visitors, and for those yet unborn who will retrace our hikes into the next century and beyond.

We will be judged not by the mountains we climb but by what we pass on to others in an unimpaired condition. Happy hiking, and may your trails be clear with the wind and sun at your back.

# Appendix A: Our Favorite Hikes

**Mountains**
> Telescope Peak (54) Central peak with magnificent view
> Thimble Peak (28) Short approach to Grapevine Mountain vista

**Sand Dunes**
> Eureka Dunes (35) Highest dunes in North America, backdrop of Last Chance Range
> Ibex Sand Dunes (1) Remote, easily accessible, with historic mining ruins

**Canyons**
> Room Canyon (8) Short approach to dramatic canyon shapes
> Mosaic Canyon (44) Colors and contours of artistic elegance
> Marble Canyon (45) Twisting walls with varied stripes and colors

**Slot Canyons**
> Fall Canyon (30) Sheer walls above narrow canyon
> Sidewinder Canyon (10) Deep, dark slot canyons with natural bridges

**Natural Bridges**
> Natural Bridge (14) Massive bridge spans the canyon
> Moonlight Bridge Canyon (33) Highest documented natural bridge in the park

**Wetlands, Waterfalls, and Streams**
> Saratoga Spring (2) Lush desert wetland, with pupfish
> Surprise Canyon to Panamint City (56) Spring-fed stream, chutes
> Darwin Falls (49) Hideaway canyon with forked falls

**Interpretive Nature Trails**
> Golden Canyon/Gower Gulch Loop (17) Geology of Death Valley
> Salt Creek Interpretive Trail and Beyond (40) Geologic changes and pupfish

**Prehistory and History**
> Hungry Bill's Ranch/Johnson Canyon (57) Farm of 1880s
> Surprise Canyon to Panamint City (56) Dramatic watery canyon with a ghost town

**Mines and Mills**
> Ashford Canyon/Mine (6) Numerous mine buildings in scenic canyon
> Keane Wonder Mine (22) Extraordinary tramway, mine, and mill
> Aguereberry's Eureka Mine (50) Site of expansive gold mine and miners' camp

# Appendix B: Recommended Equipment

Use the following checklists as you assemble your gear for hiking the California desert.

## Day Hike
- [ ] sturdy, well-broken-in, light- to medium-weight hiking boots
- [ ] broad-brimmed hat, which must be windproof
- [ ] long-sleeved shirt for sun protection
- [ ] long pants for protection against sun and brush
- [ ] water: 2 quarts to 1 gallon/day (depending on season), in sturdy screw-top plastic containers
- [ ] large-scale topo map and compass (adjusted for magnetic declination)
- [ ] whistle, mirror, and matches (for emergency signals)
- [ ] flashlight (in case your hike takes longer than you expect)
- [ ] sunblock and lip sunscreen
- [ ] insect repellent (in season)
- [ ] pocketknife
- [ ] small first-aid kit: tweezers, bandages, antiseptic, moleskin
- [ ] bee sting kit (over-the-counter antihistamine or epinephrine by prescription) as needed for the season
- [ ] windbreaker (or rain gear in season)
- [ ] lunch or snack, with baggie for your trash
- [ ] toilet paper, with a plastic zipper bag to pack it out
- [ ] your FalconGuide

## Optional Gear
- [ ] camera and film
- [ ] binoculars
- [ ] bird and plant guidebooks
- [ ] notebook and pen/pencil

## Winter High-Country Trips
All of the above, plus:
- [ ] gaiters
- [ ] warm ski-type hat and gloves
- [ ] warm jacket

## Backpacking Trips/Overnights
All of the above, plus:
- [ ] backpack (internal or external frame)
- [ ] more water (at least a gallon a day, plus extra for cooking—cache or carry)
- [ ] clothing for the season

- ☐ sleeping bag and pad
- ☐ tent with fly
- ☐ toiletries
- ☐ stove with fuel bottle and repair kit
- ☐ pot, bowl, cup, and eating utensils
- ☐ food (freeze-dried meals require extra water)
- ☐ water filter designed and approved for backcountry use (if the route passes a water source) or a non-filter system such as chlorine dioxide drops to avoid clogged filters
- ☐ nylon cord (50 to 100 feet for hanging food, drying clothes, etc.)
- ☐ additional plastic bags for carrying out trash

# Appendix C: Other Information Sources and Maps

Death Valley Natural History Association
346 Salt Pan Vista
Death Valley, CA 92328
(760) 786-2146
www.deathvalleydays.com/dvnha
The association is a nonprofit membership organization dedicated to the preservation and interpretation of the natural and human history of the park. Membership benefits include book discounts, educational programs, and periodic newsletters.

Death Valley Conservancy
PO Box 566
Death Valley, CA 92328
dvconservancy.org
The conservancy has established the Death Valley Fund to provide private funding to support National Park Service–requested in-park projects.

Death Valley websites and blogs
The most comprehensive Death Valley hiking website is Steve Hall's Death Valley Adventures (panamintcity.com). This isn't a hiking guide, but it is a good source of information ranging from safety hazards to route descriptions and photos of Steve's extensive explorations throughout Death Valley.

**More Handy Maps**
The "At a Glance" chart lists the detailed 7.5-minute topographic maps for each hike. There are also additional smaller-scale maps that are indispensable for overall trip planning and for navigating around the park to and between hikes. These recommended maps include:

- NPS Death Valley National Park Map that can be printed out from the NPS website or, better yet, obtain a copy on-site at the Furnace Creek Visitor Center, which includes excellent information about the natural and human history of the park

- Death Valley National Park topographic backcountry and hiking map, 1:160,000 scale, published by National Geographic/Trails Illustrated

- AAA map of Death Valley National Park published by the Automobile Club of Southern California

- An excellent waterproof topographic recreation map for the park can be purchased online from Tom Harrison Maps.

# Appendix D: Park and Land Management Agencies

Death Valley National Park
PO Box 579
Death Valley, CA 92328
Visitor Information: (760) 786-3280

Furnace Creek Visitor Center and Museum
Furnace Creek Resort Area on CA 190
Death Valley National Park
(760) 786-3280
(Open year-round 8 a.m. to 5 p.m. daily)

Camping reservations: Destinet, (800) 365-CAMP (2267)
Website: www.nps.gov/deva

Scotty's Castle Museum
North end of DVNP on NV 267
Death Valley National Park
(760) 786-2392
(Open year-round 8:30 a.m. to 5 p.m. daily; temporarily closed October 2015 due to flooding; check current status with the NPS)

For information about wilderness and other public lands adjacent to the park, contact:
Bureau of Land Management
California Desert District
22835 Calle San Juan De Los Lagos
Moreno Valley, CA 92553
(951) 697-5200

# Hike Index

# About the Authors

**Polly and Bill Cunningham** are partners in many outdoor adventures. They were owners of High Country Adventures, leading backpacking trips in the wilds of Montana and Alaska for nearly forty years until selling their guiding business in 2013. They now have more time to hike in their favorite places, like Death Valley.

Polly and Bill coauthored FalconGuides' *Hiking California's Desert Parks*, *Wild Utah*, *Wild Montana*, *Hiking the Gila Wilderness*, *Hiking the Aldo Leopold Wilderness*, and Best Easy Day Hikes guides to Anza-Borrego, Joshua Tree, and Death Valley. Writing about the vast and varied Death Valley National Park has been especially rewarding because long ago the authors both lived close to the California desert—Bill in Bakersfield and Polly in San Diego. They have enjoyed renewing their ties to California while exploring the state's desert regions and want others to have as much fun exploring Death Valley as they did. They currently reside in Choteau, Montana.

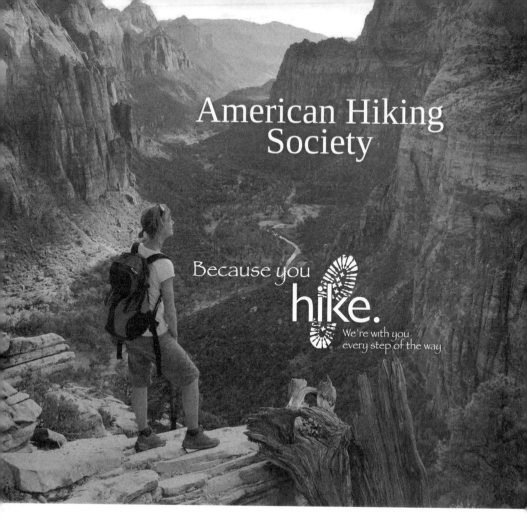

American Hiking Society

Because you
hike.
We're with you
every step of the way

As a national voice for hikers, **American Hiking Society** works every day:

- Building and maintaining hiking trails
- Educating and supporting hikers by providing information and resources
- Supporting hiking and trail organizations nationwide
- Speaking for hikers in the halls of Congress and with federal land managers

Whether you're a casual hiker or a seasoned backpacker, become a member of American Hiking Society and join the national hiking community! You'll enjoy great member benefits and help preserve the nation's hiking trails, so tomorrow's hike is even better than today's. We invite you to join us now!

American Hiking Society